# A Reformer on the Throne

# A Reformer on the Throne

*Sultan Qaboos bin Said Al Said*

Sergey Plekhanov

4

Published by Trident Press Ltd


Text copyright: ©2004 Sergey Plekhanov
Layout copyright ©2004 Trident Press Ltd



Editor: Gabrielle Warnock
Production: Paula Vine
Typesetting and book design: Johan Hoffsteenge
Photographers: Mohammed Mustafa and Mohammed Al-Rashdi.

British Library Cataloguing in Publication Data:
A CIP catalogue record for this book is available from the British Library.



ISBN: 1-900724-70-7

# Contents

*Sultan Qaboos bin Said Al Said*

# Preface

THIS BOOK ABOUT HIS MAJESTY Sultan Qaboos bin Said Al Said is in part the fruit of the author's many years of thought on the fundamental phenomena of the modern world. Over the past century the peoples of all continents have experienced social and military upheavals which have, little by little, overturned the high ideals of the nineteenth century. Revolutionary theories of all kinds bloomed and withered, leaving disappointment and emptiness in their place. Giant empires of unprecedented economic and military might collapsed, leaving no spiritual legacy. In the smoking ruins that littered the twentieth century, many people began to re-explore the past for models of fair and stable systems of private and communal life.

In coming to understand modern Oman and its structures of power, I was inspired not only by my own political inclinations, but also by my admiration for the beauty of Oman's use of its own past. Key to any understanding of the central value of the modern Sultanate – its vitality and flexibility – is a recognition of the continuing utility of its age-old institutions of power and its cultural traditions. Oman is one of those rare societies to have accomplished modernisation and innovation while maintaining a firm grip on traditional values, built up over an immense period of time. The devotion of the Sultan and the Omani people to their ancient dynasty and religion has ensured triumph over all attempts to overthrow it.

My meetings with the political figures of modern Oman, its intellectuals and its ordinary citizens, have provided me with a comprehensive picture of the country and its leader; it is clear from all that I have learned that the current transformation of this ancient land has largely been made possible through the efforts of its Sultan.

I would like to thank all those organisations and individuals, inside and outside Oman, who have so graciously contributed their time and expertise, and made this account of a great man's life possible.

I am thankful to several individuals in Oman for their time and support in many ways. I am especially grateful to the support offered to me by H. E. Abdul Aziz bin Mohammed Al Rowas, Adviser to His Majesty the Sultan for Cultural Affairs and the staff of his office; in particular, I would like to thank his assistant, Mr Salim bin Mohammed Almahruqi, Adviser for Cultural Relations. I would also like to thank the Embassy of the Sultanate of Oman in Moscow for its continued assistance toward the realisation of the project.

*Sergey Plekhanov*
Moscow and Muscat
April 2004

# A Restless Autumn

VEN FOR THOSE WITH LONG MEMORIES, the southern seashore of the Arabian Peninsula had never seemed so empty as in the last months of 1940. The small town of Salalah, situated on a narrow strip between the waters of the Arabian Sea and the green slopes of the Dhofar Mountains, rarely saw a ship of any size, even at the busiest of times; in late 1940, the naval war between Britain and its enemies ensured that the sea was deserted, but for the occasional Arabian dhow sailing from the northern Gulf and neighbouring countries and local fishing boats gliding past the old, palm-shadowed al-Husn Fortress.

Salalah had long been a favourite place for the Sultans of Oman. The local climate is quite different from that of the rest of Arabia. In summer, a monsoon from the ocean brings low, moisture-laden clouds ashore; and as they reach the slopes of the Dhofar Mountains, they release their rain onto the coast. The clouds also stop the Arabian sun from scorching the monsoon-moistened soil. This balmy period, known as *khareef*, lasts three months.

As a result, this Arabian land is covered with rich vegetation. Trees commonly seen in India or Africa abound: papaya, banana and coconut palms. Ten miles inland, on the other side of the mountain range, stretches the severe terrain of the Dhofar Plateau, relieved only by rare, gnarled little trees covered with tiny, scaly leaves. These are the source of frankincense, once a provider of wealth for the area. But the era when frankincense was the basis of prosperity ended long before imperial Rome had turned to ruins.

Sultan Said bin Taimur came to the throne in 1932 when his father abdicated and departed for British India. As in the years of Sultan Taimur bin Faisal, the sinister shadow of a world war once again darkened the horizon of history. The new Sultan must often have wondered what would be Oman's fate in such a rapidly changing international landscape. When his father Taimur had assumed the throne, the Ottoman Empire was Oman's closest neighbour. Several hundred miles from the Gulf, in Persia's Isfahan, there were Cossack units under Russian command, and it seemed that there was no force capable of stopping their approach to its shores. A few years later only small fragments of both of these huge empires remained, their lands broken up by foreign powers and riven with internal discord.

On 18 November 1940, the Sultan's beloved wife Miyzun bint Ahmed Alma'ashani gave birth to a son. The boy was called Qaboos, a rare name in the Arab world[1], and the title of Sayyid (His Highness) indicated his unique destiny as a future ruler of his people.

A belief in the sacred mission of kings is innate in all cultures and probably originated because the alternative – that an incomprehensibly capricious game of historical fate had raised a mortal to the summit of earthly power – was unthinkable. The same importance was ascribed by the people of those remote ages to the link between the name of a person and their fate. Still more importance was attributed to naming those of royal blood. Even today, names are considered magical – in naming a descendant after a great prophet, apostle, caliph, sultan or king, it is hoped that some of that force and talent which glorified previous bearers of this name will be passed on to the baby.

We can never be sure why Said bin Taimur chose the rare name of Qaboos for his son. It is unlikely that he himself was aware of all the factors that influenced his decision. We can only conjecture as to his mood when he welcomed his firstborn on the threshold of life. But the prospects for Oman were so uncertain that it would not be an exaggeration to suppose that he was looking for support from the historic past. The name Qaboos goes back to the pre-Islamic era – to the Lakhmids, the first Arab state to emerge. Shortly before the revelation of the Qur'an to the Prophet Mohammed, King al-Munzir III was ruler of

[1] The birth took place in Salalah while Said bin Taimur was in Muscat. It was to be a year before the father saw his son for the first time.

the Lakhmids. His son Qaboos commanded the army, fighting against the Ghassanid rebels. An ancient poet praised the courageous Lakhmid warrior with these words:

*He throws himself fiercely into battle,*
*His hauberk is strong, it is iron, resilient,*
*His sharpest white sword strikes ruthlessly.*

The story of the sovereign's upbringing is related in the classical text *Qaboos-nama* (The Qaboos Memoir). The main character in *Qaboos-nama* (which translates as 'the kings' mirror') is a wise monarch of the Bani Ziad dynasty who ruled a small state in the north of Iran at the end of the tenth century. Written in Persia in the eleventh century, it was widely disseminated throughout the Middle East. Oman and Iran have long been linked through alternating periods of cooperation and antagonism. From time to time large pieces of the territory have fallen to one or other neighbour, leading to an intermingling of the cultures and historical destinies of both peoples.

A highly educated man, Said bin Taimur was well acquainted with the literature of East and West and it is quite probable that he would have read *Qaboos-nama*. He may well have been attempting to bestow the wisdom and courage of this distant monarch on his new son who had been born at such an uncertain period in world history.

Said bin Taimur had seen the world. Not long before the Second World War he visited America and met President Roosevelt, then went to Tokyo, London, Paris and Rome. An observant man, he could not fail to see that the Old and New Worlds had different ideas of history and geography. On the one hand, Europe accepted the idea of the interconnection of different civilisations and of their continuity; America, on the other hand, was notable for its self-sufficiency, as reflected in one of the major symbols of empire for the West – the geographical map. From the beginning of the worldwide expansion of Western civilisation, empires struggling for supremacy saw maps as a sort of banner of their greatness. A map hung in the office of every British official at even the furthest outposts of the British Empire – and the sight of those maps on which most of the lands that had belonged to them now bore the colours of the European empires must have aroused in most Arabs a sense of injustice.

The final weeks of 1940 marked a rare historical moment when the map of the world ceased to be a mere political symbol and became a working document for monarchs, presidents and politicians of all ranks. Each day they attempted to guess the way in which the moving of small flags, representing the displacement of front lines, would affect the future of the world's political boundaries. Sultan Said bin Taimur must have spent much time observing the unprecedented struggle as the battle lines reshaped whole continents, and lands that had been the focus of civilisation found themselves on the margins of history. The destiny of the world was being shaped in the battlefields of the far approaches to the Indian Ocean. Great Britain, which not long before had been in the ascendant in these volatile regions, was struggling for its very life with a powerful and fortunate enemy who was the secret hope of all those subjugated by the British. The military and political élite of Iraq, Iran, Turkey, Palestine and Egypt impatiently devoured news of the 'Battle of Britain' being fought under the grey skies of distant Europe.

German planes were not only landing at Iraqi airports but were flying on to bomb British military bases in Bahrain; Italian boats patrolled the Red Sea, ready to attack British troop transport going towards Suez; Japan, allied with the Germans, had pushed the Britain aside in the Far East and south-east Asia and had occupied Indonesia, ending the colonial power of the Dutch. Throughout the rest of the world the two sides bitterly contested every yard of territory. History had never known such a struggle for the repartition of the world. If the Germans could avenge their defeat in the First World War . . . but no one quite dared to imagine the consequences of a thousand-year Reich.

One of the few countries of the Arab world that had preserved its independence during the long age of foreign invasions, the land of Said bin Taimur, therefore found itself near a major theatre of the Second World War. Its situation was made worse by the depletion of the treasury and other problems, inside the country and on its borders, which were growing more and more acute. Hence, when reflecting on the destiny of his newborn son who would succeed him, Sultan Said bin Taimur could not but be anxious. Instead of following the Eastern élite's tradition of studying English and the cultural and political institutions of the West, it looked quite possible that his son might have to choose another route to knowledge of the West.

# Early Impressions

THE STUDY OF THE WEST could wait – the Sayyid had first to learn about his immediate, but ever so mysterious, surroundings. As soon as he could walk, he began to make his first discoveries in the rooms of the ancient palace: rooms crammed with intriguing and enigmatic objects; ancient chests and decorated guns; long, gently-curved swords and small leather shields; Persian and Kashmir rugs; mirrors with gold-plated frames and carved bookshelves filled with fine books.

The air was always so delightfully scented; here and there he would come across brightly-coloured clay incense burners with scented smoke rising in the still air. In Dhofar each residence, from that of the monarch to the nomad's palm-leaf hut, was perfumed with frankincense.

With his first independent steps outside the palace came new, staggering discoveries: huge coconut-palm trunks reaching up to the sky; a strip of coconut palms beyond the wall forming a copse which separates the palace from the town; the smooth sandy seashore sloping gradually down to the ocean; and the ocean itself – a vast, glittering expanse merging imperceptibly with the distant sky. Sometimes the sea lay calm. More often its surface heaved, and foam-topped waves chased each other to the shore, spending themselves at the boy's feet with a muffled hiss. And the receding tide left so many treasures behind for Qaboos to examine: shells, starfish and tiny crabs convulsively burrowing into the sand.

When Qaboos was three years old, life around him changed abruptly. Not far from Salalah a British staging post was established and became one of the strategic points along the air routes from Europe to the Middle East and India. After the Allied victory over the Germans in North Africa, the Empire resumed battle against the Japanese in Burma. Heavy American aircraft transporting ammunition through Iran to the Far East and Russia started to land regularly in Salalah.

The Sayyid enjoyed watching from his window the dark grey freighters, large and ominous against the sunlight, which landed and took off with such surprising precision, and the fighter planes, swift and accurate as falcons, flashing above the wicker roofs of peasant huts.

The British military base was fenced with barbed wire; Qaboos would have seen guards with machine guns on the towers and many different types of soldiers – Africans, Indians, Gurkhas, white-skinned men in kilts, all of them ready to greet the Sayyid. Such a mixture of nationalities was not unusual in Oman, long a place of congregation for merchants and seamen from many parts of the world.

These were only his first contacts with the mysterious world of adults. The time to understand adult complexities would come later, when, with the war over, Oman found itself at the centre of a new battlefield. Sultan Qaboos, like his father, was brought up in the spiritual environment formed many centuries ago in Arabia and which continued almost unchanged until the middle of the twentieth century. Although the future Sultan's education would give him a thorough understanding of Western culture as seen through the prism of Anglo-Saxon civilisation, his personality was forged by the country in which he grew up. We can, therefore, gain a better understanding of the man by looking at the world that nurtured him.

One of the first questions to arouse the curiosity of the young Sayyid was why his country was named Oman. It was a question of more significance to Qaboos than to other children of his age, for to the heir the name of his country was not an abstract idea. In due course he would have to bear a title that would become an integral part of his own name – Qaboos bin Said, the Sultan of Oman. He learned that the origins of his country's name were obscure. It was known only that some centuries before the Qur'an was revealed, Roman historians and geographers knew of the name Oman. Arab writers at the beginning of the Islamic era tried to explain it in different ways: some maintained it was the name of a tribe, others believed that it was the name of a valley in Yemen, once inhabited by the powerful Azd who at the time occupied the south-west of Arabia. Some held the opinion that it was named after someone who had built a town there. This latter explanation was the most attractive: a small boy could well imagine a tanned, muscular leader giving orders to erect sentry walls in a barbarous, unsettled country and his fellow tribesmen repulsing the attacks of wild lions and belligerent foreigners.

Incense burners situated around the palace were probably taken for granted, but strange to think that all over the ancient world translucent resin, harvested from the bark of local trees and emitting a heady fragrance as it was heated over glowing embers, was considered a great treasure and was used in many religious ceremonies. A major trade in Oman's frankincense was well-established by the time of the historian Herodotus, and a map by the geographer Ptolemy I identifies the Salalah plain as a source for the sought after commodity; it is safe to assume that incense extracted from the Dhofar Plateau was being burned in temples throughout the known world by that time. The hardened resin from a small tree growing in sun-baked gullies was one of the most precious goods in the ancient world. Classical writers called the south-west region of Arabia that supplied frankincense to markets from China to Rome 'Arabia Felix', meaning 'happy' or 'favoured' Arabia. However, the onset of difficult times for this land was probably linked to the decline of the Roman Empire. As its gods were abandoned in favour of Christianity, the market for incense, such an essential feature of Roman pagan worship, disappeared.

Because of limited cultivable land Oman has never been densely populated. Only the foothills of the Jebel al-Akhdar Mountains and the area stretching along the northern shore of the Gulf of Oman have been favourable to the development of agriculture. Although the southern part of Oman around Dhofar is the sole area to benefit from the summer monsoons, rainfall is considerable (somewhere between 250 and 400 centimetres per annum) in the Jebel al-Akhdar Mountains, providing fresh water for irrigation of the coastal plain as well as for the numerous fruit crops that have been grown in the hills for centuries – fruits such as pomegranates, dates, walnuts and almonds. The sea, too, has always been a rich source of economic well-being for Omanis, from the oyster pearl beds that lay in the shallows close to the shore to the productive fishing grounds, easily accessed by those for whom the ocean was a second home; of particular importance has been Oman's strategic location on a key ocean transport route for merchants journeying both east and west, making the coastal ports of Oman significant international trading centres. But some 15 kilometres beyond the ridge summit the desert begins. The route from the Jebel al-Akhdar Mountains to the narrow strip of land on which Salalah lies is a waterless plain stretching for almost 1000 kilometres, virtually without vegetation. South-west of this road, in the direction of the holy city of Mecca, a vast desert lies – the Rub' al-Khali, (the Empty Quarter) – location of Wilfred Thesiger's gruelling travels during the second half of the 1940s. It is one of the world's largest sand deserts, with little water and, to the uninitiated, seemingly devoid of life. For centuries it has been an insuperable barrier to those wishing to invade Oman by land.

Many kinds of Arab vessel ply the ocean. The young Sayyid soon learned to distinguish between *bumas, ghanjahs, baghlats, jalbuts, sambuqs* and other types of boat, discovering that local fishermen prefer *badans,* and that those in search of a trustworthy new fishing boat go north, to Sur. There, the Sayyid was told, live craftsmen capable of making any kind of seagoing vessel. The Sayyid dreamt of the day when he would be old enough to go to Sur to see with his own eyes the old dockyard on the Gulf of Oman, long a major centre of the shipbuilding industry and once particularly noted for the construction of *al-ghanjah* (built for ocean passages) and *al-sambuq* (traditionally used for pearling). He could envisage dense piles of teak tree trunks – the skeletons of ships – brought from India and when he closed his eyes he could smell the freshly cut timber as the renowned craftsmen of this leading seaport worked together skilfully, silently, to build the different sections of some new vessel. The evocative sound of axes, saws and chisels as they bite into reddish-brown wood fills the air like a unique form of music. It is a strange music which carries in its notes the future journeys of those vessels which have yet to undergo their maiden voyages. Powerful waves will test the fragile-looking structure presently under construction. Its frame which now looks like the skeleton of a fish will, when clad with planks, resist destruction for many decades.

The dockyard's narrow harbour is thick with quarrelling seagulls. The round towers of forts rise above the hills. The red banners of the Sultanate flap in a sharp wind. A sea voyage of 100 kilometres or so due north into the open sea, leaving Sur astern, brought the dreaming boy to the shore on which the border between Iran and British India meets the sea. Not far from there lay Gawadar bay, belonging to Oman, but surrounded on all sides by British territory. He knew it as the last overseas territory of a once great empire. But large vessels seldom headed north. *Boums* and dhows sailed along the shore, some southward to Africa, others westward, returning to the ports of the Gulf – while those bearing a red standard were normally bound for Muscat or Sohar.

Regions of Oman differ in their handicrafts and in the character of their inhabitants. Even clothing and language are distinctive. Qaboos's respected great-great-grandfather, Sayyid Said bin Sultan spent the last few years of his long reign over Oman away from Muscat. He particularly liked the flavour of Sur, influenced as it was by cultural exchanges with Zanzibar and East Africa. Like many towns in Oman, it had its own unique character and there were frequent weddings and feasts among his followers that proved to be marvellously distinctive celebrations of the region's rich diversity.

It was true that a slave trade had existed, but despite the undoubted injustices and hardships connected with the slave trade in general, there were differences in the treatment meted out to slaves depending upon in which country they found themselves held captive. Europeans were shocked by the fact that Arabs kept slaves; they failed to draw any distinction between the terrible hardship of black Africans in the North American plantations and the treatment meted out to those kept by Arabs, taking no account of the patriarchal interdependence that existed in many Muslim communities where slaves often became like family members. Applying European notions to life in the East can be counter-productive, creating misunderstandings and enmities which still nourish arrogance in the West and fundamentalism in the East.

Compared to the West Africans who were sold into the American slave markets, immigrants from Africa probably felt considerably more at home in the town of Sur, where the local music resembled that of the coast from Somalia to Mozambique. Arab culture had long since merged with the cultures of the black tribes there, creating a strange world which spoke Swahili and danced to torrid equatorial rhythms. Was it from Africa that the famous tune of Sur sailors, *shubani*, came? Or did it come from Sur, an exotic African flavour having been added by the accompaniment of drums and *numan*, a six-cord harp-shell brought there earlier.

The child listened to the stories of the adults around him, and tried to imagine the rest of the country. He asked endless questions about the life of the people in different parts of Oman so that he could picture himself in these places, among tribes unknown to him. He adored exploring the geography of his own country and one of his chief pleasures was to study books and maps of Oman, travelling in his imagination from town to town.

If Sur evokes thoughts of unknown lands and ocean voyages, the settlements over the mountains, on the edge of the desert, bring to mind quite different images. Ancient Nizwa, nestled in a semicircle of mountains, is almost completely shrouded in palm trees. Only the outline of forts rise above the sea of green. This lush vegetation, suddenly appearing after the long journey through the desert, seems like paradise, overwhelming the traveller with trance-like thoughts of rest, peace and eternity. Such a place can steal the will to leave from those who reach its sanctuary.

Towering over Nizwa is the Jebel al-Akhdar. Reaching the summit of the highest mountain, the bare peak of Jebel Shams becomes visible. It is so high that sometimes in winter the hillsides are, according to the locals, white as if sprinkled with salt. The cold at these heights means that there are almost no villages. Only the occasional shepherd and his flock make the ascent in search of grazing. Those near the mountains seem more tranquil and less talkative than those from the south. Even their songs are different: one can hear their sadness, their affinity with the high panoramic view of the desert.

Nizwa is famous for its beautiful gold and silver engravings, various kinds of belts, scabbard decorations made from silver braids, and above all for its skilfully-crafted handles of wood, ivory and, previously, rhino horn for Omani *khanjars* (daggers).

Every Bedouin brought camels and sheep once a year to sell at the local market; then he could pay a skilled craftsman to decorate his rifle butt with silver, or inscribe a verse from the Qur'an on its barrel with inlaid silver. For his wives he would buy arm and ankle bracelets, and rings, earrings and pendants. He might also buy exquisite dates. And for the next 12 months he would recall with great satisfaction the sweet cool water from the local *falaj*. The young Qaboos was told much about this remarkable invention of the ancient Arabs, which works as well now as it did then (there are estimated to be about 11,000 *aflaj* (Arabic plural of *falaj*) in Oman, of which 4000 flow constantly). A *falaj*, similar to the Persian *qanat*, is an underground channel dug from an aquifer on a hillside down to the valley. Even on the hottest of days, the water arrives at the settlements and the fields tasting fresh and sweet.

Nizwa was known for its scholars and some Islamic law schools originated here. Students from all over Arabia studied in the local *madrasah*. The town also boasted an impressive fortress and large mosques.

The traveller who journeys from Nizwa along the mountain range in the direction of the Trucial States (the United Arab Emirates since 1971) encounters numerous small oases and old fortresses. Not far from Nizwa is Bahla, the oldest of the ancient citadels, built before the Islamic era. Even today, the enormous crumbling ruins could shelter an entire army for a long time.

A few kilometres further on lies the formidable Jibrin castle, a fortified Imam's palace, looking, from a distance, like a displaced battleship. It has an austere courtyard, some ancient cannons on wooden carriages, and giant, cracked jars in rows on the wall. Inside the palace a *falaj* flows, freshening the hot dry air of the desert. The vaults are covered with elegantly written quotations from the Qur'an; lying on a Persian carpet one can read these passages from the sacred *suras*, with their treasured revelations. From the roof, the view in one direction is of a range of low rocky hills while, in the other, a plain stretches to the horizon. In the mosque on the roof of the palace, its owner could pray to Allah five times a day, but could also hide from danger. From the narrow embrasures in the walls of the mosque a lookout for invaders could be kept. Here on the border of two worlds, at the gates of a great desert, the Imam offered up prayers for his people and here he listened to their needs.

In one of the guest rooms on the ground floor of the palace is the tomb of Imam Bal'arab bin Sultan, who built Jibrin at the end of the seventeenth century and used the fortified building to resist, for a number of years, a siege by his brother Saif. Saif's mausoleum is 60 kilometres away, on the far side of the Jebel al-Akhdar massif, protected by the Rustaq fortress.

To the west of Jibrin are many other watchtowers and forts, stretching in a chain along the old trade route. The fortifications gave protection for the crops and water supplies of the local settlements, and the caravans laden with frankincense which once passed between them sought their protection from attack by desert raiders. In a journey lasting no more than a few days, fully-laden caravans following this road could reach the Buraimi oases, some of the liveliest meeting places in Arabia. Travelling from Nizwa along the road over the mountains and down to the Gulf of Oman, one reaches the Batinah, which means underbelly, the name for the low flatlands between the mountains and the coast. The Batinah varies in width between 4 and 14 kilometres, and it follows the coast for some 330 kilometres. There, where the mountains meet the sea, lies Muscat. The very name of the city, from the Arabic word *muscat* (to fall), reflects the nature of the site: here the mountains, as it were, tumble into the ocean.

From ancient times the Batinah has been a major focus of settlement in Arabia. Plentiful rain and subterranean reservoirs of water made this fertile plain the sustaining core for all the adjacent regions. Ancient trading routes passed nearby, date palms, limes and cereals have long flourished here and viewed from the sea the area appears like a vast, luxuriant garden. Growing wealthy on agriculture, entrepôt trade and boatbuilding, this was one of the richest regions, providing a vital source of revenue for the treasury. Indeed, the very destiny of the country was inextricably linked to control of this region. Hence, from earliest times, fortresses were built all over Batinah to protect against incursions. Moreover, the capitals of Oman were usually situated here: first Sohar, then Rustaq, then Sohar again, and finally Muscat.

Sayyid Qaboos did not actually see these towns until much later, when he made his first trip to the north. His father, Sultan Said, had an aversion to heat and humidity, preferring a milder climate, and as a result the main palace, al-Alam in Muscat, was usually unoccupied. Looking through the lancet windows of the carpeted chambers on the occasion of his first visit, the Sayyid observed that although a finger of the sea came right up to the walls of the residence, the rocks crowned with powerful forts which clustered round the bay and the rocky island opposite the palace concealed most of the open sea from the sight of those within the palace.

Those qualities that provided Muscat with its excellent fortifications and a strategic defensive location had the unfortunate effect of endowing the place, sandwiched as it was between sheer sided cliffs and deep sea, with a sense of physical confinement. Said bin Taimur favoured locations that were more open, less claustrophobic. In former times many foreigners sailing along the coast of this part of Arabia did not even suspect the existence of Muscat's sheltered harbour secreted by rocky cliffs. Nor was it easy to approach the capital from the mainland, since the narrow mountain passes that gave access to the bay were defended by small forts.

Sohar, midway along the Batinah coast, is, by contrast, exposed to wind from every direction. This town was the capital of Oman for almost 1000 years. If one stands on the wall of the fort, which was built in the eighteenth century when the al-Busaidi dynasty took power in Oman, one can see both the distant horizon of the sea and the golden chain of the Jebel al-Akhdhar Mountains. A particular pleasure is to hear, while lingering on the sandy shore in the cool evening air, the haunting sounds of the oboe and to see local men in white *dishdashas* dancing rhythmically, while singing the *lewa*. An added strand of the enjoyment for the listener lies in the sense of African rhythm which is so prevalent in both the dance and chants of this area.

The residents of Sohar had a reputation for being good navigators. Many of the country's most respected captains of the dreaded black *ghurabs* came from here. It is also a place where traditions have flourished right up to the present time. One such tradition is the *malid,* and no festival or wedding is complete until the inhabitants of Sohar have united to sing their unique version of this chant of praise to the Prophet.

Not far from Sohar, just within the foothills, lies Rustaq. As in Nizwa, many of the traditional crafts of Oman, such as the forging of *khanjars* and fine silver work, began here. The best Omani *halwa* and pressed dates come from here and the local market attracts people both from the Batinah and from the mountains. Rustaq was, for many years, the centre of resistance to Intermittent Persian occupation.

The first Imam of the al-Busaidi dynasty made this town his capital. From a robust citadel, surrounded by palm groves, one can see the mausoleum of Saif bin Sultan I, a powerful Imam from the previous Ya'ruba dynasty. When in the presence of the body of Saif bin Sultan, the founder of the new dynasty probably meditated more than once on what would happen to his own descendants. Saif bin Sultan II, the grandson of the country's great administrator, turned out to be a poor ruler, who almost lost the country its independence.

Stories about different parts of Oman enthralled Sayyid Qaboos as much as his history lessons. He was naturally drawn to the ordinary people. Whilst encounters with those in the royal entourage – courtiers and servants – were predictable and therefore lacking much interest, his encounters with desert dwellers, fishermen and merchants were far more rewarding. He was avid to learn about his people and the country and quickly realised that these were the best teachers. His peers often commented on the close attention the young Qaboos paid even at chance meetings with his countrymen during his all too infrequent trips outside the al-Husn palace.

Oman's position on the perimeter of Arabia has given it a great diversity of tribes and peoples. The ancestors of the Arabs were the first to inhabit this land. These dusky-skinned people were strong and bellicose. Modern scholars have recognised the people of the Dhofar Plateau, which rises above Salalah, as the probable descendants of these ancient inhabitants.

At the base of the tribal structure of Oman were two mighty branches: the Hinawi and the Ghafiri. The former believed themselves to have originated from Yemen and the latter traced their kin from the Nejd and al-Hijaz Arabs. From time immemorial the ability to consider the interests of the various tribes has been the major tool of policy-making among Arab leaders.

On the Arabian Peninsula the well-founded tribal structure of Arabia which provided centuries of existence free from tyranny and nurtured an independent and proud people has survived, to a greater or lesser extent. Throughout Europe, Russia and the Far East, countries have tended to build up central power by forcing the submission of individual tribal leaders, thereby causing the gradual dissolution of the tribal structure as a whole. Arabs, on the other hand, particularly those in Arabia, have long looked upon the tribal segmentation of society as an excellent basis for the formation of a state; tribal rule once performed many of the social functions now reserved for the state and constituted the basis of the military forces. The tribal structures which evolved on the Arabian Peninsula resulted in a system based upon debate and popular choice, marking the origins of a unique style of democracy whose principles are well established in the Arab psyche.

In ancient times chiefs and kings entered the battlefield ahead of the army, which is why history contains so many accounts of the loss of monarchs killed in battle. This necessity to prove one's right to power through acts of personal courage and hardiness died out long ago in the West, but in Arabia the image of the warrior king remains a powerful concept even now.

Sayyid Qaboos's father was a believer in education, having attended an English college in India – Mayo College, Ajmer – followed by a period at a similar college in Baghdad. He was a striking figure, impeccably dressed and courteous, but he also possessed a sternness and strength that belied his appearance. A great shot, he often practised his aim by targeting lines of bottles arranged along the palace wall.

Sultan Qaboos's early education took place within the al-Husn Palace, under the tutelage of local teachers from the al-Madrasa al-Sayyidia School, Salalah's only educational establishment; this was to provide an excellent basis for his future studies in England.

For the young Sayyid, these early years in the palace were the most carefree; but the carefree period ended sooner for him than for others of his age. Royal offspring generally have a shorter childhood, unavoidably aware from an early age of their own significance and schooled from birth to succeed to power. If history is an abstract to ordinary boys, to a future ruler the study of history is an essential introduction to his own future role as leader.

The fragmentary information about the past that Sultan Qaboos acquired in his first years in school and during his meetings with people of different nations and tribes, gradually coalesced into an attractive but incomplete picture of his country. He needed to look at the detail, at the entire sweep of Oman's history and at the nation's place in the world. So the heir began to study his country more thoroughly, supervised by a talented tutor chosen by his father.

# Oman's Ancient Centrality

ERHAPS SAYYID QABOOS, like his father and his grandfather, more than once asked himself why nations that seemed to be at the centre of the world shared the same colours on the map as countries at the very edge of Europe; or why those who were not even Muslims were playing the master on the shores of Arabia, the native land of Islam. How had they achieved a position where they controlled the riches of the world and held such incredible power? These were questions the Sayyid's tutors preferred not to answer directly: instead, they sought to motivate the boy to seek his own answers from the events of the past. The sages have said that history is the educator of kings and I have tried to imagine in what way the future ruler discovered how far back the history of his country stretched. Local knowledge was not always reliable. When passing by the many ruins around the palace and in the coastal villages close to Salalah, the young prince never failed to ask the age of the ancient buildings, but he was not always given accurate answers. He asked for the names of natural boundaries and settlements, but often those around him could only make helpless gestures with their hands. He would therefore have had to turn to more scholarly sources of information.

For a boy as curious as the young Sayyid, the information being uncovered about his country by archaeologists would have been a source of particular interest. Archaeologists continue to uncover evidence of ancient cultures at many fascinating archaeological sites in Oman, though the record is by no means complete. The settlement at Wattayah in the *wilayat* of Muscat, the oldest so far identified, dates back to the Stone Age, while a burial ground at Ra's al-Hamra, a site with evidence dating to the fourth millennium BC, revealed 220 skeletons, buried in foetal position, facing the sea. Clasped in the hand of one of the skeletons was a pearl, one of the earliest pearls to be discovered in the region. Had they been discovered, the Sayyid might have longed to visit the beehive tombs of Bat, a world heritage site which together with neighbouring sites forms 'the most complete collection of settlements and necropolises from the third millennium BC in the world'. Salalah itself is situated in a region dense with archaeological interest – perhaps the young Sayyid visited the tomb of the prophet Job (mentioned in the scriptures of Muslim, Jew and Christian) located only 40 kilometres from Salalah at Jebel Eiteen. Did he wonder about the lost city of Ubar and guess at its location?

Oman may seem isolated from the ancient centres of the world, yet the history of this territory stretches back so far that already the first written reports on Magan (the name the Sumerians used for the north-east of the Arabian Peninsula) speak of an 'ancient' culture and copper artefacts from Magan were found in the tombs of the first kings of Ur.

For the founder of the first empire in the history of mankind, the Akkadian ruler Sargon the Ancient (twenty-fourth century BC), Magan was an important commercial partner, for it was a main supplier of copper, a major component – with tin – of bronze, and thus a strategic material in antiquity. On an important trade route, midway between the Indus valley and Mesopotamia, where the first civilisations emerged, Magan was a commercial crossroads in the true sense of the term. The population grew rich on navigation and commerce, making the country a tempting prospect for ambitious conquerors. The successor of Sargon, Naram-sin, was probably one of the first foreign rulers who tried to add Magan to his dominions.

In an inscription found by archaeologists, a Mesopotamian king mentions an expedition to Magan and the capture of its king, who bore the Semitic name Manium. Thus, the remote ancestors of modern Arabs ruled what they saw as the land of copper.

Over the centuries other peoples came from the depths of Asia and settled on the shores of the Gulf. Some gods were forgotten, while others triumphed. Periods of plenty alternated with centuries of poverty, when commerce dwindled because of lengthy wars and the degradation of ancient realms, but throughout the inevitable fluctuations of economic, social and political fortune, cultures survived or were replaced. The empires of Darius, Alexander the Great and Rome progressively extended the known limits of the civilised world to the edges of the giant continent of Eurasia. Other new countries and peoples were becoming involved in world trade, and the sea road from India to Mesopotamia remained the major thoroughfare for the exchange of goods between East and West.

Long before the beginning of the Christian era, just when the modern territory of Oman was being settled by Arab tribes, an ocean route from the Arabian ports to India was discovered. Prior to this time, sailing vessels had rarely ventured far from the coast for fear of piracy; the establishment of the new route to India led to an immediate improvement in the prospects for mercantile navigation. The discovery of this route, as important as the discovery of a sea route from Europe to the Indian Ocean 1000 years later, is accredited to Omani sailors.[2]

In those distant times sea trade was already the basis of life for the coastal tribes. Despite the gradual depletion of copper deposits in the spurs of the formidable mountain range later to be known as the Jebel al-Akhdar (the Green Mountain), Magan continued to thrive, due mainly to its increasingly substantial income from incense production. The more the south-east of Arabia became involved in international trade, the more the welfare of its inhabitants came to depend on events taking place in distant lands. Thus, the decline and fall of the great empires in Europe and Asia reverberated in Magan itself, by that time known as Oman.

It was a gradual transition, however, with an almost imperceptible decline in the incense trade and a reduction in size of the once great camel trains. The decline of the incense trade attacked a vital source of wealth for the tribal rulers, and it became increasingly difficult for them to afford to maintain the elaborate irrigation systems that provided the means of survival for all their people. When the famous Ma'rib dam started to break up (it was destroyed around 600 AD), a vast territory

[2] T. Shumovsky, a Russian historian and the first to study the ancient Arab sea routes, has written: 'The monsoons of the Indian Ocean, as well as its rains and cyclones, are very regular. The seamen have found out that every year there is a southwesterly monsoon from the end of March until the middle of July. The cyclone season lasts from June to the middle of October, and navigation ceased completely during that period. In November, it is the opposite – a north-east cyclone, which lasts till the middle of March, begins to blow. Observant seamen from ancient times realised that ocean winds do not blow chaotically, but follow a certain meteorological rule, the reasons for which they did not know. After having ascertained the existence and the periodic changes of the south-west and north-east monsoons, they used this discovery mainly for long ocean crossings. Their confidence in

turned into desert. The most populous area of Arabia, once a dependable source of food, suddenly became unable to support its own inhabitants – who departed in mass emigrations. To escape hunger and want, the Arabs invaded the lands of neighbouring empires and certain Arab tribes from the Ma'rib region of Yemen settled in what is today known as Oman. Whilst the region was already governed by Arab kings, and had been since the beginning of the Christian era, the inhabitants belonged to several ethnic backgrounds, reflecting its proximity to a number of culturally distinct groups. The arrival of this new wave of immigrants from Yemen created a dominant Arab culture for the first time in Oman.

By the seventh century, the Arab takeover of Oman had become irreversible and the region adopted the religion of Mohammed while the Prophet was still alive. In addition to the Arab tribes from Yemen, which provided the foundation of the population of modern Oman, significant numbers of migrants also came from the central regions of Arabia (Nejd). In the interior of the country, separated from the ocean by a rugged mountain range, numerous tribes settled – forming a tribal union (*azd*) that spread its influence from the Hadramaut to what is now Nizwa.

Recollections of the proud Azd, which can be found in the Qur'an, refer to one of these clans. The Azd built the 'multi-columned Iram', which was destroyed in a disaster as punishment for their rejection of the preaching of the prophet Hud, who called for the tribesmen to renounce polytheism. The eleventh sura of the Qur'an is entitled 'Hud', and it speaks of the verdict that awaits everyone on Judgement Day. Though Hud did not succeed in converting his tribe to Allah, his name is spoken with respect, and today many pilgrims still gather at his tomb in Dhofar. The magnificent town of Iram, whose residents did not acknowledge him, was long thought to have vanished without trace, until archaeologists discovered its ruins in a now uninhabited region of Dhofar.

the constancy of the weather and the inviolability of meteorological phenomena was so strong that their ships, which went to sea only when the sky was clear, had no facilities to protect them against rain or storms. The Arab seamen were the masters of the monsoons of the Indian Ocean, a fact exhibited in their navigational supremacy and the high level of marine commerce which has long linked Arab ports to all the shores of the Indian Ocean. An admiral of Alexander the Great, Nearchos, rediscovered the north-east monsoon and used it during his campaign from the Indus to the mouth of the Euphrates; the character of the monsoon is emphasised by the duration of the operation – 326/5 BC, indicating a meteorological period from November to March. T. Shumovsky, *Araby i more (The Arabs and the Sea)* Moscow, Institut Nardov Azii (1964) pp. 7–9.

The ancient beliefs of the Arabs retreated rather peaceably in the face of the new religion, though some cultural practices survived for many years. Arab historians call the period preceding Islam *Jahiliya* (the time of ignorance), which corresponds to the abrupt division in the West between the pagan and Christian eras.[3]

Mazin bin Gadhuba al-Tae, a native of Oman, became an apostle of the doctrine of Mohammed in his own land. A witness of the events of the first years of Islam, Abu Naim, calls Mazin a custodian of the idol Bajir, who was worshipped by the Azd in Sama'il. During a sacrifice Mazin heard a voice ordering him to give up his faith in the idol and listen to the messenger of Allah. After a second visit to Medina, the Omani underwent a transforming vision of the Prophet, an experience which caused him to destroy the statue of Bajir and to devote the rest of his life to the conversion of his fellow countrymen.

A letter from the Prophet of Islam to the Omani kings, the co-rulers Jaifar and Abd, sons of al-Julandi, preserved over the centuries, reads:

> *In the name of Allah, the Beneficent, the Merciful . . . from Mohammed bin Abdullah to Jaifar and Abd, sons of al-Julanda, peace is upon him who follows the way, now and thereafter . . . I am calling both of you, in the name of Islam. You will be safe if you submit to Islam. I am the Messenger of Allah to all of the people. I bring news of Islam to all the people, and will fight the infidels. I hope you will accept Islam, but if you do not, then you will lose your country, and my horsemen will invade your territory, and my prophecy will overtake your country.*[4]

The letter of the Prophet to the Omani kings was delivered by one of his comrades in arms, Amr ibn al-A'as. Speaking to the rulers of the country, Amr conducted himself as if he actually were a deputy of Mohammed. On behalf of the messenger of Allah, Amr promised that they would stay on the throne if they converted to Islam, and also called for a tax on the rich to benefit the poor.

---

[3]  J.C. Wilkinson, a modern English scholar of the history and theory of the Imamate in Oman, maintains that: 'For a good Muslim, history has a different conceptual framework from our own, for it has a moment of perfection: pre-Islamic history is *Jahiliya*' the time of ignorance before the revelation; whilst post-Islamic history is precisely that, events that have led, more or less, to a divergence from the Islamic state which the Prophet created.' J.C. Wilkinson, *The Imamate Traditions of Oman*, Cambridge, Cambridge University Press (1987) p. 7.

[4]  *Oman in History*, London, Immel Publishing Ltd (1995) p. 120.

News of the death of Mohammed arrived when Amr was with the Omani rulers; the Prophet's associate hurried back to Medina. A representative delegation of tribes, headed by Abd al-Julanda, followed him. The Omanis met with caliph Abu Bakr, who had inherited the mantle of Mohammed. The caliph greeted his guests and declared that voluntary submission to Islam would be seen as a credit to the people of Oman.

For Sayyid Qaboos, as for any Arab, his first notions of writing were connected with the history of Islam. The workaday alphabet had recorded what the Almighty had dictated. The letters traced by the schoolboy's insecure hand had once been chosen to inscribe the spiritual code of Muslim civilisation. That is why the view of calligraphy as a supreme art permeates Arab history. Written in an elaborate cursive script, the 99 names of Allah decorate palaces and huts alike. On the walls of mosques, bazaars and public buildings and on the doors of homes, quotations from the Qur'an are skilfully carved or drawn. Even nowadays Arabic calligraphy often takes the place of other types of figurative art and for many centuries beauty has been embodied in these written characters. A line of calligraphy can look like an agitated ocean surface or like the contours of sand dunes. It can also look like a flock of sheep stretched out along a path. Single letters can be recognised in the silhouette of a seagull, in a fore-and-aft sail, in an isolated cloud, in a crescent moon above the horizon. Was this the way Allah inspired the first inscriber of Arab characters on the sand?

The library at the palace in Salalah holds a large collection of books, some of great antiquity. The beauty of the calligraphy in those ancient, leather-bound books is in itself an aid to contemplation, and it would have been natural for the young Sayyid to gaze at the exquisite characters and long to understand their meaning. As his understanding developed, the very first lines of each *sura*, arranged so carefully, would have captured his attention with their concepts of singular wisdom, and his desire to know more would have urged him forward. Qaboos's first teacher of calligraphy promised him that he would one day be able to read all the books in the palace library.

An ancient collection of parables, *Kalilah and Dimnah*, became one of the favourite books of the young Qaboos. Although the origin of this work is unclear, its first known appearance in written form was in India during the fourth century, at which time it was entitled *Pancha-Tantra*.

It was then translated into Sassanid Farsi, and when Iran became a part of the Arab Caliphate, an Arab translation appeared. In translation the book underwent many metamorphoses – chapters were added, names of heroes changed their pronunciation, and small interpolations resulted in alterations to the meanings of the parables. The main modification was that *Kalilah and Dimnah* began to reflect the monotheistic ideology brought to Sassanid Iran by Islam. Thereafter the book was repeatedly rewritten and widely disseminated in the Muslim world, becoming a king's book in the true sense of the word: its major topic was the proper use of power. Animals and birds, the heroes of the parables, discuss honour and dishonour, justice and tyranny. Each thesis is examined from different points of view, and it is up to the rulers of the animal kingdom to make balanced decisions.

The predilection of the young Sayyid for analysis surprised and pleased his parents and tutors. Thoughts about life and about relations between people began to interest the royal child at an early age. Among the many books he read, a collection of Shakespeare's tragedies compiled by a famous Arab writer, Kamal Kalani, impressed him most. Having learnt to read at the age of five, the future Sultan enjoyed immersing himself in a complex world of human passions. His father nodded approval when the child retold him the stories he had read. Said bin Taimur himself liked to season his conversation when appropriate with a quotation from Shakespeare, which more than once enchanted his guests and advisers.

But the most important book that the heir to the throne discovered for himself, as soon as he learnt the art of reading, was the Holy Qur'an. At every stage of his life Qaboos bin Said has said that it has been his true spiritual fulcrum.

Religion comes into the consciousness of a child even before he learns his alphabet. Initially the child's religious consciousness is a world of naïve images, but when the word pronounced by others and the word read by him merge together in the child's soul, images emerge of ideas for which there is no correspondence in the visible world.

Oman, which bordered exclusively on other Muslim nations, and which had never been enslaved by adherents of another creed, had one of the most traditional societies on earth. Probably in the childhood years of Sayyid Qaboos, every day in that country seemed another moment of an everlasting history, and the past a long dawn of that day.

# Oman and the Spread of Islam

N EVENT WHICH WAS TO BE momentous for the history of Omani civilisation occurred in the year 622 of the Christian era. Many lunar years separate us from the moment when the Prophet Mohammed set out for Medina, driven out of Mecca by his fellow countrymen. This emigration, the *Hijra*, is a triumph of the spirit and a lesson for Muslims and is widely seen as a defining moment in the formation of Islam, to the extent that all events coming before that year are categorised by the faithful as occurring during the time of ignorance, *Jahiliya*. The thousands of preceding years, when the territory of Oman experienced a kaleidoscopic sequence of races, peoples, cultures and religions, can, on such an interpretation, be considered a pre-history, and the Islamic calendar dates from the year of Mohammed's arrival in Medina. Today, according to the calendar of this civilisation, we are living in 1425. The faith that several dozen people shared with Mohammed would become the main religion of the Arabs during his lifetime. Even Christian Arabs would recognise it as an expression of Arab identity. In the twentieth century one of the fathers of modern Arab nationalism, the Syrian Christian Michel Aflak, would declare Islam to be a synonym for Arabism.

Oman, which accepted the faith of the Prophet in the eighth year of the Hijra calendar, can be considered one of the major strongholds of Muslim civilisation throughout its history. Oman's uninterrupted existence makes it possible to view its fourteen-century Islamic history as a whole, and to see present events (whether beneficial or negative) as the results of events in the country's Islamic past. Not many countries possess such a homogeneous historical and cultural heritage as Oman. In the historical memory of the majority of peoples there are hiatuses due to foreign invasions and upheavals in social patterns.

Everything that happened during the life of the Prophet and under the first inheritors of his earthly power is directly linked with the political history of Oman, even in the twentieth century. The religious stream that emerged a quarter of a century after the death of the Prophet became both the foundation of the country's originality and the source of its principal problems right up to recent times.

Two groups gathered at the deathbed of the Prophet Mohammed – his closest relatives and his associates. The groups were virtually synonymous, as in Arab society those from the same tribe are all interrelated to some degree, due to the long tradition of arranged marriages within the extended family. The Prophet had four daughters by his wife Khadija and no direct heir, as all his sons had died very young. Only Fatima, his daughter from his first marriage, – an imperious and intelligent woman, who married Mohammed's cousin, Ali ibn Abi Talib – bore sons. Thanks to her, Mohammed had two heirs: Hassan and Hussein were the hope of the whole community. These, and many more of Mohammed's closest relatives and associates, came to grieve at the passing of the Prophet. Fatima's husband was an important presence at the deathbed. Many of the Prophet's associates thought that Ali should inherit both the temporal and spiritual power of Mohammed. A devout and honest man of deep faith, he had stood side-by-side with the Prophet through all his military campaigns. He was the very image of the ideal ruler.

Also present were other relatives from the Bani Hashim clan and his wife's relatives, including the 60-year-old Abu Bakr al-Siddiq, whose daughter Aisha was married to Mohammed. Aisha had taken on an important role in the community in the last years of her husband's life.

In the first days of his mortal illness, the Prophet had entrusted Abu Bakr to lead public prayers in his place. This provisional deputisation later became an hereditary title (caliph) for the sovereigns of what was to become a large empire – which at its peak included the greater part of the territory of ancient Rome. Another father-in-law, Omar bin al-Khattab, also arrived at the house of the Prophet. Only Othman bin Affan (who was married to one of Mohammed's daughters) was away from Medina.

It was clear that with his passing it would not be easy for the community of Muslims, which in the lives of one generation had turned into a powerful state, to choose an equally authoritative leader. Each of the four had a realistic chance of becoming the Prophet's successor.

The following three generations were not challenged for power, so each in turn eventually became caliph. But their rule brought about many tragedies with major historical consequences.

For 29 years one after the other ruled: Abu Bakr, 632–634; Omar, 634–644; Othman, 644–656. Only Abu Bakr departed peacefully. Omar was killed by the sword of a Persian slave in a mosque. Othman was killed amidst the chaos of civil war by the people of Abdullah, son of Abu Bakr. A fatal role in the destiny of the Othman caliphate was played by the fact that he ordered the dismissal of the vicegerent of Egypt, Amr bin al-As, who can be called an apostle of Islam to Oman – an act which led directly to his murder. After Othman's death, Ali became caliph. In his fifth year of rule he was murdered by an extremist.

The harsh laws of the desert operated in that world. 'Some are killed here, others perish in forays . . . Only a coward lives to old age,' wrote Abid bin al-Abras, a sixth century Arabian poet.

Ali stood out for his kind-heartedness and gentleness. He did not contest the election of Abu Bakr as caliph. He did not incite his supporters when the élite of the Muslim state preferred first Omar and then Othman. It was only when revolts broke out all over the caliphate that the old guard of Mohammed made Ali take the reins of power. His mildness, which some have called indecisiveness, indirectly led to his death.

The vicegerent of Syria, Muawiya bin Abi Sufyan, the son of an old enemy of Prophet Mohammed, who had accepted Islam only under duress, refused to recognise Ali as caliph and came out against him with a large army. When the two forces met in Siffin on the upper Euphrates, military fortune smiled on Ali. The troops of Muawiya, beleaguered by a fierce charge from the caliph's men, wavered in confusion and were ready to flee. At that moment, above the lines of the losing side, lances with scrolls bearing inscriptions from the Qur'an were raised as an appeal to resolve the conflict by way of arbitration (*tahkim*). Ali ordered the cessation of hostilities and agreed to negotiate. Amr ibn al-As was elected as one of the arbiters. Indignant that the caliph had refused to press his advantage, some of his partisans left the battlefield. They were given the name Kharijites, and became one of the most intransigent sects of Islam. Five years later one of the Kharijites stabbed Ali with a dagger as he was walking out of a mosque in Kufa.

One of the basic tenets of the first Islamic dissidents required the rejection of dynastic forms of rule. They believed that sovereign power belonged to the Muslim community, who might choose to delegate the implementation of communal decisions to a caliph. The dissidents believed that anyone who followed the Qur'an and the Sunnah, and who was righteous and capable of taking up arms against a sitting tyrant, could be elected to this role. The origins of the aspirant to the supreme position were not important – such a person could even be a slave – while a caliph could be dismissed and even executed for misconduct. Centuries before any impeachment procedure was adopted anywhere, the dissidents developed and strictly adhered to this idea.

On the basis of their own understanding of Islam as a democratic or even a socialist doctrine, the Kharijites, however, regarded all of the caliphs after Omar as usurpers, and struggled implacably against them.

As the twelfth century Muslim theologian Ash-Shahrastani testifies, one of the Kharijite postulates was: 'Everything that Allah the Almighty has created is common and not private, for he ordered it to a believer and to a non-believer. In the Qur'an there is no concept of 'privacy'.' Rejecting the arbitration that ended the battle of Siffin, the Kharijites insisted that the decision on the legitimacy of the transfer of power belonged to Allah, and not to the people. Their motto was: 'There is no judicial decision, only a divine one.' According to them the divine verdict had been rendered, because Ali had gained the upper hand over Muawiya, and to initiate talks with him after that was tantamount to flouting that verdict.

All purist organisations give rise to subgroups which train their hypercritical eyes on 'deviations' from the spiritual and moral norms of the organisation. People of this sort also sprang up among the Kharijites and founded numerous extremist movements that shook the caliphate for several centuries. But followers of the Muslim school headed by Jaber bin Zaid (630–710), a native of Oman, though not denying the stern moral principles of classic Islam, rejected the way of aggression initiated by their recent comrades-in-arms. It was probably not by chance that this enlightened theologian, who was the chief architect of this propitious doctrine, had grown up in the atmosphere of tolerance and benevolence that existed in Oman.

Jaber was born in the village of Farq, near Nizwa, a city which later became the capital of Oman and one of the centres of Arab achievement. This learned young man set out for Basra to enhance the knowledge acquired in his homeland. He was destined to become one of the luminaries of first century Islam. Guided by the associates of the Prophet, he studied the Qur'an, *hadith* and *shari'a*. He spent most of his life in Basra, where he wrote his highly original encyclopaedia, *Diwan Jaber*.

Jaber was well known in the centres of scholarly erudition – Mecca and Medina – as an expert in Islamic law. He was one of the creators of the theory of the Islamic state according to the pattern established by the pious caliphs Abu Bakr, Omar, Othman (at the beginning of his rule) and Ali bin Abu Taleb (before the arbitration).

Though Jaber bin Zaid spent almost all his life in the south of Iraq, he gained many pupils and followers in different parts of the Islamic world, especially in Oman. Basra attracted idealistic young people and all who were dissatisfied with social injustice. One of Jaber's pupils was Abdullah bin Ibadh al-Tamimi, a member of the influential Arabian tribe of Tamim who lived near Basra. An important school of Islam, Ibadhism,[5] was named after him.

The history of early Ibadhism is inseparable from the political history of the Middle East. Emerging when a fierce struggle for power was taking place in the Arab Empire, it attracted many supporters because it gave answers to the most relevant questions of the time: 'Is the power of the Umayyads, which they exercise in the same way as the opponents of Islam, Persian sovereigns and Byzantine emperors, lawful? What is the ideal Islamic state? Is the fate of a man predestined by the Omnipotent or do some things depend on his own spiritual efforts? Is it sufficient for a Muslim to believe in Allah, or is it necessary to demonstrate this faith with works? Should the death penalty be imposed for dissent?' Clearly those who asked such questions became an embarrassment to the powers that be.

[5] Ibadhis strongly believe that they are not a branch of the Kharijite sect. Historian Ahmed al-Maamiri wrote: 'The Ibadhis do not accept that they are Kharijite. Ibadhism as a sect was born in Basra but it was essentially conceived in al-Madinah. The Omanis have a saying that 'The egg was laid in al-Madinah, it was hatched in Basra and [the bird of knowledge] then flew to Oman.' Ahmed H. Almamari, *Oman and Ibadhism*, New Delhi, Lancers (1980) p. 48.

Discontent with the patriarchal rule of the Umayyads brought revolts. The grip of the state grew weaker with increasing distance from the centres of power. For over half a century the descendants of Julanda, who ruled Oman, did not really notice the heavy hand of the caliphs. While paying several types of taxes, they continued to enjoy complete freedom in their internal affairs. After the death of caliph Ali the question of power was resolved in favour of the Umayyads.

The capital of the empire moved from Kufa to Damascus. From there Oman seemed a faraway province and the centre of the caliphate could not be seen very clearly from the south-east of Arabia. No wonder that when Muawiya acceded to the throne, Julanda's descendant stopped paying *zakat* to Damascus.

This continued for some decades until Abd al-Malik became caliph. He wanted to centralise and establish order in the empire, which was debilitated by internal disturbances. The man he appointed Amir of Iraq and Islamic Mashriq, al-Hajjaj, sent a military expedition to punish the disobedient Omanis. But the naval invasion was a failure, and the commander of the caliphate army was killed. The *wali* (governor) of Basra then personally directed another punitive expedition. An army of 40,000 succeeded in crushing the forces of Said and Suleiman, the descendants of Julanda. Both rulers escaped to East Africa, and an officer appointed by Damascus became the ruler of Oman.

By that time the Azd, who had dominated Oman for several centuries, had also gained considerable influence in the south of Iraq, the main centres of which were Kufa and Basra. Since the Arab conquests of the seventh century, many tribes had been obliged by the Islamic state to serve in the army. Thus, the bellicose Azd became participants in distant military crusades. Lower Mesopotamia was the first to be subjugated by the Arabs, during the war against the Persian state. It is believed that the lands in this rich region were awarded to the tribes for meritorious acts.

When under caliph Omar the new town of Basra was built, the Azd came to live there. Many natives of Oman settled in the vicinity of Basra under Othman, and by the end of the century their influence was dominant. During a bloodthirsty struggle against the Kharijites, commander al-Muhalab, a member of one of the more influential tribes in the area, rose through the political ranks. His raids deep into Persian territory destroyed the main forces of the extremists, which in turn brought about the progressive collapse of the hitherto powerful opponents of the Umayyads. In gratitude for this, the caliphs first appointed al-Muhalab *wali* of Ahwaz, and then *wali* of Khorasan, the easternmost province of the empire. His son, Yazid bin al-Muhalab, later became *wali* of Basra, and then made his brother Ziad *wali* of Oman. But in 720 Yazid stirred up a revolt against the new caliph, Yazid II, probably in response to the anti-Omani projects of the monarch.

The Azd who moved to Iraq maintained strong and extensive contacts with those who remained in the land of their ancestors. For a long time, this apparently permitted Oman a good deal of independence in the conduct of its own affairs, since the deputies of Basra, the major strongpoint of the Umayyads on the shores of the Gulf, could not neglect this powerful tribe.

Indeed the balance of power threatened to tip toward the Azd. Attempting to limit the influence of the wayward Azd on Iraqi affairs, the Umayyad authorities resorted to intervention in Oman in order to undermine their support. After the failure of the first naval expedition, al-Hajjaj began to wage war against the Azd of Basra. Apparently he planned to prevent them from supporting Oman. After 13 centuries it is not easy to judge the real motives of that war. In any case, the fall of the independent dynasty of the descendants of Julanda coincided with the beginning of the decline of the Azd.

The dispersion of the Azd played a large part in the destiny of the socio-religious school founded by Jaber bin Zaid of Oman. One can sympathise with the opposition of the Azd, who were, after all, oppressed by the Umayyad authorities. Obviously a talented preacher could find numerous followers among his fellow countrymen. From them, anti-Umayyad heresy would have quickly spread among their kin in Oman. And the ground had already been laid by the invasion of foreign troops, who subjected a previously free land to the harsh control of the caliphs.

When in 720 the Azd left the surroundings of Basra and returned to the homeland, the spiritual autonomy of Oman had already become a reality.

While the Umayyads had succeeded in suppressing discontent across Iraq and western parts of Arabia, in the faraway mountainous regions of Oman and Yemen they could scarcely maintain their control. It was here that the Ibadhis demonstrated their might for the first time.

The rebellion of the Yemeni tribes in the 740s brought the Ibadhi Imam Abdullah bin Yahya to power and his sixteen-month rule was an attempt to create a just Muslim state. As with any genuine revolution, this first Islamic revolution sought to expand its sphere of influence. The warriors of the Imam took Mecca and Medina and were ready to spread the light of truth further afield. But the Umayyad caliph Marvan II was still strong and managed to overcome the Imam.

Abdullah bin Yahya died in battle. But this was the last major victory for the Umayyad dynasty on the internal front. Just three years later it was swept away by a more powerful religious revolution, the revolution of the Abbasids.

After the accession of the Abbasids considerable changes took place throughout the vast empire. The first, short-lived Ibadhi Imamate in Yemen, as it turned out, left a deep impression on the consciousness of the people. The legends of the pious life and just rule of Abdullah long outlived him. After the fall of the Umayyads, power passed smoothly into the hands of the Ibadhis in Yemen.

A short time later this also happened in Oman – in 751 the first legitimate Ibadhi Imam, Julanda bin Masud, was elected there. Five years earlier he had been present at the inauguration of Imam Yahya, testifying to his important role in the Ibadhi movement in the time of the Umayyads.

After the dissolution of this dynasty by the Abbasids, the Ibadhis did not become loyal supporters. The new governors' immersion in internal affairs did not enable them to establish their control immediately over the remote parts of the empire. But the first Abbasid caliph, as-Saffah, decided to subdue Oman because it lay on the most important route to India, the major target of the caliphate's expansionist ambitions. The Omanis were defeated and Imam Julanda was killed. Thus the first Ibadhi Imamate lasted just two years. For nearly four years the Abbasid deputies, called 'tyrants' (Jababera) by the local population, reigned in Oman. Then some local dynasties and elected Imams succeeded one another. From time to time there were disturbances and internal struggles, and it seemed that power was definitively passing to secular rulers. As it turned out, however, the Ibadhi ideals had been sown in favourable soil, for the Imamate unfailingly revived, notwithstanding a lengthy series of subjugators and civil wars. Something in the nature of Ibadhism seems to have been consonant with the Omani national character, and it became an integral part of the local identity, determining for many years that country's destiny.

There was a period in history when Ibadhism was a noteworthy force on a wider scale, and Ibadhism gained numerous followers thousands of miles from Arabia. In 777 the Ibadhis came to power in the North African Tahart (now Algeria), and the Imam they elected, Abd Ar-Rahman bin Rustum, founded the Rustamid dynasty. This state existed for over 100 years and played an important role in the history of Maghreb, being renowned for its scientific and cultural achievements. To this day there are Ibadhi communities in the Algerian oasis of Mizab, on the Tunisian island of Jerba, and among the tribes of Jebel Nefusa, Libya.

The example of North Africa, where Ibadhism was supported by the Berbers, the local population of this region, testifies better than anything else which ideas were closer to the people of that era. The proclamation of the equality of all peoples and all races before Allah, and the refusal to acknowledge any privilege, attracted people then, as now, to the Ibadhi preachers across a larger geographical area.

The destiny of Oman always depended directly on the affairs of the Islamic metropolis. As soon as the state became stronger and once again declared its authority over the life of Muslim peoples, the troops of the caliphate marched into Oman. But even when the power of the Abbasids grew weaker, there were new contenders for this strategically important region. And once again Oman became a battlefield.

At the very beginning of the tenth century, the Gulf was dominated by the Carmathians, who created their own state centred in Bahrain. This religious sect had emerged at the beginning of the ninth century in Lower Mesopotamia, the same place where not long before the Kharijites had operated (Kufa and Basra, as well as their surroundings, had long been a hotbed of revolutionary movements). Often the Carmathians and the Kharijites disagreed deeply on fundamental matters, but they resorted to a surprisingly similar repertoire of radical methods of combat. If the Kharijites were irreconcilable enemies of Ali and his descendants, the Carmathians became an extremist branch of Shiism who acknowledged Ali as their forefather and idolised him.

The new sectarians showed their strength during the revolt of the black slaves, the *zinj*. The preacher of one of the Shia groups, Hamdan Qarmat, was the intellectual force behind the rebels, and his followers were therefore called Carmathians. For some decades the Abbasids had fought against the slaves and the state they had created. During this period heresy became widespread, largely among Bedouins and the inhabitants of the cities.

Using guerrilla war tactics, the Carmathians caused considerable damage to the government forces, while remaining invulnerable themselves. The extraordinarily mobile army that emerged in this struggle gradually managed to take control of the entire east coast of Arabia. Naturally, the Carmathian state then directed its attention to its closest neighbours. In 905 the Carmathians made their first attempt to take over Oman, but failed.

Movements like this have existed in other religions – in Reformation Europe, in medieval China and in the pre-Columbian civilisations in America. Social and political egalitarianism, prohibition against lending money at interest, and an extensive network of welfare provision – these features of Carmathian society made it attractive to supporters of the original simplicity of Islam. But Carmathian rejection of some of the prohibitions of the *shari'a* made them outcasts in the Islamic world.

The Carmathian state lasted several centuries and had an aggressive foreign policy, but eventually it collapsed. Interestingly, the region – greater Bahrain and bordering with greater Oman – later became the native land of a new ascetic movement in Islam, the Wahhabis. And for a long time they were the major opponents of the Ibadhi Imamate.

The democratic ideology conceived after the battle of Siffin coalesced only after the founding of the state. Only by putting into practice the ideal of a just Islamic world order could certain political principles be worked out. From the very beginning the Ibadhi repudiated the supremacy of the aristocracy and the imperious regime of the Umayyads, so the way to achieve democracy became the principal subject of their reflections. A tribally-structured society facing a strong state could not develop an efficient apparatus of power. To keep the balance, the Imam constantly had to oversee and coordinate the interests of the tribes. He could not substitute his own tyranny for that of the Umayyads.

This fundamental contradiction jeopardised the rise of an effective and vigorous state in Oman. The natural isolation of the interior regions of the country prevented for many centuries the formation of a stable society. Time after time, tribal discord doomed to failure the attempts of different governors to legitimise the dynastic form of rule.

Meanwhile, a new opponent of Omani independence arose on the northern shore of the Gulf. The Shiite dynasty of the Buwayhids, which had taken Baghdad and had begun to rule on behalf of the nominal holders of power, the Abbasid caliphs, set to conquering lands according to the old imperial formula. A son of the founder of the dynasty, Oudhd ad-Daula Fana-Husrau (949–983), was the most fortunate of these conquerors. The enfeebled country capitulated to his threat of force and he took control of Oman without needing to fight a single battle.

Over the next half century Oman was ruled by a Persian dynasty. Before the downfall of the Buwayhids in 1050, however, Imam Khalil bin Shadhan re-established Omani independence and began to rule without taking instructions from Baghdad. About this time the Abbasids were transformed into a shield for a new invader, the Turkish Seljuks. The caliphate returned to life only with the weakening of Seljuk power at the end of the twelfth and the beginning of the thirteenth century. But the revival was short-lived. The last remnants of the Abbasid state collapsed under the onslaught of the Mongols in 1258, and the pagan Khan Hulagu killed the last caliph in Baghdad, al-Mustasim.

Invasions, rebellions and foreign overlords constituted the harsh reality of coastal Oman. Invaders seldom reached the interior, and here a theocratic regime was preserved – an Ibadhi Imam exercised both spiritual and secular power, according to the Islamic principles based on the Qur'an and the Sunnah. For the inhabitants of south-west Arabia the ideal state had existed in the past, and the Imams always aspired to the model of a Muslim community in the times of the Prophet.

Imams were never regarded as infallible. Some were deposed by the community; others were given the opportunity to pass their authority on to their descendants, although the putative heir always had to be approved as Imam by his co-religionists. As the spiritual leaders of the country, many Imams showed themselves to be outstanding statesmen. One of them is remembered as an architect of the navy; another did a great deal for the development of irrigation and fortification; yet another succeeded in creating a worthy system of Islamic education.

In those stormy centuries Oman knew periods of decay, but also more than once became a powerful state, defining the culture of the whole region, as history and geography testify. A Persian traveller, Nasir Khasraw, who visited Basra in the middle of the eleventh century, called the entire Gulf region 'Omani'. Not a native of Oman himself, he was simply repeating what he had heard from the local Arabs, which indicates how dominant a role Oman played at that time.

However, Omani society was unstable. Its tribal structure was often a source of sharp contradictions which led to conflicts. Frequent invasions by alien forces interrupted the natural development of the country, brought about the end of dynasties, and sapped the vitality of influential clans.

Destruction of a nation's élite naturally awakens authoritative ambitions in forces that have previously been outsiders. The gradual weakening of the Julanda clan, due to the loss of its most important members, led to a lengthy power struggle between the tribes. The Imams were unable to curb it and it brought to the forefront secular rulers from the Nabhan tribe who, as some, perhaps not completely objective, historians say, sank Oman for centuries in a morass of tyranny and turbulence. With the death of Imam Mohammed bin Khanbash in 1161, a period of Bani Nabhan absolute monarchy began. The Imamate was restored only in 1406 with the election of Malik bin al-Hawari, head of the Ibahdi community. Some historians believe that a number of rulers from the Bani Nabhan bore the title of Imam during that period and at the same time remained kings in those territories where the Ibadhis were not in the majority.

In any case, the period of Bani Nabhan rule is called 'a dark chapter in Omani history', and not only for its violence and devastation. Because virtually no documents for that period have survived, a complete picture of events cannot be constructed. Only fragments of information have been preserved – the names of rulers, the odd comment on inter-tribal battles and invasions from overseas, etc. It is probable that that period also saw competent rulers and periods of relative calm, but in the general confusion no traces have been left of isolated good deeds. The very fact of centuries of darkness following a well-documented period testifies to the country's historical catastrophe. It is a pity that its lessons cannot be used to instruct new generations. Only bitter proverbs have survived to bear witness – for example, 'The house of the tyrant is converted to ruins'.

During the period of Bani Nabhan supremacy (1161–1624), Oman focused on internal affairs: it seems that Omanis simply did not have the resources at that time for an active foreign policy. The only notable spheres of activity available to Omanis were the navigation of the Indian Ocean and the gradual colonisation of East Africa. In the first centuries of Islam a chain of commercial settlements from Mogadishu to Zanzibar was formed, and by the time the first European conquerors (the Portuguese) arrived, a unique culture called Swahili had come into being, with its language of the same name, a mix of Arabic, Persian and local African dialects.

The unstable position of the Bani Nabhan rulers, the result of continuous internal dissension, made Oman's neighbours think that the country, or at least part of it, would be easy prey. The rulers of the Hormuz state, which had arisen on the northern shore of the Gulf of Oman, organised various military campaigns against the adjacent territory of the Nabhan kings. They wanted to move the most important commercial centres from the ports of Oman to Hormuz. Practising the same trade on the sea as the Bedouins along the camel routes – offering protection and compelling commercial middlemen to use their harbours – the authorities of Hormuz gradually succeeded in changing the age-old sea routes. A celebrated Russian merchant from Tver, Afanassy Nikitin, visited Hormuz in 1467 and wrote in his notes: 'Hormuz is a great quay. People from all over the world go there; it has all sorts of goods. One can find everything on Earth there.' After ten days at sea, Nikitin saw Muscat, then one of the main ports on the trade route from the Red Sea to India. After more than five years abroad he turned back to Russia, pausing in Muscat to celebrate Easter in 1472.

But Hormuz was soon supplanted by a new enemy. When the Portuguese first appeared in the Indian Ocean in 1498 (the expedition of Vasco da Gama), they did not reveal any aggressive intentions. Their aim was to explore a sea route to India. It was the Omani navigators, knowing better than anyone else the river estuaries and hidden harbours, the direction of the winds, and the islands capable of supplying fresh water and convenient anchorages, who helped them in their search. When the newcomers mastered the necessary knowledge, they began to build proper ports on the East African coast and methodically to destroy Arab coastal cities. Their objective was to gain control over commercial routes, and thus undermine the economy of the Arabs and of the Ottoman Empire. After seizing territories in India, they began to look for fortifiable points along the route from Portugal to the new colonies. Hence Oman came under their scrutiny. In 1507, making the most of the weakness of the local rulers, the colonisers, under the command of Alfonso

Albuquerque, fired from ship-based cannons on Muscat, Sohar, Sur and Quriyat, and captured these ancient trading cities.

Portugal was the first Western state to begin assembling a colonial empire. Situated at the very edge of Europe, on the Atlantic seashore, it was the nearest European country to Africa and actually controlled the sea route to the south. It was also closest to the Cape of Good Hope, beyond which opened out the route to India and to the Spice Islands. No wonder the Portuguese led the way. And there were other reasons for Portugal's military expansion besides its geographical location. It was the first country to set itself free from Arab dominance: the Reconquista had been completed in 1270.

Their centuries-long war against the Iberian Sultans fashioned a special mentality among the Portuguese élite. Messianic ideas about their destiny and their hostility to Islam, even after the withdrawal of the Arabs from Portuguese territory, predetermined the mindset of those who set out for the East.

Of course, the Arabs on the east coast of Africa had nothing to do with those who had once occupied the Iberian Peninsula. But the Portuguese raged against them as if they were the minions of Satan himself. The colonisers notified the Holy See of their victories, continually declaring their resolution to carry out the Reconquista on a global scale.

But with a population of only one and a half million, Portugal was unable to consolidate its victories, and its garrisons could control the coastline only at certain points along the route to India. Apart from the coast, those countries that had become targets of Portuguese expansion, including Oman, remained beyond their control. The Portuguese burned Muscat, Qalhat, Tiwi, Darsait and Julfar – and utilised such methods of terror as mutilation to control the local Arab population, cutting off the ears and noses of those who dared to oppose them.

Internal dissension prevented the Omanis from ousting the Portuguese. The tribal leaders once again proved incapable of rising to the historical occasion. Arrogantly, they frustrated every attempt by the Imams to restore an ideal Islamic state.

A society based on the model of the Azd had obviously outlived its usefulness, and Oman had to choose either to become a state in a true sense of the word, or fall victim to upstart plunderers intent on carving up the world as they saw fit.

# Intrusion
# from the West

T HE PORTUGUESE WERE ABLE to rule the Omani coast for almost a century and a half. This was partly because of division among the tribes, with some fighting on the side of the Nabhan kings, and some on the side of the Imams, and also because of lack of unity within the Islamic world.

Instead of uniting against the common enemy, the Ottoman Empire was waging war against the Persians and the Egyptian Mamelukes, and the Arab sheikhs of the Gulf were in conflict with one another. But the Christian world was also divided. The Venetians, to mention just one example, were forming an alliance with Mamelukes against their Portuguese brothers in Christ. In the end, this spelled defeat for the Portuguese.

The Portuguese garrisons located along both coasts of the Gulf of Oman (Hormuz had also been subjugated) brought trade in the region completely under their control. All spices travelling to Europe from the East passed through Portuguese customs. The resulting monopoly lasted for more than 100 years, driving up prices and arousing the discontent and envy of other European countries, who coveted the spoils of India with equal intensity. This clash of interests inevitably put the big powers on a collision course with one another.

The British and Dutch East Indian Companies, founded on the eve of the seventeenth century, represented in the eyes of local people nothing more than militarised commercial bodies, quite capable of piracy at sea and aggression ashore. Their trading routes became heavily defended shipping lanes where naval flotillas cruised in order to protect their own interests. They were in conflict with both local vessels and, of course, the Portuguese. One of their flotillas defeated a Portuguese fleet near Hormuz in 1625.

Nonetheless, expelling the Portuguese from their territories was to prove difficult, for the Portuguese had established formidable bases, such as Fort Jesus in Mombasa (which still stands on the Kenyan coast), all along the route from Europe to India.

In Oman, the site of the main Portuguese fort at Muscat seems created by nature for defence against both land and sea attacks. The mountain range that slopes down almost to the Gulf of Oman leaves only narrow gaps that can easily be plugged by 100 soldiers, while the two rocky promontories which dominate the harbour present a formidable obstacle to any adversary approaching from the ocean, exposing them to the danger of fire from above. The Portuguese found these rocks already crowned with two mighty fortifications: to the left (looking seaward), Fort al-Mirani and, half a mile to the right, Fort Jalali.

Restoration of the ancient bastions, which had earlier resisted the bombardment of their own Albuquerque flotilla, was one of the first tasks undertaken by the Portuguese, but these marvellous constructions (which still adorn the capital) failed to secure them a permanent position in the region, although their final expulsion was many decades away.

Foreign domination always stimulates a national self-consciousness, and the appearance of a man capable of harnessing this fragile move towards nationhood was timely at this juncture. The election of Nasir bin Murshid, from the Ya'ruba family, as Imam in 1624 coincided with the beginning of open conflict between the Portuguese and their opponents in the Gulf. The new Imam made it his goal to expel the intruders but, realising the difficulty of this task, he went about it gradually, winning back, step by step, one territory after another.

The first of these territories was the village of Nakhl, situated at the very foot of Jebel al-Akhdar near the coast. Here the Imam gained a beachhead from which it was possible to take Portuguese-controlled Batinah.

His main task, however, was to unite the tribes from the part of Oman not under Portuguese control. Local leaders, who for no good reason had proclaimed themselves kings and princes, ruled the oases which stretched in a long chain beyond the Jebel al-Akhdar range. They were the main obstacle to unification. Hatching plots and orchestrating revolts against the Imam, they more than once threatened his life and his momentous mission. His superiority was evident to his adversaries – his wisdom and his loyalty to the idea of national salvation gave his deeds a consistency and foresight which his antagonists, driven by naked self-interest, sorely lacked.

The Imam showed great skill in consolidating his position of dominance. Having taken a city and its suburbs after armed struggle, he moved wisely and cautiously, organising the administration of the region in such a way that demonstrated to neighbours the benefits of the Imamate. Nasir did not try to settle scores with those he defeated, but showed them benevolence and charity. Against the background of constant, bloody civil conflict, to which inland Oman was accustomed, such a policy created a positive image of the Imam and of the order he personified. After subduing Nizwa and Dhahira, the Imam succeeded in gaining control of a group of oases, which are now called Buraimi, establishing there a further base for his struggle against the Portuguese.

Having secured his position in these key areas, the Imam was ready to transfer his theatre of military operations to Batinah. The first fort his forces managed to take was Liwa; they then laid siege to Sohar, an important Portuguese base in the Gulf of Oman, securing their own position there through the construction of a fort opposite that of the Portuguese. By 1643, Sohar was mainly in the hands of the Imam's forces. By 1649 only the Sohar Portuguese fortress and a fortified region of Muscat–Matrah remained under colonial control.

It was at this crucial point that the Imam died. Although he was unable to complete the task he had set himself, his efforts had done much to unify what had been a disparate collection of tribes into a far more powerful collective force. Fortunately, the new Imam, Nasir Sultan bin Saif (1649–1680), turned out to be a good strategist and politician, quite capable of progressing Nasir bin Murshid's policies, and the Portuguese were to be disappointed in their expectation that Oman would once again sink into the abyss of strife between clans and tribes. The perceived benefits of unity and the appearance of a series of leaders strong enough to command respect from the most important of the tribes ensured the continuing ability of the Omanis to work together for a common cause – the expulsion of the colonialists.

As 1650 drew to a close, scouts informed the Imam that the garrison of Muscat had been weakened by the transfer of some of its soldiers to India.

In a surprise assault the Omanis succeeded in taking the fort of Jalali, and then the entire city. Two naval vessels anchored in the adjacent port of Matrah were also captured, which neutralised the remaining Portuguese forces in Muscat. The Portuguese sent a huge fleet from their Indian colonies in an attempt to re-establish control over the Omani coast, but failed.

Now it was the Portuguese who had to drink the cup of humiliation, which a century and a half earlier they had forced on the Arabs. The Omanis, fortified by their success in freeing their own coastline from Portuguese control, adopted a far more aggressive policy towards the occupiers and a fleet assembled under the Imams of the Ya'ruba dynasty began to pursue the foreigners. Almost every post of Lisbon's colonial empire on the shores of the Indian Ocean became a target for Omani naval arms.

Several decades after liberating their own country, the Omanis delivered the entire African coast from Somalia to Mozambique from Portuguese occupation. In 1661 the Omani fleet attacked Bombay, which was then under Portuguese control. In 1668, 1670 and 1676 it assailed nearby Dio. In 1698 the Omanis took Mombasa and shortly afterwards gained control over Pemba, Zanzibar, Patta and Kilwa. The enemy did not want to surrender its supremacy in the Indian Ocean and in 1729 the Portuguese simultaneously attacked Muscat and Zanzibar. But this attempt to regain their colonies was also unsuccessful.

The internal unity of Oman, restored by the first Imam of the Ya'ruba dynasty, was the main foundation of the nation's power during the rule of Imam Sultan bin Saif. When the Imamate passed to his son Bil'arub in 1680, social stability was preserved and the people enjoyed peace and prosperity. But then a challenge came from the Imam's brother Saif, who was supported by some of the tribes. Some of the élite were devoted to Saif and proclaimed him Imam. War broke out and shortly thereafter a large part of the country came under the control of the adversaries of Bil'arub. But the rebels could not take Jibrin castle, where the legitimate Imam took refuge for many years. Only after the death of Bil'arub was Saif able to command the allegiance of all the tribes. In 1691 he was proclaimed Imam for the second time.

The 20 years of Saif bin Sultan's rule was one of the most successful periods in the history of Oman. The powerful fleet he created drove out the Portuguese from the majority of their East African colonies and forced other colonial states to take account of the developed role of Oman in the region's affairs. The growth of the Omani empire increased government revenues, which was reflected in all aspects of the country's life. Under Imam Saif many new *falaj* and irrigation networks were built and considerable progress was achieved in agriculture. New schools were built. His devotion to the well-being of the Omani people earned the Imam the title 'the Earth's bond'.

The rule of Sultan bin Saif II, who succeeded his father in 1711, was equally successful. In the seven years of his Imamate, Oman became a significant power in the Gulf region, establishing control over part of its northern coast, over Bahrain and over other Arab lands as far as the Red Sea. Eastern Africa and Western India also came under the sphere of Omani influence.

But although the Imamate of Sultan bin Saif II was a time of great achievement for the Ya'ruba state, it was followed by yet another period of instability. Yet again, the issue of the transfer of power fatally told on the destiny of the country and its people. With the death of Sultan bin Saif II in 1718, forces opposing the dynastic principle arose once more.

Saif, the son of the deceased Imam and grandson of the great Saif bin Sultan, was underage, and the religious leaders decided that he was not eligible to become head of state as, according to the Ibadhi conception of political justice, the leader of a secular authority should also be the head of a religious community.

Such logic made it impossible to acknowledge the boy as the supreme authority in questions of a religious and moral nature, and the *ulema* decided to choose a new Imam from the family of the late Sultan bin Saif. His son-in-law Muhannah bin Sultan was judged the most acceptable. Not everybody accepted the new Imam. Some continued to defend the dynastic rights of Saif bin Sultan.

Muhannah governed for less than three years, until he was killed in an uprising of the followers of Saif. This intensified the unrest, with various tribal groups promoting their own candidates, and the struggle stopped only when Saif bin Sultan came of age. The religious leaders declared him Imam in 1727 and the people breathed a sigh of relief, hoping that peace would be restored.

But Saif, the person at the root of the struggle that had lasted for almost ten years, did not live up to expectations. He was accused of deviating from the *shari'a*, and after five years was forced to resign by the council of *ulema* and sheikhs. Bil'arub bin Himyar was elected the new Imam, but was thwarted in his leadership by Saif bin Sultan, who sought allies in neighbouring countries against the authority of his new superiors. He first went to the Baluchis on the Makran shore in the northern part of the Omani Gulf, to enlist their support, but Bil'arub destroyed his army. Then Saif turned to Persia.

Nader Shah had just come to power in the neighbouring state and was one of the most efficient and ambitious rulers of that time. In his eleven-year reign (1736–1747), Iran greatly expanded its territory at the expense of its neighbours. Saif's fortuitous appeal for help enabled the Shah to pursue his plans to gain control over the Gulf. When in 1737 Persian troops landed near Sohar, the Iranian commander Latif Khan did not have the slightest intention of fighting for the cause of Saif.

Meanwhile Omani tribal and spiritual leaders, alarmed by the scale of the civil war, attempted to restore stability. They persuaded Bil'arub bin Himyar to resign and brought Saif back to power. Saif bin Sultan was for the second time proclaimed religious and secular leader of Oman.

However, another few years of 'legitimate' rule did not bring peace. The trials had taught Saif nothing; he remained arrogant and wayward and was again accused of neglecting the *shari'a*. In 1741 Saif was removed from power once more, and Sultan bin Murshid al-Ya'rubi was elected Imam.

Probably the only good deed performed by Imam Saif was the appointment of Sheikh Ahmed bin Said al-Busaidi to be governor of Sohar. This man was destined to play a decisive role in the fate of Oman.

Meanwhile, the dismissed ruler again went to Nader Shah for help. This time the Persians demanded a promise from the now bankrupt Saif to pay taxes to the Shah's Treasury. The vast Persian army invaded Oman and laid siege to Sohar and Muscat. During this nine months' siege, Sultan bin Murshid was fatally wounded. The death of Saif bin Sultan followed. The Omani leaders tried to fill the power vacuum by electing a new Imam from the Ya'ruba dynasty, and once again Bil'arub bin Himyar became Imam. But this time most of the tribes and the towns refused to recognise him. Thus, the story of the dynasty, at the roots of which stood a great man and which had been glorified by outstanding and confident rulers, ended. Nevertheless, the miserable role played by Saif bin Sultan failed to annul the remarkable achievements of his ancestors.

# The Birth
# of a Dynasty

*T*HE PERSIAN INVASION in the middle of the eighteenth century completed a cycle in Omani history, described by the British scholar J.C. Wilkinson as an 'Imamate cycle'. According to Wilkinson, the Imamate reflected tribal expectations of social structure, and was a quasi-state. Every attempt to create an authentic state and establish a dynastic rule was met with resistance from the tribal élite, inevitably leading to civil war. The destruction of the semi-states within the Imamate weakened the country and enabled foreign occupation of strategically important coastal territories.[6]

Ahmed bin Said al-Busaidi was born into a family of merchants in the small village of Adam, on the border of the desert and the foothills of inner Oman. He did not belong to those clans that traditionally supplied

---

[6] Wilkinson explains the reason for the cyclic nature of the phenomenon thus: 'Their apparatus of statehood was minimalist also, aimed only at a gradualist progression towards re-establishing the true Islamic state founded by the Prophet. The institutions Ibadhism put in place in Oman, therefore, were too weak to force basic change in the social system, so that government authority remained largely decentralised and dependent on the tribes. Above all, its power to collect revenue was absolutely controlled by the Islamic constitution, and the tribesmen ensured that it never exceeded this power, at least at home. Together, Ibadhis and tribalism prevented the development of capital, whether in the form of a capital in an urban hierarchy, which itself would have elicited changes in the agricultural production system (cf. for example the difference between the expansion of cultivation incited in its hinterland by the internationalisation of Sohar in the 10th and 11th centuries AD with the static or declining agricultural area of the Imamate capital of Nizwa), or of a capitalisation of the land production system, or through the development of a market economy, or through a centralised bureaucracy. Any attempts to centralise power automatically triggered off resistance in the two institutional frameworks which governed the social and political system of interior Oman. And so the "Imamate cycle" might exhibit periods of expansion or contraction, but never enough change to explode or collapse the basic socio-political order. Hence apparent "timelessness" in Omani history and also "closure" of the social "system".' J.C. Wilkinson, *The Imamate Traditions of Oman*, Cambridge, Cambridge University Press (1987) p. 6.

the country's rulers: he was Omani by origin (of the al-Azd). He made a fortune trading in Sohar and became a distinguished person in the city. The Imam appointed him *wali* (governor) of this important commercial centre. As the governor of Sohar he gained authority over the people and the part he played in repulsing Persian intrusion made him an acknowledged leader of the national resistance.

The dynasty that Saif bin Sultan had bankrupted could no longer be trusted; but the strong character of Ahmed bin Said al-Busaidi seemed to offer hope of reviving the tortured land.

The Persians were gradually driven out. Ahmed bin Said proved to be a skilful politician, guided by common sense, reflecting the popular Omani saying: 'travel a long way, but come back safe'. Realising that it was impossible to vanquish a strong enemy in one military operation, he signed a peace treaty with the commander of the army of Nader Shah. Thus, the influence of the Persian forces was significantly restricted, and their control became limited to the Muscat forts. By repeatedly delaying the agreed payment of taxes and supply of stores to the Persian garrisons, Ahmed bin Said seriously weakened and dispirited the enemy.

This nerve-wracking war might have continued indefinitely but for a dramatic course of events in Persia. Nader Shah, an outstanding military commander and the builder of a huge empire, was killed in a conspiracy in June 1747. The Persian soldiers despaired and when the commanders of the Muscat fortresses received an order to evacuate, the army responded without protest, unaware that they had been deceived and that the order originated not from their own superiors but from Ahmed bin Said himself.

Majid bin Sultan, a relative of the dead Imam Saif and the Shah-appointed governor of Oman, had been shipwrecked and captured near Sohar. It is supposed that he submitted to Ahmed bin Said and surrendered the government seal used to authenticate the order to hand over the forts. The order to which the Persian soldiers responded so unquestioningly was delivered to Muscat on behalf of Majid by one of Ahmed bin Said's men. The demoralised Persians returned home without further ado.

The death of Imam Bil'arub and Imam Saif had left nobody capable of uniting the tribes; the unchallenged leader of the resistance, Ahmed bin Said, was therefore elected Imam unanimously, an expression of confidence which gave him the authority to start reforming the country immediately.

Most modern historians agree on 1744 as the most reliable date for the commencement of the new Imamate, though some postpone the investiture of Ahmed bin Said to 1749. The precise timing of the ceremony is only of academic interest, since the election merely authenticated the *de facto* leader. Ahmed bin Said possessed the judgment of the best of those to whom he was successor. Realising that a leader from outside the ruling dynasty would be subjected to the harshest scrutiny, he was careful to avoid any appearance of excess in his assumption of power. The ceremony to proclaim the new Imam was extremely simple, symbolising the democratic character of his power and the avoidance of veneration for the bearer of the highest authority. The investiture itself was far from lavish: the country was devastated by the war, and festivities were inappropriate. The new Imam's modesty and common sense were highly appreciated by the pragmatic Ibadhis.

There were those who nurtured the hope that an ideal Islamic state, the ultimate aim of the Ibadhi doctrine, would at last be built. The accession of this new Imam seemed as though it might herald a revival of the Golden Age of Mohammed himself – that time when simplicity and democracy without dissension had held sway within the Muslim community. But the preceding cycle of dynastic power, collapse and civil strife had not prepared the ground for the years of peaceful leadership envisaged by the proponents of the tribal semi-state. The real drawback of the established ruling system was that it reflected the realities of an underdeveloped state. Anarchic groups opposing the creation of a structured, efficient system of state power tried to justify their stance by recourse to the Ibadhi ideology, although any link between their actions and their ideology was questionable. And every Imam conscious of the necessity to reform the feeble governmental structure was up against the *ulema*, the guardians and upholders of the now defunct tradition.

Under Ahmed bin Said the fifth dynasty since the beginning of the Islamic period moved forward. Previous dynasties, such as Julanda, Nabhan and Ya'ruba, had, through failing to curb the tribal element, lost their leading role in Omani society.

For the young Qaboos, the figure of his great ancestor was of particular importance. No image of the Imam has remained, but the boy tried to imagine his appearance, scrutinising portraits of later dynastic Imams. Though separated by two centuries they had much in common.

Imam Ahmed came to power after many years of administrative decay. Devastation and misery surrounded him. The great history of the country had already begun to fade from memory and to restore the dignity of Oman, the people's faith in the possibility of renewal also had to be restored.

Qaboos asked his mentors about the deeds of the founder of the dynasty and slowly reconstructed a picture of the epoch in which Imam Ahmed had lived. It was a difficult period, and had required in its leader a well-developed gift of foresight and the ability to recognise potential allies, while remaining prepared to confront mighty states when necessary.

By that time political reality in the Gulf depended on interrelations between states far removed from that region. Competition between France and Great Britain in Europe was leading to the formation of spheres of influence in the East. In an attempt to weaken the position of the French in the Mediterranean, the British had long ago become associates of the Ottoman empire. The French had, therefore, sought collaboration with Persia as a counterbalance to this alliance.

As Persia had been the main adversary of Omani independence down the centuries, alliance with the Ottoman Empire was natural to Oman. But Ahmed bin Said was not inclined to follow primitive logic. Instead of a union with Great Britain and opposition to France – which seemed reasonable in those circumstances – the Imam preferred a policy of equal distance from both states. This wise position manifested itself in one episode that the young Qaboos heard of during a history lesson.

During the Seven Years War (1756–1763), the French navy frequently attacked the English, trying to damage communications between Great Britain and its Indian trading stations and the Omani Gulf was often the battle arena. More than once, in pursuit of British ships, the French navy attacked them in the proximity of the Muscat forts. Coastal arms then opened fire against the French on the grounds that they were violating the freedom of the seas.[7]

The position taken by the Omani government reflected not only the need to protect the country's commercial interests, hampered as they were by such maritime piracy; it also reflected traditional Arab hospitality which enjoined that every guest should be protected.

[7]  *Oman in History*, London, Immel Publishing Ltd (1995) p. 442.

When the French captured an Omani ship transporting British goods, the Omanis in reply detained a French ship in Muscat. However, Ahmed bin Said subtly tempered the incident by inviting French King Louis XVI to open a French mission in Muscat, thereby persuading him of his friendly intentions.

Relations between Oman and Mysore also improved. The Sultan of this state, Khaidar Ali, controlled the Malabar shore of India, where such important ports as Mangalore and Calicut were situated. His son, Tippu, who acceded to the Sultanate (1782–1799), became one of Oman's major commercial partners. The two countries successfully collaborated in the struggle against pirates, and when monsoons made navigation towards India impossible, much of the Mysore fleet regularly laid up in Omani harbours.

Having reduced custom taxes from 10 per cent to 6 per cent, the Imam achieved dominance in trading with the rich Sultanate of India. Sandalwood, pepper, ivory, materials and rice were imported from India, while Muscat exported saffron, salt, horses, pearls and raisins, and carpenters built vessels for the Sultans of Mysore.

The utterly pragmatic foreign policy of Ahmed bin Said succeeded in making the country stronger and assured its economic prosperity. Possibly because he came from a family of merchants, the founder of the Al bu Said dynasty thoroughly understood economic trends and this became the strongest feature of his reign. During his rule, Muscat was transformed into a flourishing port, one of the richest in the Indian Ocean. The combination of a reasonable tax policy and internal stability drew merchants to Oman from all over the world.

The Imamate of Ahmed bin Said, lasting nearly 40 years, was a triumphant period of revived glory. From being a country unable to protect itself, Oman became, during that period of renewal, a powerful state, capable of defending its interests at sea and on the mainland. When the Persians besieged Basra in 1775 the military assistance provided by the Omani navy enabled the Turkish commander-in-chief to avoid defeat. The Persian ruler, Karim Khan, was equally unsuccessful in his aggressive policies towards Oman, finding the impressive fleet assembled by the Imam a force too strong to engage with and defeat. Ahmed bin Said had possessed only a handful of old ships at the beginning of his rule, but over the years he had succeeded in organising the resources both of the country and of private ship-owners in such a way that he could, if necessary, mobilise thousands of armed vessels. While the most outstanding Imams of the preceding Ya'ruba dynasty had depended on a strong navy, a characteristic of Ahmed bin Said's epoch was a new reliance on the commercial fleet. For the first time in the history of the country, the power of the state was based on a well-grounded economic policy.

The reforms touched all spheres of life in Oman. The administrative system became less rigid and more dynamic. The Imam paid particular attention to the choice of regional governors. He assigned the posts of *wali* to his sons so that they could practice the art of government and, to distinguish them from the country's élite, the Imam introduced the name Sayyid, as a term of respect.

But, as with a number of his predecessors, there was one crucial matter which Ahmed bin Said overlooked: the mechanism of succession. After his death this issue was to lead to further turmoil and political instability.

# Holding the Balance

THE SEVEN SONS OF THE FOUNDER of the dynasty and many of his grandsons were drawn into internal conflicts. As the eldest son, Hilal, had died before his father, the Imam declared his third son, Said, to be his successor. Omani law at that time did not clearly specify how a new Imam was to be selected, which allowed wide latitude for interpretation; Ahmed bin Said's solution was to separate secular from spiritual authority. While Said was appointed Imam and focused on spiritual leadership, Ahmed's son Hamad was granted the powers of a *de facto* governor of a state. Part of the country's territory remained under the control of Qais, the eldest living son. In order to avoid provoking a conflict with Hamad, the other two brothers respected his sphere of influence: Saif went to East Africa, and Sultan to the interior of Oman, where he attempted to establish his own sphere of control, supported mainly by nomadic tribes. When Hamad died in 1792, Sultan rushed to Muscat, where, backed by Qais, he took secular power into his own hands.

Stability and prosperity marked the eleven years of Sultan bin Ahmed's rule, though relations between the members of the ruling family were far from harmonious. Imam Said bin Ahmed was still in Rustaq and Qais ruled the part of Batinah centred on Sohar. When the Sultan set out on the *Hajj* in 1803, his nephew Badr, a son of Saif, who had died in Africa, tried to seize power in Muscat. The plot failed and Badr escaped to the Muwahhidun of central Arabia, who more than once had sought to conquer Oman.

Despite the seeming impossibility of maintaining political stability in such circumstances, civil war was avoided. It was probably Sultan's personal qualities and the inherited disposition towards consensus of the

Omani aristocracy that ensured the peaceful resolution of conflicts during his rule, despite the obvious tensions within the royal family. Though the authority of the actual ruler had never been acknowledged *de jure*, both tribal heads and the *ulema* recognised the leadership of Sultan.

Impressive new forts and a vast palace, Bait al-Alam, which remained in existence until the 1970s, became symbols of the power of the Omani ruler. Although Sultan Qaboos had the buildings (by then in a state of advanced disrepair) demolished shortly after his accession to the throne, a new palace, built on the same site, retains the name Bait al-Alam and the image of the palace, along with the Omani flag, remains the symbol of state power.

Thanks to internal stability and economic growth, Sultan bin Ahmed undertook a pro-active foreign policy with the aim of pre-empting challenges. He carried out military expeditions to the Makran coast of the Gulf of Oman (opposite Muscat and Sohar), to Hormuz, and to the island of Qishm, not far from the Iranian coast of the Strait of Hormuz. He also tried to take over Bahrain, which in previous centuries had been controlled by Oman. But the Bahrainis asked the Muwahhidun for help and frustrated Said's plans, sharply aggravating tensions between Oman and its bellicose neighbour.

The vicegerent of the Ottoman Empire was also preoccupied with the Muwahhidun threat and it seemed therefore logical that Sultan bin Ahmed and the Pasha of Baghdad should attempt to strengthen their ties, the better to combat a growing menace. A debt of gratitude already existed, as evinced by the annual tribute the Turks continued to pay to Oman for the help it had once given them during the Persian siege of Basra. So in 1804 Sultan decided to sail with a fleet to Basra.

We can presume that the Muwahhidun came to know of the circumstances of his visit and the substance of his negotiations with the Ottoman authorities. In any case, the small Omani fleet was attacked off the island of Qishm, as it was returning from Basra, by a fleet sailing from Ra's al-Khaimah. Sayyid Sultan was killed in the ensuing battle.

Said bin Sultan bin Ahmed now became ruler and managed to succeed where so many of his predecessors had failed: he created a state that was respected by some of the most powerful countries in the world. For the first time since the downfall of the caliphate, a new Arab empire emerged, created not by force of arms, but by the commercial shrewdness of the monarch (although Sultan Said more than once, particularly during the first half of his reign, called upon his army and navy to defend the state's interests).

The commercial needs of this new empire, which spanned thousands of kilometres from India to Mozambique, were served by a huge fleet that was second only to that of the British. The Omani ships were attractive prey for privateers, who since time immemorial had fed on the trade routes. A particularly high tribute was paid by trading seafarers to the inhabitants of the coasts next to the Strait of Hormuz. Here, as in the times of Sultan bin Ahmed, the Qawasim dynasty was in control. Its head, Sheikh Saqr of Sharjah, who ruled from 1803 to 1866, challenged not only his neighbours, but the British as well.

Sharjah's fleet, which consisted of several hundred ships of all sizes, was making its presence felt in the Gulf, damaging Omani state interests. When the British freighter *Minerva* was attacked on its way to Basra while transporting a cargo worth more than 100,000 rupees, the British intervened. Mutual security interests resulted in Said bin Sultan and the British forming an alliance that lasted long after the immediate threat had subsided. The Sultan had once said: 'I am nothing but a merchant'. This was not a casual remark, but expressed the true feelings of the head of the enormously successful commercial enterprise which his empire had become. In this respect his mentality was like that of the monarchs of Europe – driven by a mercantile spirit.

Said bin Sultan undoubtedly forged these coalitions for pragmatic reasons, for he preferred to have mighty friends and not powerful enemies. But his allies' victories did not always benefit Oman. After Ra's al-Khaimah suffered two humiliating defeats, the sheikhs of what the British had somewhat controversially labelled the 'Pirate Coast' were obliged to sign a Common Peace Treaty (1820) which was later confirmed by a Sea Armistice (1853) and an Unlimited Sea Armistice (1853). From then on, the 'Pirate Coast' was known as the Trucial Coast or Trucial Oman (the latter name lasting until 1971, when the seven emirates forming the Trucial States united to establish a new independent state: the United Arab Emirates). For centuries the Omani state had nurtured ambitions to extend its power over the Gulf region, but the treaties signed with the British and local sheikhs brought these moves to an end. Now the state turned its attention to Africa.

# All the Riches
# of the Earth

AYYID SAID BIN SULTAN'S POSITION as ruler was underpinned by traditional systems of government and an acceptance of dynastic succession that found widespread support at all levels of society. But not everyone was in agreement. During the more than 50 years of the Sultan's reign there were many tribal revolts and appeals for restoration of the conservative systems of government characteristic of certain periods of the Imamate. But these attempts to contest the Sultan's plenary powers had little impact, despite complaints of economic difficulties, social injustice and national humiliation. Said bin Sultan's country was generally regarded as a model state whose economic progress had supported fundamental improvements in the well-being of all classes of society and turned Oman into a major player on the international stage.

Once the young Sayyid Qaboos had learned the fundamentals of the dynasty's history, he began to focus on the achievements of his great ancestor, in particular, his transformation of Oman into one of the great states of the Indian Ocean. He studied all the different facets of Said bin Sultan's political life, because, from an early age, he dreamed of matching his ancestor's great triumphs. The world in which Sayyid Qaboos lived was very different to that in which Said bin Sultan had carried out his far-reaching policies, but the country's essential characteristics and people had not changed and the same potential for success existed. The sky and the earth remained the same, the same people continued to live on the ocean shores, in piedmont oases and in the desert space – why, then, should one generation blossom, while another struggled for survival?

As he explored the characters and policies of all his predecessors, Qaboos came to understand that the truly outstanding men of the past had in common more than intelligence and competence; they also possessed the capacity to dream and the passionate desire to realise their dreams.

Qaboos was fascinated by Said bin Sultan's own personality and the romanticism that accompanied descriptions of his exploits. It was easy to imagine his majestic figure, his proud bearing and his noble face, authoritative in the heat of battle somewhere in the deserts of Arabia or the savannahs of Africa, or amidst raging waves during a skirmish with pirates. The name Said bin Sultan evoked for the young Sayyid images of distant territories and towns of legendary beauty that had once belonged to Oman.

Zanzibar held a particular fascination for Qaboos and he was intrigued by old images showing elegant ornamented houses – their wooden carvings creating facades quite different to those with which he was familiar. Zanzibar was a place of cool walkways, the narrow streets protected from the worst of the sun by the tall stone houses which flanked their sides. Ships from all over the world crowded its bays – vessels of all sizes, from dhows and *sambuqs* with fore-and-aft lateen sails to many-masted frigates and vast steamers with their imposing smokestacks. Sometimes Qaboos came across illustrations showing throngs of people in loincloths, and, standing slightly apart, Arabs in Omani dress, *dishdashas* and sandals, with silver *khanjars* under their belts . . .

Said bin Sultan was not the first sovereign in the history of Oman to understand the importance of sea power and to fix his eyes on the rich lands of East Africa. Arab forts and trading houses already established at intervals along the coastline for thousands of kilometres southwards from Cape Guardafui, the north-eastern extremity of Africa, attested to an existing network of well-developed commercial links.

From the first centuries of Islam these lands had attracted enterprising seafarers and merchants from the Gulf. The Omanis were among the first colonists from Arabia. So the contacts between this region and the land of their ancestors grew ever stronger. Flicking through the books in the palace library, beside an open window with a view of the ocean, the shortest route to Zanzibar – it was easy for an imaginative young boy to forget the present and imagine himself transported with the Arab seamen to those alluring shores.

At the beginning of the tenth century, a prominent medieval historian and geographer, al-Masudi, visited East Africa. In his book, *Gold Refining and Mining for Precious Minerals*, he writes: 'The *zinjes* have settled in this locality, their lands bordering Sofala – and these are the outskirts of the country of the *zinjes* . . . This is a land rich in gold, rich in luxury goods, fertile, hot.' One can picture the verdant country of long ago, where caravans of black porters bore elephant tusks, leopard skins and rhinoceros horns from the interior for sale to the merchants who gathered in the ports to purchase these exotic goods for distant markets. In the white city on the green coast with its vibrant trading atmosphere, gold, silver and iron, extracted from the depths of Africa, change hands. Buyers and sellers speak Swahili, the language of the coast, a language containing many Arabic words.

When the Portuguese arrived, they were amazed by the wealth, beauty and comfort of the Arab towns of the African coast. Nevertheless, this did not deter the new invaders from wreaking destruction, and the lovely settlements were brutally devastated. A German, Hans Mayer, who was on the flagship *San Rafael*, witnessed the assault of Kilwa, the major trading city on the coast, in 1505.

It is all the more dispiriting to learn that an Arab ruler, Malindi, helped the Portuguese to gain a foothold on the East African coast. He hoped that the newcomers would aid him in his conflict with the neighbouring town of Mombasa. The ships of Admiral Vasco da Gama received water and provisions, enabling them to continue on their voyage. And, most importantly, an excellent pilot, Ahmed bin Majid – Omani by origin – was seconded to help them. It was he who showed the European colonisers the way to India. When, years later, he realised that he had brought wolves in sheep's clothing to the pastures of Arcadia, he bitterly lamented:

> *In the year of Nine hundred five the Portuguese sailed down to India,*
> *They settled there, they began to strike up acquaintances,*
> *relying on the governors.*
> *People distrusted them . . . Oh, if I had known what they were up to!*
> *People were astonished by their deeds.*

Despite sustained efforts by local communities to resist the Portuguese, they were cruelly suppressed by the Portuguese garrisons, billeted in impregnable forts such as Fort Jesus in Mombasa.

A century and a half later, when news of the collapse of Portuguese rule in Oman reached the Arab settlements in East Africa, the hope of freedom was rekindled.

In 1646 the inhabitants of Pemba Island, just north of Zanzibar, rebelled against the Portuguese and were supported in their rebellion by armed forces drawn from towns on the mainland. Realising that they could not hope to achieve the expulsion of the Portuguese on their own, the rebels called on Oman for help. The Imam responded to the appeal by despatching his warriors as soon as the winter monsoons got under way, but it took several decades for the combined forces of the Imam and the local militia to oust the Portuguese. Only in 1699 were the last Arab towns of East Africa freed, and all along the coast, up to Mozambique, the power of the Imam was recognised.

When the state of Ya'ruba fell, many local rulers made the most of the opportunity and proclaimed independence. Even the powerful Ahmed bin Said, the founder of the new dynasty, could not re-establish Omani sovereignty in the East African territories. To achieve this historic task the country had to replenish its army and its fleet and repulse external threats. This became a reality only in the first half of the nineteenth century, when a new state, shaped to a significant degree by the character of its ruler, was formed.

Under the power of the Omani Sultans and Imams, Zanzibar became a centre of importance in East Africa and a base for economic development in this part of the continent. Arab merchants had penetrated the region of the great African lakes much earlier than the Europeans. Nineteenth century travellers, such as Livingstone and Stanley, were surprised to find old Arab settlements in the depths of the 'virgin lands'. During Sayyid Said's reign the Arabs extended their involvement with this region beyond the traditional trade in ivory, gold and slaves to become agriculturalists, growing cash crops for sale in Zanzibar markets.

It seems initially curious that Sultan Said made no attempt to seize territories and create a colonial empire similar to those of the Europeans. But the Arab settlements, which stretched in a loose chain from Oman to Mozambique, had long been centres of Arab culture and trade, magnets for the Africans of the interior. Relations between them had been based on mutual advantage, and not on dominance and submission. What need had the Sultan of Oman to change this relationship when he had achieved what mattered most – a united country, basking in peace and prosperity?

In 1828 and 1829 Said bin Sultan personally directed the military operations of the Omani fleet in East Africa. For the first time he visited Zanzibar, and, understanding its commercial and strategic military importance, decided to construct the empire's second capital there. Within a few years, the relatively small Arab settlement had become a major town. The local population called it 'Stone Town', because the Arabs used techniques of construction hitherto unknown in those parts. Indeed, never before had even the Arabs built on such a scale and with such refinement. The use of wood, the major building material of past centuries, was developed in Zanzibar to embellish its houses with exquisite inlays resembling intricately ornamented brocades on doors, doorjambs and balconies. These highly decorative buildings represented the highest expression of Swahili culture. The festive atmosphere of this city of white walls and skilful carvings reflected the openness and hospitality of the Omanis, seafarers and merchants, people of great learning and curiosity.

The narrow, shaded streets were designed so that air could circulate freely, and the temperature within the city was always lower than that beyond the boundaries.

Said bin Sultan grew to love this city, the embodiment of his dreams. Having spent many years making the annual voyage between Muscat and Zanzibar, he finally decided to settle in Zanzibar permanently. From 1840 he resided mainly in his African dominion, taking an active part in the provision of utilities to the villages, in the organisation of spice plantations, and in the management of Zanzibar's expanding industrial base.

On the orders of the Sultan, a marvellous three-storied palace, with many adjoining buildings for servants, was built in Mtoni, a suburb of Zanzibar. In the centre of the palace were situated luxurious Persian baths, generously adorned with pictures and mosaics. Here numerous members of the Sultan's family passed their time reading the Qur'an or Arab poetry and listening to the local music (ta'arab).

Not far from this residence, completed by 1834, the Sultan ordered the construction of another, more splendid palace. The site he chose was a headland jutting out into the ocean, with a magnificent view of small green islands surrounded by reefs. At the end of the day the sun set in the midst of them. The Sultan, who relished poetical moments when alone by the seashore, imagined himself saying farewell to the setting sun from the terrace of his new palace, Bait al-Ras.

Construction continued for almost ten years, but the Sultan did not live to see the building completed. His descendants did not maintain the palace and it fell into ruin. Nowadays palms sway above it, saying farewell to the sinking sun, the rustle of their leaves like the murmuring of poetry remembered from the days of the Sultan.

An enormous volume of goods passed through Zanzibar in those years. The ports could not keep up with the unprecedented commercial boom. A German traveller, Karl Klaus von Decken, who visited the island between 1859 and 1861, wrote:

> *The outward appearance of the customs house does not correspond at all to the amount of treasure that passes though the hands of the banyan, [Indian merchant] and which is then loaded for further shipment or is sold here, on the spot. Lately there has been some transformation and addition. Some neighbourhoods even now are nothing but miserable little huts, yet inside them life is busy and effervescent from morning till night; crowds of people, coming and going, move ceaselessly like waves, and Europe, Asia and America exchange their treasures with Africa.*

Books describing Oman's former dominance and sophistication aroused a determination in the young boy that his country would once again realise its marvellous potential. Said bin Sultan was to remain Qaboos bin Said's model of greatness throughout his childhood and beyond. Many of Sultan Qaboos's own decisions would have something in common with those of his great ancestor.

In contrast to the Imams of the Ya'ruba dynasty, who had also governed Zanzibar and the neighbouring territories but had regarded those lands as peripheral, Said bin Sultan realised their strategic importance and great economic promise, which exceeded that of the Arabian lands of the empire. Being an ardent patriot of his native country, however, he concentrated his efforts on developing the economy of Zanzibar and adjacent domains, showing himself an assiduous ruler and adept at predicting market trends. On his initiative plantations of new crops, especially cloves, were established on Zanzibar, thus reorienting the island's agriculture to meet the demands of overseas markets. The Sultan also instituted a policy of 'redevelopment', which aimed at a closer integration of the economies of East Africa, in order to ensure the sustainable development of Oman.

By the end of his first period of rule (1822–1840) he had gained full control of the coast from Mogadishu in the north to the frontier with Portuguese Mozambique in the south.

Forts were built in those port towns that were the endpoints of trade routes through the continent. For instance, Dar es Salaam was the terminus of the great caravan route from what is now Uganda, Rwanda, Burundi and the Congo, and Kilwa was a starting-point for caravans to Njasa and beyond (through what is now Malawi and Zambia). A unique administrative system was introduced. The local authorities were in the hands of superiors (*kadhis*) and deputies (*walis*).

Forts were also built along the ancient trade routes, which enabled Arab colonisation to make deeper inroads into the continent. Sayyid Said personally supervised the new construction sites, because he thought that government revenues could only increase if the security of commerce could be assured.

He proved to be correct; the flow of ivory, turtle shells, palm oil, skins and furs grew year by year. The labour market also expanded, because demand for manpower in the French island colonies of the Indian Ocean increased sharply and the development of spice plantations in Zanzibar created favourable economic conditions as well.[8]

The more young Qaboos learned about the life of his great-great-grandfather, the more he admired his gift of foresight. He had achieved things that even a century after his death seemed applicable to modern Oman.

---

[8] J.C. Wilkinson makes some interesting comments on the economy of Zanzibar: 'Cheap labour was used for three main tasks: as gatherers of natural products, as cultivators and as porters. The main production involving the first was copal (Burton 1860, Appendix 1), used for lacquer and varnishes. So great had the demand become that it became Zanzibar's chief export by mid-century and Speke (1860) estimated some 19 million lbs were exported annually, the cargo for some 12 or 13 large ships. Copal was produced on the mainland coast, up to some 30 miles inland, and along the coconut plantations and copra estates (which developed in Lamu, Malindi and Mombasa in the 1860s; cf. Miege 1982) lay in the domain of the Sultan of Zanzibar and his coastal subordinate sheikhdoms. The great product of the island state of Zanzibar and dependent Pemba was, of course, the clove, which Sd. Said encouraged but in no way started. From beginnings around 1820 Zanzibar was exporting nearly 5 million lbs by the end of his reign and nearly five times that figure after the Second World War, when it produced some four-fifths of the world's trade. Unlike copal gathering,

Throughout the empire he had established a kind of free economic zone with 5 per cent duties. As a result, ships from every country with commercial interest in the Indian Ocean preferred the ports of Said's state. Realising the importance of stimulating trade, the Sultan conducted a simple and effective monetary and credit policy, aimed at substituting the Omani currency for the foreign currencies dominant in the region. The success of this policy was reflected in a sharp rise in the number of Omani coins in circulation. The income of Zanzibar in the period of Said bin Sultan's rule increased ten-fold. Arabs from Yemen and Oman, attracted by the economic boom, flocked to the Sultan's African dominion. On Zanzibar alone, the population doubled.

Many things written about the times of Sayyid Said are strikingly topical. His statecraft, similar to that of the leaders of the most developed countries in the mid-twentieth century, seemed to Sayyid Qaboos to provide a suitable template for transforming Oman into a significant power once again: what he saw around him seemed backward when compared to conditions during the epoch of the great Sultan. He admired particularly the Sultan's dedication to the principle of direct and frequent consultation with his people.

Despite commanding a vast and powerful state, the Said bin Sultan appeared to Qaboos to have been neither arrogant nor despotic. Representatives of the population gathered in his palaces on Fridays and Mondays and his espousal of democratic freedoms made him extremely popular with his subjects, as did the interest he took in their personal affairs. Hearing of a sad or joyful event in their lives, he would visit them with words of consolation or congratulation. The famous traveller, Sir Richard Burton, who knew Sayyid Said, said of him: 'One felt that one was before a majestic personality, religious but not intolerant, kind and noble.'[9]

cloves were produced entirely with slave labour on plantations, and it was on this that Arab fortunes were primarily based. This specialisation in cloves, along with other plantation crops like sugar, in turn tended to push out more local standard produce, rice and coconuts (thereby also reducing the African and Shirazi land holdings in favour of the Arabs) and this, coupled with the growing consumption of Zanzibar's own population, incited greater productivity elsewhere for staples. So a dhow trade developed up and down the coast in grain: similarly there was an increase in the exploitation of timber, some of which was also exported to Arabia. Imports also increased, notably textiles, grain, dates and salt. Some of these, it should be noted, were products of Arabia, so that home production in Oman itself was becoming geared to the African market in the middle of the nineteenth century, but the main demand was for Indian rice which was always considered higher quality than African.' J.C. Wilkinson, *The Imamate Traditions of Oman,* Cambridge, Cambridge University Press (1987) p. 59.

[9] R. F. Burton, *The Lake Regions of Central Africa,* London (1860) vol. 2 pp. 194–195.

One of the factors creating social stability in the empire of Said bin Sultan was the lack of discrimination against any national, religious or social group. During his reign, Indian merchants gained total commercial freedom and became a major feature of economic life from Mozambique to Arabia. The good relations between India and Oman in that period created a valuable reservoir of goodwill on which both countries were still able to rely many decades later.

Contacts with East Africa, which had existed for over a millennium, became particularly strong in the days of Sayyid Said not only because of increased trade but also because of the rapid spread of Islam. History has recorded the names of many Omanis whose proselytising fervour penetrated the depths of the African continent and converted many tribal leaders, kings and ordinary tribesmen to Islam. This activity was encouraged by the monarch, who did much to create a system of Islamic education and to develop a judicial system based on *shari'a*. This new culture built on Islamic values, having taken root among the people, also became a basis for close relations between Oman and the peoples of Africa – relations which were to survive into the post-colonial era.

So deeply embedded were the changes wrought by Said bin Sultan that his immediate successors were able to continue effortlessly in the implementation of his policies and ideas. One hundred years after his death, his distantly connected descendant recognised their undiminished relevance and began to undertake transformations, similar to those of the creator of the great state of the Indian Ocean.

When on 19 October 1856 Said bin Sultan died on board the *Victoria* en route from Muscat to Zanzibar, his empire was flourishing. Who could have thought that not many years after his death not even a trace would be left of that glory and that this empire would be riven once again by war and revolt?

For the future Sultan Qaboos, the stormy century that followed the death of his celebrated ancestor was too pertinent to be viewed as 'history'; rather it was the crucial precursor of the world in which he now lived. The Industrial Revolution and the collapse of the old empires had forced the birth of a new world, one which endorsed new ideals and which was awaiting new leaders.

# Far from Home

QABOOS KEPT LOOKING out of the window of the military transport plane departing for Britain. The variety of landscapes within his native country, seen for the first time from high above, was striking. The whole of Salalah, with its streets, palm groves and gardens, was visible. Even from above, the old palace seemed taller than the other buildings. Far away, by the edge of the shore, stood Taqa, the home of his beloved mother.

The higher he flew, the more boundless seemed the ocean. Its silken surface was empty all the way to the horizon, where the water merged with the air in a pearly mist. The plane banked to the left and, when it straightened its course, the hilly brown plateau of Dhofar, crossed by deep *wadis*, stretched out below.

For century upon century the sun has shone relentlessly on the Arabian land. It has baked the stones and dried up the beds of ancient streams – from high above, the work of the millennia lay bare in all its awe-inspiring magnificence. In this expanse, any shrub was seen as a gift from God, given as protection from the light of the 'fire that severs day from night'. How Qaboos was to miss that fire later, under the grey skies of Europe!

When Qaboos bin Said arrived in London, the sensitive young man was overwhelmed by the contrasts. Everything aroused a burning interest – the vegetation, the buildings, the people, the vehicles.

As a car rushed him from the airport, he looked all around, trying not to let anything escape his gaze: bulky red buses, the hurly-burly of pedestrian traffic, the endless variety of advertising slogans and images, the rich green parks, the faded green of the bronze statues, the mellow stones of the ancient churches and the steel-grey waters of the Thames. After the calm of Salalah this huge city seemed an infinite and mysterious labyrinth.

The Sultan, Said bin Taimur, had chosen the county of Suffolk, lying north-east of the British capital, as the place for his son to begin his studies abroad. It is a land of fields, coppices, marshes and small rivers. Leaving behind the red-brick London suburbs, the train rushes past rounded hills overgrown with shrubs; compact towns with identical single- or two-storey houses, and with chimneys protruding from the tiled roofs; ancient cottages next to overgrown ponds; flocks of large black birds scattering the fields; herds of cattle, sheep and horses in green pastures.

High-voltage lines, railway tracks going off in all directions, freight trains laden with coal, smoking factory chimneys – all these ordinary sights of the landscape were viewed by the Sultan's heir with the same enthusiasm as tourists generally view the famous monuments and palaces of London. There was nothing like this in Oman at that time. Even telephone poles were a wonder in Salalah.

In the middle of green fields there were often goalposts; sometimes one saw teams of children or adults running after a ball. Everywhere there were people strolling with unusual creatures that could just about be described as dogs. But it was not long before the Sayyid started to distinguish greyhounds, setters, dachshunds and the other breeds so dear to the English heart.

At first Bury St Edmunds seemed rather gloomy to Qaboos and much less attractive than he had imagined. But on closer inspection the town began to reveal its charm to the Sayyid. There were many nooks and crannies which made every new exploration exciting. Everything here was different from his homeland.

Entering beneath the mellow arches of the ancient abbey's gate gave the Sayyid the sense of travelling backwards in time. Within that serene enclosure, everyday bustle fades away. Among the ancient pines, oaks and maples, among ruins that jut out like grey fingers above the green grass carpet, time itself slows down. Under the chestnut trees are simple wooden benches, placed there by residents of the town in memory of their parents, their names inscribed on copper plates. The hours spent there reading books could seem like days. The sounds of modern civilisation did not penetrate the walls of the monastery. All that could be heard was the hubbub of geese and ducks by the river that flowed through the abbey, and the sound of the ancient fountain with its water trickling down its stone tiers.

There were so many unfamiliar things to delight in – the Angel Hotel, covered in crimson Virginia Creeper, the word 'Saxon' in the names of shops and pubs, reminding the locals of their ancestors. Even the shop windows were entrancingly different, with pasties shaped like saucepans and frying pans, platters of large iced buns each crowned with a little red cherry, and spice cakes in the shapes of little men in chocolate hats. Amidst the commercial commotion of the central square, his gaze would rest upon a monument to the fallen in a faraway, bygone war. Its stone figure of a soldier, sitting wearily on a boulder, evoked the vanished age of the great empires.

The inviting cries of traders, the sound of music and people's voices retreat into the most secluded corners of consciousness while the images conjured by a simple monument cluster inside the mind. Around the pedestal are inscribed column upon column of the names of local citizens killed in the Boer War. How many, he wondered, still remember how, and for what, the children of the farmers, traders and workers of Bury St Edmund fell? If one multiplied the number of the victims in this one location by the hundreds and thousands of similar English localities, it was clear that this war, now so remote in time, must once have been the biggest event in the lives of millions.

Qaboos experienced such fragments of the past intensely, grieved as he was by the historical oblivion into which his own homeland had sunk. Only a hundred years before, the great empire of Said bin Sultan, alive with the rich colours of the many cultures of Asia, Africa and Europe, was known in the remotest realms. And now . . .

The young man blushed each time he was called upon to explain where Oman was. Eventually, he bought a pocket atlas in a bookshop and used it to show the location of his native land. It is probable that dissatisfaction with the situation in the Sultanate had already begun to take root in Qaboos's mind, and Oman's apparent insignificance to countries outside Arabia would have accelerated his resolution to revitalise his country.

Even before his arrival in England, Sayyid Qaboos knew how keenly interested in the events of the Arab world its citizens were. The London newspapers delivered to Salalah were full of large headlines reporting the risky actions of Colonel Nasser: the purchase of arms from communist Czechoslovakia, the nationalisation of the Suez Canal. But in tranquil Salalah itself it seemed that events taking place in distant Cairo and the other Arab capitals did not concern Oman at all.

The failure of the ill-trained and haphazardly armed troops of the Arab rulers in 1948 not only provoked discontent among officers but also led to a military coup in Egypt and anti-monarchical plots in Jordan and Iraq. The generation of Arab politicians, whose formative experiences took place in the second half of the 1950s, concluded that the failure of rulers in 1948 to evaluate the global situation correctly in the light of local interests meant that the chance of exploiting the changes in the disposition of international power was missed. Sultan Qaboos, avidly absorbing new political theories and practical knowledge, turned out to be one of the ablest young Arab leaders. He succeeded in learning the lessons of those turbulent times.

Fifteen years would pass and the world would become even more complicated and confrontation would reach an unprecedented scale; Sultan Qaboos's foreign policy, aimed at averting threats, would be one of the foundations for the independent development of Oman, with the well-being of the army and its readiness for combat the lynchpin of that policy.

But for the time being, the pupil of a private school in an ancient English town followed current events on television (an unknown luxury in Oman), soaking up reports from the Middle East, listening to the predictions of new wars and hearing the scarcely concealed anxiety in the voices of commentators; few of them were optimistic. The bitter aftermath of the Suez adventure was still fresh.

As soon as Israeli troops had invaded Sinai, as soon as British aeroplanes bombed Port Said, reporters filled the airwaves and newspaper pages with victorious communiqués. For some days it seemed that the empire was being revived, and the hearts of Her Majesty's subjects were overwhelmed by patriotism. But how pitilessly these illusions were shattered. With a shameful defeat, a government crisis and the triumph of Nasser, the outdated dogmas of empire were swiftly washed away.

The prestige of Nasser, who after the events of Suez became an acknowledged leader of Arab nationalism, rose enormously. The 38-year-old colonel became an idol for youth of all social classes from Morocco to the Indian Ocean and his portraits adorned the dwellings of poor men and princes alike. Before 1962, when a group of officers launched a coup against the Imam in Yemen and Nasser provided Egyptian troops to aid the conspirators, few people in the Arab world had the courage to criticise him. Sultan Qaboos's father was one of the rare exceptions.

The creation of a United Arab Republic in 1958 aroused enthusiasm everywhere in the Arabic-speaking world. The kings of Jordan and Iraq, whose wish was to create an Arab federation to counterbalance the Egyptian–Syrian state, were accused of being Western agents.

Centuries of colonial domination, first by the Turks, then by the European states, came to an end. Many now believed that the Arab world had entered an era of dynamic development, and that political independence would be accompanied by the improvement of life in all respects.

But the first visible sign of the new era was instability, provoked by the struggle of different political groups for power. Cairo was the organisational headquarters of the propaganda war against unfriendly regimes, and it directed all of Nasser's followers.

In revolutionary Iraq, clashes between communists and nationalists erupted. The Ba'ath movement, dissatisfied with the revolutionary leader General Kassem's opposition to Nasser, made an attempt on his life. Prominent in this action was the 22-year-old Saddam Hussein. Disturbances in Bahrain continued. A war of national liberation was heating up in Algeria. Oman too was suffering the first tremors of disruption.

From the reaction of the British press and public opinion (so fearful of a reigniting of the Suez embarrassment), Qaboos gained a lively impression of the instability of the situation back home. But looking through the window of his room at boarding school, seeing the tiled roofs of the ancient town, the gothic needle of the cathedral church of St James rising into the overcast sky and the grey stone of the gate tower of the Benedictine Abbey, it was difficult to wrest his imagination from this serene little world and transport it to the sun-baked lands of the Middle East.

In his years at Bury St Edmunds, Qaboos became accustomed to Western culture. The very atmosphere of the venerable town, named after the shrine of the last king of the east of England, inspired him to plunge into the world of ancient lore and architectural antiquities. Bury, notwithstanding its insubstantial size, has a glorious history, epitomised in the town's motto, 'A king's shrine is the cradle of the law'. Apart from the fact that King Edmund (killed by the Vikings in the ninth century) became one of the major saints of England, the abbey that bears his name was the birthplace of the first constitution. Before its high altar, a group of barons swore revolt against King John should he refuse to sign the Magna Carta.

Qaboos was fascinated by photography and took a camera everywhere, trying to capture the remarkable places and scenes. When he had mastered the fundamentals of photography, he started to experiment with chiaroscuro. He took close-ups of flowers, plants and leaves. He planned his shots carefully in advance. He was especially fond of landscapes and tried to find an attractive background, even when photographing people. Suffolk charms with its subtle beauty. Flat valleys are relieved by gently sloping hills, their crests adorned with modest country churches, windmills, forests and villages; quiet, rural cemeteries set in trees, their clusters of white gravestones looking, from a distance, like flocks of birds; large herds of thickly-fleeced sheep, quite unlike the sheep that nibble the tough grass on the mountains of Dhofar. The camera shutter clicked at every hour of the day, preserving for ever a beautiful sunset, oak trees bent under the wind, a swirling, multi-layered cloud lit by the setting sun. In this region of England, as an English poet has said, there is a mile of sky for every inch of land. One can gaze at the sky for hours as an invisible force in the heavens erects and destroys aerial castles, forms bizarre faces and drives fleets of shape-changing celestial ships effortlessly from one end of the world to the other.

Classical music was another of Sayyid's pastimes. His natural love of music had been fostered by the songs and dance melodies which were so much a part of his childhood in Oman. Music was an integral part of the many festivals held in Salalah during Qaboos's childhood – not just the music of Oman itself, but music brought to Salalah by merchants and sailors from throughout the East. Songs from Yemen, India, Iran and Indonesia pervaded the streets, the houses and the palace itself.

In England the Sayyid became more deeply acquainted with the music of the West, studying composition and the particularities of different musical genres. This growth of musical awareness was of service later when he began to play classical pieces himself and was instrumental in his decision to inaugurate the first symphony orchestra in Oman.

During his two years in Great Britain, he came to a much better understanding of the problems of the modern world. Armed with only the most rudimentary grasp of European civilisation at the beginning of his sojourn, he had, on departure, a thorough knowledge of the history and the culture of the West.

His political interests likewise changed. As his horizons widened, he grew to realise that to confine his interest to the affairs of his homeland and the Arab world was not only politically naïve, but impossible to one who had grasped the fact that all these events were links in the same chain. It was precisely for that reason that Said bin Taimur sent his son to study in the West. He himself had received an excellent education, and cultivated a wide range of interests, and though he maintained an isolationist foreign policy, he was capable of realistically evaluating the geopolitical balance of power. It was his capacity for realistic evaluation which made the Sultan so sceptical of pan-Arab nationalism at a time when all the other Arab rulers continued to pay tribute to this ideology. Events were to show the prescience of the Sultan. The gradual devaluation of Nasser's political stock and the resulting isolation of the revolutionary leaders demonstrated that the dominant tendency in the Arab world was still that of strengthening national sovereignty. The idea of integration acquired new life in forms completely different from those envisaged by the ideologists of pan-Arabism in the 1940s and 1950s.

Qaboos was influenced by the respectful attitude shown to him as a representative of Oman by officials, teachers, military officers and fellow pupils. His country was one of the few that stood by Great Britain in difficult times. Most ex-allies changed orientation and sided with the United States or the Soviet Union, but his father acted in accordance with the Omani proverb, 'Better old silk than new wool'. Despite his firm desire to act independently, he never resorted to underhand deals and never plotted against London, though other Arab countries would surely have welcomed such actions.

As the United Kingdom entangled itself in economic and financial difficulties, its obligations towards the Gulf countries and their neighbours became an unbearable burden. Even before the Suez collapse, the withdrawal of Great Britain's armed forces from the region was a topic of discussion in the upper echelons of power.

The Baghdad Pact, uniting Turkey, Iraq, Iran and Pakistan, occupied a special place among the treaties sponsored by the West. Pakistan was regarded as playing an important role in the defence of the region, as it maintained a pro-British orientation. In such circumstances, the loss to Pakistan in 1958 of the last overseas dominion of the great Omani empire, the Gawadar enclave on the Makran coast of the Gulf of Oman, was not surprising, given the strategic importance of Pakistan to Britain.

From 1947, the newly-created country of Pakistan surrounded this enclave of the Sultanate of Oman. The leadership of the young Muslim state saw in Gawadar a fragment of the colonial heritage, and did not conceal its intention of absorbing this strategically important piece of land into Pakistan by whatsoever means might be necessary. From the beginning of this dispute, Britain put pressure on Said bin Taimur, urging him to start negotiations concerning Gawadar's cession.

When the Sultan visited London in the summer of 1958, the question of the enclave was one of the main issues in his meetings with the British leadership and Sayyid Said agreed to start discussions with Pakistan on the matter. In July 1958 a resolution was finally reached and a special relationship between Gawadar and Oman was defined.

If some immediate effect had accrued – the improvement of water supplies, say, or the institution of a basic healthcare service – this would have increased the Sultan's popularity. But although the British offered these and other benefits, including projects to develop the Omani education system, Said bin Taimur declined all such proposals.

During the decades of revenue shortfalls, when he spared no effort to keep his country out of debt, he regarded extravagance as the cardinal vice of a ruler. Such an approach may have been justified in difficult times, but it became a hindrance when the financial prospects of Oman finally improved. The Sultan was incapable of altering his engrained habits and continued to economise on everything.

It was while Sayyid Qaboos was studying in England that these negotiations between his father and the British government took place, his father staying, as he sometimes did for several weeks at a time, in the Dorchester, the famous 1920s hotel overlooking London's Hyde Park. During the visit, Said bin Taimur was constantly busy with meetings and negotiations with politicians, military personnel and businessmen and saw little of his son. The heir wanted so much to ask his father about what was happening in Oman, about his plans, about their relatives and acquaintances. But the questions remained unasked. The letters of his mother were more informative; though they did not say much about political events, they helped Qaboos to retain a sense of connection with his home and country.

The bond between mother and son grew stronger with the years, while relations with his father cooled. At first Qaboos wondered at the reasons behind this, but as he grew older he began to understand that the Sultan's growing fear of change made him suspicious and distrustful.

Sultan Qaboos remembered how much his father talked about his wish to improve the lives of his subjects, how often he mused aloud about the day when fountains of oil would gush forth from the Omani sands. But his father gradually lost his interest in optimistic projects. The unstable political situation altered his character. He felt an outsider in the world, where the voices of new leaders were drowning him out. All his efforts to declare himself an autonomous leader met with resistance. Time after time, Arab countries blocked his attempts to enter international organisations – the Universal Postal Union, the World Health Organisation, the Food and Agriculture Organisation. It became more and more difficult for his British friends and their allies to restrain the attacks in the UN on the Sultan's regime. In the hands of Nasser and his followers in the Third World, the so-called Omani question turned into a weapon of political blackmail. The countries of the communist bloc voted for every anti-Omani resolution submitted to the Committee on Decolonisation (established in 1961) and the General Assembly.

Said bin Taimur's reactionary image was, to a great extent, the creation of his opponents, whose condemnation of the Sultan's regime, combined with a refusal to recognise their own deeply reactionary nature, ensured both the Sultan's increasing withdrawal and his mounting distrust of intellectuals – the main exponents of the nationalist, leftist ideals so dear to his critics. The fall of the ruling dynasties in Egypt, Iraq and Yemen as the result of plots by pro-Nasser officers heightened his fear of change.

Any ruler is first of all a human being and the Sultan's isolation, together with the hostility he experienced from those whom he might in happier times have seen as his associates, could only feed his suspicion and mistrust of those around him. Such conditions induce political paralysis. There was, in a sense, no right move for the Sultan to make, for while doing nothing left him open to accusations of neglecting the welfare of his people, any attempts at reform might have been interpreted as the manoeuvring of a politician and derided as such.

The Sayyid's studies in Bury ended in the summer of 1960. His private tutors considered that the heir to the Omani throne had mastered English sufficiently well to begin a course at the Royal Military Academy at Sandhurst. The Sayyid was very excited. For the first time he had to immerse himself in the world of professional soldiers, very different from the hothouse of Salalah and Bury. The closer he got to Sandhurst, the more unusual everything around him seemed, even the landscape – so different to the quiet idyllic sceneries of Eastern England. Situated on the Berkshire border, 50 kilometres from London, Sandhurst is one of the best-known and most respected military schools in the world.

On being admitted to Sandhurst in the autumn of 1960, Sayyid Qaboos was given a British military identity card, on which his name was preceded by 'HRH'. In every other respect it was a standard army document. But to the young heir this rectangle of paper seemed a great treasure and many times he took it out to admire the photograph glued to the card, in which he sported a cadet uniform and unusually short hair.

Qaboos bin Said had learnt English well in his two years at Bury St Edmunds, so lectures on military history and other special subjects did not present the difficulties for him that they did for many of his fellow students from Asia. Although military service was tough for everyone, it was particularly difficult for one who from birth had been brought up to be a ruler. From the moment Qaboos entered the school, he had to forget everything he had been accustomed to from childhood – the deference and the privilege – and learn the formative art of submission himself.

Potential regular officers undergo a two-year course. In six thirteen- or fourteen-week terms, a cadet has to master an intense programme of military education. The enormous physical and psychological load of the first term makes it the most difficult time for the recruits. During this period, three-mile runs are conducted daily in full marching kit. Drill on the parade ground, cleaning rooms, assembling and stripping weapons, cleaning ammunition, washing uniforms – all this is drilled into young men accustomed to an easy life.

Sergeants castigate the unskilful at every slip; senior students pour out torrents of abuse. As the tutors say, the purpose of the first term is to knock all the nonsense and laziness out of the recruits; not until then is it possible to turn them into effective commanders. This is the basis of every military school throughout the world: without learning to submit, a person cannot become a part of the military machine.

This system develops tenacity, precision and determination in its students. It is not by chance that so many political leaders have had a military education. The monarchs of the East have long appreciated the merits of the British military school and have willingly sent their sons to Sandhurst, the motto of which is 'Serve to lead'. Many years later, speaking to the graduates of the school, Sultan Qaboos bin Said himself would say: 'I learned that with responsibility comes obligation.'

On the walls of the Royal Military Academy one can read the roll call of those who became the pride of their countries. Among the British pupils of Sandhurst are Sir Winston Churchill and Field Marshal Montgomery. The latter visited the school many times while Qaboos was studying there. The old soldier (he was over 70 then) was a distinguished character with remarkable poise. The legendary victor over Rommel at El-Alamein seemed to the students to personify the British military spirit. Rarely did a week go by without a VIP visit. Members of the royal family, foreign leaders and military delegations showed up during lectures, sports sessions and at the firing range for Sandhurst was (and remains) a showcase for the British system of military education and a custodian of rich army traditions

A visit to the museum was a must for every guest. First-year students also began their life at Sandhurst here. Crossing the threshold of the old building, they found themselves in a temple to the dedication and courage of generations of the British army. Pyramids of ancient guns at the entrance, crossed lances on the walls, banners and canvases depicting famous battles created in everyone a thirst for heroism and glory. Every now and then, while strolling along the building's long corridors or sitting in the reading room, a student's gaze would fall on the majestic faces of celebrated generals. Their portraits, and those of British monarchs in ceremonial dress, made the young men feel part of a great historic process. The years would pass. All of them would follow their own destiny; but in each one of them an officer's manner learned at Sandhurst would be recognisable.

Qaboos visited the school museum many times. He liked to examine the beautiful collections of porcelain, the generals' coats of arms on the walls, the ancient maps and the towns depicted in drawings and old photographs. There was an especially large number of exhibits connected with the expansion of the British Empire to the East. One of the most precious of these was a wooden chest in which the treasures of Tippu, the Sultan of Mysore, had been kept. After his capital was taken by the British in 1799, the contents of this chest were distributed between the regiments of the Coast Army. Tippu who died in the fall of Seringapatam, had been an ally of Qaboos's ancestors, Ahmed bin Said and Sultan bin Ahmed, a fearless and noble warrior and one of the most powerful rulers in the East, but his courageous opposition to the advance of the British could not prevent what was, in effect, a decisive step in the creation of the British Raj in India.

Said bin Sultan, who came to power some years later, chose another strategy, and thanks to his alliance with the British he managed to create his own empire. If he had not drawn the right conclusion from the story of Sultan Tippu, his chests might have ended up next to Tippu's in Sandhurst's museum, where so many exhibits testify that the right choice of friends and allies can be decisive for a country and a dynasty.

There are trophies of the First World War, many of them taken from the Turks. For a long time the Ottoman Empire had allied itself with Britain, and this strategy extended its life for a good century. But it crumbled shortly after it had changed sides and joined forces with the Austro-German bloc, and became only a memory.

After lessons in the classroom and on the parade ground, or after several hours in the library, Qaboos liked to sit alone in his room and daydream, listening to music. One of his favourite pieces was Handel's *Water Music*. It appeared to the young man that this work, composed by the famous German during the years of his service to the English royal court, captured the spirit of the English landscape – that quiet, soft-toned beauty he had grown to appreciate. But it captured more than that; for Sayyid Qaboos the music of Handel seemed to identify an unchanging essence at the heart of British culture – something sensed by Handel in 1717, and still sensed by Qaboos in the twentieth century.

There were boys from many countries and diverse cultures at the Academy; they all spoke English, but for many, music formed one of the warmest, most relaxing bonds. Songs and melodies from many native lands found a place at Sandhurst. Differences in tonality, style and mood was no barrier to communication, because music doesn't need a translation.

The commanders and teachers made no class distinctions among their cadets, whether British or foreign; Sayyid Qaboos received no preferential treatment on account of his royal background. This rare anonymity offered Qaboos a unique opportunity to understand what it was to be a soldier, a lesson which was to serve him well in the future – his ability to share the difficulties of camp life with the soldiers of his army made his name a symbol in the war that defined the future of Oman.

Another important lesson of Sandhurst is the self-control it teaches. A leader should be able to read the battlefield as a professional footballer reads the situation on the pitch – automatically, from intensive, disciplined training. First, a cadet was presented with a theory, then its realisation was demonstrated in practice, and finally the student was required to perform the task by himself. Frequent repetition made these actions second nature, so that in extreme conditions the cadet could give orders calmly and keep control. The ability to control emotions and keep his composure at difficult moments would more than once be useful to the future Commander-in-Chief of Oman.

The crisis of world communism was still very distant and during the two-year course at Sandhurst the global political situation often encouraged students to believe that their knowledge would soon be put to practical use. The world was being shaken by the Cuban crisis and the blockade of West Berlin, while in Algeria and in Vietnam international conflict was brewing.

It was during these years that the balance of power began to shift. Some Western powers, most notably Britain itself, had undergone major reductions in influence; Britain, from being a great power, was now a country reliant on overseas allies. These transformations took place within a single generation, which meant that those teaching in military academies were having to prepare their students for a world very different to the one that they themselves had experienced.

Although the regime at Sandhurst was very demanding, the students made the best use of what free time they did have. Foreign students found England to be a far more cosmopolitan place than they might have anticipated before their arrival. Whether they were just sampling the local eating places (where Chinese and Indian restaurants outnumbered those providing British cuisine) or visiting London's theatres, museums and exhibitions where art from every continent was displayed, students were assured of finding congenial pockets of society in which an enormous variety of cultures were recognised and celebrated.

Sayyid Qaboos's years at Sandhurst were brightened by the fact that other Arabs suffered the hardships of military service at his side. Many of them represented their countries with dignity and enjoyed authority in the student milieu. For example, Saudi Prince Abd Ar-Rahman Al Faisal, who was at Sandhurst at the same time as the heir to the Omani throne, was a good sportsman and captained the fencing team. Qaboos bin Said's circle of friends was not, however, limited to Arabs; many Englishmen figured among them.

Finally the day of their graduation arrived. Assembled on a parade ground in navy blue dress uniforms with stand-up collars and white belts, the students waited for the signal to begin a passing-out parade. Bugles and bagpipes began to play, followed by drum rolls, and the students moved forward on command, with measured steps. They turned, and in even rows the students marched through the main entrance to the Old Building, followed by an adjutant on a white horse. Qaboos bin Said received his lieutenant's epaulettes and his studies were over. Even after many decades, the Sultan of Oman remembers this event with great delight and considers it one of the major landmarks in his life.

After Sandhurst, Qaboos could have left for his homeland right away, but he preferred to put his knowledge into practice, and, like the majority of graduates, received orders for active service in the British army. The only difference between Qaboos and his fellow students was that he was allowed to choose where he would serve.

Qaboos chose the Scottish Cameronian regiment, one of the oldest regiments in the British army, part of the 11th Brigade, stationed in Germany. The Cameronians attracted his attention not only because these élite units had fought on the side of the Sultan of Oman in the fierce battles of 1958–59 in Jebel al-Akhdar, but also because the future

Sultan hoped that the traditions of the Scottish riflemen would serve as a valuable model for building a new army in Oman.

Qaboos had learned the history of the Cameronians while still at Sandhurst. The regiment had been formed in 1689 as the Earl of Angus's regiment. During its long history it changed its name more than once – the 26th Regiment of Foot, the 90th Perthshire Light Infantry, the Scottish Rifles. A five-pointed star, framed by two thistle stalks (the emblem of Scotland) and a bugle, stood out vividly on the regiment's coat of arms, symbolising a readiness to answer the summons to battle and to seek military glory. A new arrival who noticed the copies of old battle paintings in the officers' club could be certain that the Cameronians had more than once lived up to the symbolism of their coat of arms.

The names of the cities of Blenheim, Ramillies, Oudenard and Malplaquet, decisive battles of the war of the Spanish succession at the beginning of the eighteenth century, had the resonance of names recalled from some epic poem, while the list of countries in which the Cameronians had fought – Egypt (1801), Martinique (1809), Spain (1809), Guadeloupe (1810), China (1840–42), Crimea (1854-55), India (1857–58) and Abyssinia (1867–68) – revealed the spread of Britain's interests in the nineteenth century.

In darkened pictures and yellowing prints, it was possible to glimpse the horror and the exhilaration of long-gone battles in European valleys, in stifling jungles or beneath the walls of ancient Asian cities. The puffs of smoke, close ranks with bayonets at the ready, bodies of the killed and wounded scattered on the earth – how many generations passed through fire and blood for the glory of the empire banners? Some of the most heroic deeds made grim subject matter for the military artists – but they did not flinch. They painted as duty demanded. Other paintings showed the brutal superiority of British arms against the lances and the arrows of the tribe of gaikas in the South African wars (1846–1847) and against the people of Zulu (1877–1879). And who could fail to succeed when armed, as were Lord Kitchener's troops in Sudan, with machine-guns against an opposition supplied with nothing more powerful than smooth-bore arms and swords? (An assault by the Khalifa on Anglo-Egyptian forces in September 1898 resulted in the death of a mere 48 Anglo-Egyptians; during the same five-hour period, 11,000 Mahdists died.)

In his thoughts on his country's history, Sayyid Qaboos had already come to understand that it is only the strong who matter in a world where many are eager to take advantage of a backward neighbour. He was already determined to transform the Omani army into a modern and disciplined force, capable of responding to any challenge.

The barracks of the 1$^{st}$ battalion of the Cameronian regiment were on the outskirts of Minden, a small town in north-west Germany. Its ancient, narrow streets were almost always empty. The officers of the British Army of the Rhine, when they had any free time, loved to stroll along the banks of the river Weser. A huge bridge, carrying a canal, spanned the river and Qaboos bin Said, now a lieutenant of the 1$^{st}$ battalion, was transfixed by the technical power and beauty of this impressive spectacle. The area around Minden was most attractive. Close to the town one could admire the Porta Westfalica – the point at which the Weser breaks through the last mountain barrier and meanders as a broad ribbon through pine-covered lowland.

The last rapids of the Weser could be seen especially well from the height on which the grandiose monument to Kaiser Wilhelm I stood. The emperor, immortalised in bronze and stone, had previously gazed at another majestic monument – Bismarck's tower. Now only 129 steps and a plinth, topped by a TV mast, were left. The victorious Allies had forced the Germans to pull down their memorial to the Iron Chancellor. Nevertheless, post-war efforts to demilitarise the German landscape were difficult; monuments to battle abounded. Not far from Minden, in Teutoburg forest, ancient Germands led by Arminius had beaten the Romans and on Saturdays it was the habit of families to picnic at the feet of the giant bronze leader.

The Army of Occupation brought the officers and the soldiers to the town museum, with its diorama depicting the Battle of Minden (1759), at which the united German and British armies routed the French. This victory of the Seven Years War was particularly resonant for Qaboos, as the British and the Germans together had opposed a new common enemy in the East.

Sayyid Qaboos was accustomed to learning things thoroughly, so he was not satisfied with a superficial acquaintance with Germany and its culture. He admired the compositions of Bach and Brahms, but although music can communicate the emotions of the soul across cultures and languages, the Sayyid recognised the necessity of learning German if he was to gain a political understanding of the country. He therefore began to teach himself the language. Unfortunately, his stay in Germany turned out to be too brief for him to progress beyond the elementary stages.

The atmosphere in which the army was living was very different from that which had prevailed in Britain. Frequent practice alarms and manoeuvres kept them on the alert and, from the intensity with which the Soviet bloc was discussed, it seemed to Qaboos and the other officers that a confrontation must be imminent. The enemy's possible theatres of operations, techniques and tactics were the subject of constant analysis, and samples of communist propaganda were passed around the officers to illustrate the way in which party dictatorship in communist countries was functioning.

At the time, this hypothetical adversary seemed to Lieutenant Qaboos bin Said to have little to do with Oman; nevertheless, he studied their doctrines attentively. Some years later, this knowledge would turn out to be crucially apposite. For the enemy that had previously threatened the murky plains of Westphalia was in fact just a gunshot away from the Sultan's palace in Salalah.

The seven months in the Rhine Army were as beneficial to Sayyid Qaboos as his years in school. Not only did he command a motorised rifle unit, he also took part in manoeuvres involving many types of troops. Only after this short but intensive period of training was he able to tell himself and his father that he knew what comprised an effective modern army.

When his service in Germany was over, he returned to Britain. Said bin Taimur thought that the time had come to show Sayyid Qaboos the world in all its variety. The Sultan believed a three-month round-the-world trip, known as the Grand Tour, would make his son aware that the Western model of development was not the only possible option. As a young man, he himself had been to the major capitals of the world and considered the experience important to him as a ruler.

In European countries, the scions of wealthy aristocratic families did the Grand Tour to become acquainted with Europe's art and culture. It was the last stage of a young man's education. By the twentieth century, speedier means of transport made trips around the world feasible. Sayyid Qaboos's journey around the world was one of the stages of his growing self-awareness. With every new country he felt himself becoming more and more versatile. If his five years in Europe had made it comprehensible and familiar to him, the East still remained a mystery. Paris, Rome, Athens and other points of the round-the-world voyage surely made a great impression on the heir, but his wide reading and his deep understanding of the spirit of the Western world had already prepared him for wider experiences.

And even the great world capitals paled in the heir's memory as, one after another, the historic cities of Turkey, Iran, Pakistan, India, Japan and other Asian countries appeared before him. He was overwhelmed with enthusiasm and reverence for the power and originality of the ancient cultures, the basis of human civilisation. He photographed the ancient monuments and the ruins, trying to imagine scenes of modern life against this background. He continued to be attracted by a combination of art and nature.

In Iran, he photographed a stork standing on one leg in a nest built around a minaret; in India, he photographed the Taj Mahal framed by trees and water. In the course of his journey, Qaboos considerably broadened his knowledge of the traditional music of various peoples and learned to appreciate many musical styles he had not known before.

A meeting between the prince and his grandfather, which took place in Bombay, was one of the seminal events of this trip. After his abdication in 1932 in favour of his son, Taimur bin Faisal lived in India. He was well into his seventies at the time of the meeting, but had retained his royal bearing and a youthful brilliance in his eyes. When Qaboos came to see him, the old man was deeply moved. They embraced each other and for a long time neither was able to speak.

During lunch, the ex-Sultan watched his grandson almost constantly, nodding appreciatively while the prince told him of his years of study and service. One could detect pride in the grandfather's eyes at his grandson's thoughtful observations on policies and culture which proved that his descendant was a worthy inheritor of the crown. And the grandson looked at his grandfather with equal approval – this admirable and fascinating man, about whom he had thought so frequently, emerging as if from the mists of obscurity. It seemed miraculous to be able to sit down with this elderly man and to put to him questions about his own youth.

The conversation flowed freely, from the events of the past to the near and far future. Taimur bin Faisal believed passionately in the possibility of a bright future for Oman – now that separatists had been defeated, nothing could prevent the revival of the Sultanate's former glory. Like his son Said, Taimur linked his hopes for the improvement of the country's financial situation to oil exploration.

Some photographs were taken of that meeting; years later, the sight of them still had the power to make Qaboos bin Said tremble, for that one rendezvous with his grandfather had put him in living contact with the history of his dynasty.

His Asian impressions pushed the European ones into the background. When the prince left Japan, he could scarcely remember the beginning of his trip – it was as if years had passed. He found himself in Hawaii, and then went on to San Francisco. The New World won him over with the magnificence of its nature and its space.

Passing over the Rocky Mountains, crossing the Great Plains of Canada and the United States, visiting the Great Lakes, Qaboos found once again that his previous impressions had grown dim. New experiences were rapidly replacing earlier sights, and only months later would the Grand Tour fall into perspective as a balanced and harmonious picture.

New York turned out to be a fitting site for the end of the tour. Everything seen previously became a prelude to his encounter with this city, a symbol of the might of modern civilisation. It was wholly appropriate to proceed through all the stages of the development of human culture, beginning with the ancient ruins of Mesopotamia and the Indus valley and concluding with this kingdom of concrete monoliths on the shores of the Atlantic. Looking from the Empire State Building at the concrete jungle of Manhattan, every foreign guest involuntarily compares their own nation's level of development with that of America. There, in the final days of 1963, the heir to the Omani throne was probably realising how much the Sultanate would have to be transformed.

Some days later, a huge ocean liner, the *Queen Mary*, sailed from New York for Great Britain. Standing on the first-class deck, Sayyid Qaboos stared at the Statue of Liberty and reflected on all the cities he had seen in his three-month journey. None of them resembled the citadel of capitalism, its skyscrapers guarding the gates of the New World.

It was an imposing and faintly disturbing image of the future. People brought up in ancient cultures, in countries with long histories, are troubled when they think of America: is it possible to keep up with this dynamic giant? But this question also stimulates a fervent will to work, and suffuses the soul with cheerfulness and optimism. This was the mood in which Sayyid Qaboos returned to England.

Now he had to learn in detail the organisation of state and municipal services and the functioning of economic mechanisms. The Sayyid spent a whole year in Hampshire, south-west of London, where he studied local government administration. He dedicated a great deal of time to studying government institutions, taking a course in management and visiting factories, banks and company boards of directors. He was already forming an idea of what was required to transform Oman into a modern state.

Pride in his native land's history did not blind Sayyid Qaboos to the misery into which it had fallen after a century of decay. He was well aware of the dismal statistics which showed the Sultanate lying near the bottom of the world table in education and public health. But the desire for change did not translate into a desire to reconstruct everything according to a European model. He appreciated the wisdom of the proverb recollected from his childhood: 'Better a raw thing made with your own hands than a ripe one made with the hands of another'.

By the end of 1964 he had completed his programme of preparation for state management. The time had come to return to Oman and put into practice the knowledge he had acquired over the previous six years.

# The Autumn
# of the Monarch

OLLOWING HIS RETURN TO SALALAH, Qaboos quickly realised that his father was in no hurry to introduce him to state affairs. Even trips around the Sultanate were refused him on one pretext or other.

Said bin Taimur reacted coolly to his son's observations on the principles of social organisation which he had learned in Europe; he then announced that Sayyid Qaboos must complement his education with a thorough study of the Holy Qur'an, of Islamic law and of the history of Oman under the guidance of authoritative theologians and *qadi*.

Said bin Taimur's style was naturally authoritarian and with the passage of time he had grown increasingly petty and domineering. Virtually no decisions were taken without his approval. He even dealt with entry visas himself, which naturally provoked discontent among the Sayyids in charge of the major departments.

Tariq bin Taimur had always been offended by his elder brother's refusal to grant him much responsibility for affairs of state. His position as mayor of Muscat did not give him any real influence. In a sign of protest he left Oman in 1960 with his family and went to live in Germany, where he had once lived with his mother.

Ahmed bin Ibrahim, nephew of Imam Azzan bin Qais, served Said bin Taimur faithfully as the head of the Ministry of Internal Affairs for several decades, but was also restricted in his authority, since he had the unstable status of one 'who oversees matters pertaining to the Interior'.

The Sultan's uncle, Shehab bin Faisal, was responsible for the armed forces of Batinah, for police and for prisons. He dealt with the issuing of passports, and also represented the Sultan in Muscat when the latter was abroad, but without the requisite authority.

The *walis* of the different regions of Oman, though formally under the rule of Sayyid Ahmed, regularly received orders from the Sultan and were summoned to him for reports. Since Said bin Taimur rarely left Salalah, high-ranking officials had to make long journeys south to submit every essential decision to the monarch for his approval.

After his experiences in England and in other progressive countries it was difficult for Sayyid Qaboos to adjust to the confined atmosphere of a huge family ruled by a form of extreme paternalism. The whole of Oman was the family, and the Sultan was that stern paterfamilias. He considered no one autonomous and vetted all types of decisions. All subjects, regardless of their age and position, were regarded as children under his personal supervision. Tales of his obsessive rules and regulations have passed into folk-lore. It is said that on the Sultan's orders a telescope was installed at the window of his rooms in the palace, so that he could keep his subjects under surveillance. Since al-Husn palace rose high above the buildings of Salalah, the streets, the courtyards of other dignitaries, the market and the ocean coast itself were visible to the Sultan. The sight of a smoker or a person with a prohibited umbrella, or, God forbid, with a transistor radio, was sure to trigger an order from the Sultan for that person's immediate detention and punishment. Throughout the city only one person had permission to ride a motorcycle – an Iranian healer, Ahmad Shofig, a favourite of the Sultan.

Not satisfied with surveillance of ordinary Omanis, Sultan Said bin Taimur tried to regiment all the behaviour of his officials, thereby depriving them of initiative and giving them a fear of responsibility. Such forms of rule were characteristic of countries where tribal life or large, patriarchal families were still influential.

After a wave of anti-monarchical revolutions in the 1950s, many educated people in the Third World began to regard monarchy as an outdated relic, and in some strata of society it was felt that political systems from remote ages should give way to new, more efficient systems. Even Western democracy seemed obsolete to many.

In the countries that had just been liberated from colonial domination, different nationalist and socialist ideologies, from Maoism to Négritude, were gaining adherents. But for Omanis, who for many years had been isolated from the rest of the world, even the abolition of royal power in Egypt in 1952 and in Iraq in 1958 did not seem prophetic.

Many of the Sultan's subjects had scarcely even heard the names of the revolutionary theories that were arousing so much interest in other Arab countries, and their first direct experience of the results of revolution came in 1964, when refugees from Zanzibar arrived in Oman. Notwithstanding the Sultan's prohibitions, many of them settled in regions inhabited by tribes to which their ancestors had belonged.

After 70 years of rule on behalf of the Sultans of the al-Busaidi dynasty, Britain agreed to grant Zanzibar its independence. The territories on the African continent had been lost, and on Zanzibar itself the position of the Arab dynasty had become very unstable. Nationalist parties that had grown up in the shade of the colonial administration and whose far-ranging powers had assured the hegemony of the black majority were preparing to seize power once the British left.

If the sovereign rulers of the Omani empire and the Zanzibar Sultanate had tried to impose cultural and religious uniformity on their subjects, Britain had always skilfully exploited tensions among nationalist and ethnic groups and preferred to act as an omnipotent arbiter. This widened the breach between nationalistic groups and favoured the emergence of organisations such as the Afro-Sherazi Party (ASP), whose purpose was to drive the Arabs off Zanzibar.

On 9 December 1963, the independence of Zanzibar was proclaimed, and as early as 12 January the following year an armed rebellion of black nationalists ousted the last Sultan, the 18-year-old Jamshid. An atrocious massacre ensued, which resulted in the death of around 20,000 Arabs. Those who managed to escape from the ASP gangs fled Zanzibar.

Many refugees appeared in the coastal towns and the interior of Oman seeking shelter among their fellow tribesmen. As Omani tribes had been emigrating to the overseas dependencies for centuries, almost every tribe had numerous members on Zanzibar and on the East African coast. Listening to the stories about what was happening on the faraway equatorial island, Omanis came into contact for the first time with the harsh realities of xenophobia and racism.

Sayyid Qaboos's return to Oman coincided with the Zanzibar tragedy, so he constantly thought about the destiny of monarchy in the modern world: is it capable of resisting extremist forces armed, not only with guns and mines, but also with trenchant populist slogans that bewitch the masses with utopian dreams of equality and prosperity? A lesson not then fully grasped was that revolutionary leaders who come to power turn into tyrants much more often than do hereditary rulers. He who ascends to the throne according to the law of succession is much less preoccupied with competitors and can dedicate all his energy to the country and its people. He has, after all, been schooled for his position. From earliest childhood, a legitimate heir to the Sultanate is provided with the requisite education and special preparation necessary to equip him for rule. The representative of a dynasty feels a weighty responsibility bequeathed him by his ancestors; he tries to deliver the state to his successors safe and sound, like a solicitous father who leaves a well-cared for house to posterity. It is because of this that few hereditary rulers are inclined to risky ventures, whereas so many of those who seize power by revolutionary means end by throwing the country they profess to love into chaos, destroying its cultural heritage, its people and all that makes it unique.

As we have seen, Said bin Taimur expressed a wish that Qaboos study more thoroughly the history of Oman and Islamic theology. If initially this may have seemed reasonable as a means of familiarising the heir to the throne with his native traditions and culture after his long years in the West, as the years passed and Said bin Taimur yielded no authority to his son, the wish seemed to impose a gratuitous penance.

Mulling over various events in the history of Oman, Qaboos came to the conclusion that its most successful Imams and Sultans did not follow the beaten path, but made decisions that vastly accelerated the country's development. He was especially impressed by the example of Said bin Sultan, who had courageously restructured both domestic and foreign policy priorities. Instead of continuing the struggle for domination in the Gulf that had been draining the lifeblood of Oman for years, he channelled the energy of the tribes into the development of East Africa and fearlessly pursued close contacts with Great Britain, whose expansionist potential he clearly understood. He did not attempt to legitimise his command in the eyes of conservatives, but managed to reduce their power base by improving the welfare of the common people.

Qaboos was not able to find any parallels between the reign of Said the Great and the rule of the second Said, his father. Both struggled with insurgents and resisted the expansion of neighbouring countries, but if the first succeeded in transforming the country into one of the most influential states of its time, the second had yet to convince the world of his nation's worth.

By 1964, considerable oil reserves had been discovered in three fields, Natih, Yibal and Fahud. With oil in commercial quantities, Oman had the potential for rapid development. These oil fields could become for Said bin Taimur what Zanzibar had been for Said bin Sultan. But Said bin Taimur apparently did not have the will for change that was necessary at that crucial moment of history.

Laying out on a carpet giant photographs of Qur'anic texts that had been made to his order in the Cambridge University library, the Sayyid studied, for hours at a time, the works of ancient calligraphers and assiduously read explanations by Islamic theologians. Sometimes he was distracted from his studies and remembered his visit from Sandhurst to the library of that ancient university. Touching the old folios with his hands, he could not have imagined then that these books would be his main interlocutors for many years.

He was overwhelmed with ideas and it seemed that time was passing away fruitlessly like water running through the fingers. Several hundred miles away, new life was in ferment – new towns were being created, roads were being built, huge aeroplanes were taking off from brand-new airports. But Oman seemed unable to shake off a century's drowsiness. The heir venerated the works of Muslim scholars of previous ages, but he was not born to labour over folios. He loved his country and he knew he had the capacity to change the life of his people for the better. He could not understand why his father did not entrust him with at least a minor role in state affairs. Though Qaboos was now 25 years old, he had never seen Muscat; he did not really know the country that he would probably have to lead.

Instead, the days succeeded one another, each one just like the last. Long hours spent over books on history and theology were interspersed with walks beside the ocean. Sometimes the tide was in, sometimes it was out and the sandy beach swarmed with small crabs and snails, ready to gorge themselves on fish left stranded by the waves, while flocks of birds – seagulls, ducks and flamingos – flew over the water, calling raucously, even as the sun began to dip behind the Jebel al-Kamar. Occasionally Qaboos used a palm leaf as a mask through which to follow the sun's swift disappearance – watching as, in scarcely a minute, the disc was reduced to no more than a tiny fiery stroke and then was gone, marking the end of another day, though, even then, light lingered on, as the sky continued to flame with ever decreasing intensity until finally the night took full command. But the daily walks, the birds demonstrating the perfect freedom of flight, the endlessly repeated sunsets, each one so beautiful, were drained of some of their quality when they seemed only to emphasise the endless repetition of Qaboos's own curtailed existence.

Music relieved the heir's monotony a little. Of all the instruments, the prince was most attracted to the lute. Once, before the headlong development of keyboard instruments at the end of the seventeenth century, it had been a favourite instrument of European musicians. Its amazing versatility enables a player to perform both difficult classical works and folk tunes.

The West learned about the lute from the Arabs in the time of the Crusaders. The 'ud, with four or five pairs of strings stretched above a broad, thick fingerboard, engendered many kinds of plucked instruments. If in Europe the lute gradually became a rarity, in Arab countries its cousin, the 'ud, was – and still is – one of the most popular instruments.

Sayyid Qaboos not only played famous melodies, he often improvised, trying to express his mood and the thoughts that possessed him in the language of music. Those thoughts were not at all serene – the growing discontent in the soul of the Sayyid sought an outlet in action. And that was what the Sultan feared.

In effect under house arrest, Qaboos bin Said was vigilantly watched by palace personnel and by the guards. The only hobbies that he could openly practise were horse riding and photography. The father forbade the prince to be given newspapers. Had it not been for his mother, who regularly smuggled *The Times*, concealed in her clothes, into her son's rooms, the future ruler would have remained ignorant of events in the world.

Sometimes a man has to take a bitter medicine or even resort to surgery in order to restore his health, and his relatives resort to these harsh measures not because they do not love him, but, on the contrary, because they do. And for the sake of one's country, one sometimes has to disregard one's natural affection for one's relatives.[10] In pondering the destiny of his

---

[10] *The Times* reported Qaboos bin Said as saying, 'I had to forget my personal relations because the question was bigger than father or son. It is a nation at stake and I had to forget all my personal affection.' *The Times* (1 August 1970).

homeland, Sayyid Qaboos gradually came to understand that his father was already too tired to stop its decay, a process which was becoming more and more apparent. Within a year or two, the same fate as had befallen Yemen might befall Oman. In 1967 the hereditary rulers of many small sultanates found themselves forced to flee from new, strong revolutionary authorities – abruptly rejected in their own countries.

During his first audience with Brigadier John Graham, appointed at the beginning of 1970 as the commander of the Sultan's Armed Forces (SAF), Said bin Taimur spoke apprehensively of 'wicked and dangerous' Dhofaris who had to be 'eliminated'. Having learned of the state of the armed forces, the Englishman concluded that they were too weak to subdue the guerrillas to whom the Sultan referred. In any case, Graham considered Said bin Taimur's proposed tactics both uncongenial and counterproductive. He had no desire to conduct a war of extermination, seeing quite clearly that an enemy armed with a fanatical devotion to an aggressive ideology could only be defeated by political means. A new approach was needed – success in the battlefield could not be achieved without winning hearts and minds.

# A New Age Dawns*

MAN RAPIDLY FOUND OUT about the changes that had taken place on 23 July 1970: the young Sultan's declaration spread through the country with the speed of lightning. All the news agencies of the world published the text of the Sultan's address to the people. It was permeated with such sincerity and with such trust in his fellow countrymen that it straightaway won the hearts of the people. Omanis everywhere read and reread these words from the appeal:

> I promise you to proceed at once with the task of creating a modern government. My first act will be the immediate abolition of all the unnecessary restrictions on your daily lives. My people, I will proceed without delay to transform life into a prosperous one with a bright future. Every one of you must play his part towards this goal. Our country in the past was famous and strong. If we work in unity and cooperation, we will regenerate that glorious past and we will take our rightful place in the world.

The people were especially impressed by the new Sultan's frank description of the former regime's inability to use the new-found wealth of the country for the needs of its people. Such resolute language was uncommon not only in Oman, but elsewhere. Usually when the leadership changed hands, comment was limited to platitudes, and the new ruler carried on affairs as did his predecessor. This time everything looked different: in every word of the new ruler's appeal an unfeigned hunger for change was manifest.

All over the country these words from the appeal were repeated:

> *My people, my brothers, yesterday was dark, but with God's help, tomorrow will be a new dawn on Muscat and Oman and all its people.*

In the final lines of his appeal the Sultan promised to come to Muscat soon and meet his people.

The ministers of Said bin Taimur were dismissed. All of a sudden those who had been dignitaries (to say that they had been in power would belie their status under the former Sultan) were no longer of any significance. Although officials were perplexed as to how the new Sultan should be received, they need not have worried; the citizens of Muscat themselves spontaneously set about preparing for his arrival. Flags which had been made 15 years earlier to celebrate the victory over the Imamate were taken out of mothballs. Stocks of red material were snatched up within a few hours. Every house, every tree, every vantage-point was decked with flags and circled with ribbons. Men fired rifles into the air. Women drew designs on the palms of their hands with henna and donned their most festive attire.

The next day an aeroplane from Salalah landed on the runway close to the Beit al-Falaj fortress. The door opened and the figure of the new Sultan appeared, wearing a dark, semi-transparent *bisht* over a simple white *dishdasha,* and an *amama assaidiya* – a red, blue and gold turban. The unusually hot and humid air immediately made His Majesty, who had never before seen the capital of his country, gasp for breath – though it was possibly not the heat and the humidity but his own emotions that were to blame for the constriction in the Sultan's throat as he surveyed the scene on the airport runway. It seemed that all Oman had assembled to greet him. Thousands of rifles fired continuously, and their sound echoed through the barren mountains surrounding the airport. Drums thundered, hundreds of trumpets and pipes resounded. A multitude of people in white *dishdashas* and multicoloured *kummas* (headdress), dancing and brandishing swords, ran towards the plane. A silver *khanjar* shone at each waist.

Making his way through the crowd in an ancient limousine, the slim, black-bearded Sultan waved unceasingly to the people. The joyous cheers of women, arrayed in unbroken black lines behind the walls of houses and on roofs, mingled with the rumble of gunfire and musical instruments.

The streets along which the Sultan's entourage passed were strewn with carpets. People waved palm branches and flags – red flags were everywhere, decorating the houses, the forts and even the trees. The sea of red against the ascetic white of the buildings lent a rich sense of occasion to the city.

The Sultan stared at the majestic forts rising above the deep-blue waters of the bay, at the austere rocks calling to mind the many ships that had sailed past the city during the last century. Muscat charmed him.

Small clouds of white smoke rose above the forts. The sounds of artillery volleys, echoed and multiplied by the mountains, dominated the festive cacophony. Crowds accompanied the monarch right up to al-Alam palace.

Only when the voice never before heard by the people of Oman was projected by loud speakers, reverberating throughout the palace forecourt, did the music and the gunfire fall silent. No one wanted to miss a single word. The Sultan's speech was direct and clear:

> We hope that this day will mark the beginning of a new age and a great future for us all. We promise you that we shall do our duty towards the people of our dear country. We also hope that each one of you will do his duty in helping us to build the prosperous and happy future that we seek for this country, because, as you know, unless there is cooperation between the government and the people we will not be able to build our country with the speed required to free her from the backwardness she has endured for so long. The government and the people are one body. If one of its limbs fails to do its duty, the other parts of the body will suffer. We hope that you will think well of us and at the same time we hope that we shall think well of you.

The sense of brotherhood and unity in those heady days was so unusual that everyone wondered whether it could possibly be true – were they dreaming that all at once hundreds of seemingly immutable prohibitions had turned to dust? City gates were no longer closed at dusk; no one asked you to walk with a lantern at night; shopkeepers no longer asked to see your permit if you wanted to buy a radio or sunglasses. Smokers spilled out onto the streets, saluting with clouds of smoke the abolition of the law against smoking outdoors. The deposed Sultan had ordered that a stiff dignity be maintained, even during weddings, but now those who had musical instruments played them at every spare moment and young men strolled along dusty streets within the city walls until late at night. Gathering in groups, they devoured the news of which they had been deprived for so long. The glow of cigarettes stretched in an unbroken chain along the road to Matrah, a road which just a few days ago had emptied at dusk. Music sounded from portable radios. The voices of speakers from capitals near and far raced along the airwaves to bear news from an outside world that had so recently seemed hostile to Oman, and which was now responding to the Sultan's words with sympathy and hope.

The Sultan called for expatriate Omanis to return and devote themselves to the renewal of the motherland. The prisoners in Fort Jalali, who had been confined in horrible conditions for many years, were liberated. An amnesty was proclaimed for those who had taken up arms against the old regime.

The old palace, which Said bin Taimur had not visited since 1958, was declared to be unsuitable for human occupation. A temporary but more comfortable residence was found for the new Sultan – a small modern mansion built for Major Chauncy, a British counsellor, who had served under Said bin Taimur. Shortly thereafter the decision was taken to demolish the old palace and erect a new official residence in its place.

After some days in Muscat attending the popular celebrations, Sultan Qaboos bin Said set out for his first trip around the country. His objective was to meet ordinary people and tribal leaders and to hear at first hand of the problems that needed to be resolved.

For Sultan Qaboos this voyage was also the fulfilment of a longing to see with his own eyes those places he had read and heard so much about during the many years he had spent studying Omani history. His very first impressions proved deeper and richer than he could have imagined. It seemed to the Sultan that the past itself was coming alive before his eyes as he visited the streets, palaces and forts where his predecessors had lived, rejoiced and suffered.

In ancient Nizwa, the image of an earthly paradise to everyone who set their eyes on it, the young Sultan was received with the same jubilation as in the villages of Batinah. After many decades of living under the Imamate and then a bitter war with Muscat, local people might have treated the new ruler with suspicion. But the cogency and sincerity of Sultan Qaboos's speeches dispelled their mistrust. Celebratory fire from every kind of weapon and the deafening euphony of wooden flutes, brass cymbals and small drums showed how the people's taste for songs and dancing, their longing to express their feelings openly, had survived even the long years of priggishness in the citadel of the Imam. Everyone had the same desire: for antagonism and intolerance to be buried in the past.

Looking down from the height of the fortress's main tower, in the aftermath of the celebrations, at the bright green sea of palms below, Sultan Qaboos took advantage of the silence to appreciate the view and the overwhelming sense of place he was experiencing as he moved around this deeply known, but also astonishingly new, country.

In the short journey around the interior of Oman the young Sultan found a way of addressing his subjects that later acquired the importance of a major rite. His annual tours around different provinces would enable the Sultan to renew his acquaintance with practically all the authoritative people in Oman. Over the years, Sultan Qaboos became the best-informed person in Oman. For one who until the age of 30 had been cut off from others and who knew his land only from photographs and descriptions, this lifting of the informational embargo probably had a deeper impact than the sudden liberation from tyranny had had on other Omanis. Sultan Qaboos bin Said, like any of his compatriots, was enjoying his freedom, but he was even more delighted that he finally had the chance to make good use of his knowledge and boundless energy.

Later there were other meetings, other towns, and other discoveries. It was as if a curtain had been pulled aside. Qaboos had spent many years studying the spiritual heritage and history of Oman and he knew his country deeply, but all his knowledge was filtered as though by a screen through which no more than a glimpse of the present actuality could be seen and through which he was completely invisible to his people; now his country was lying open before him, and he, too, was no longer hidden from view. The world tour that Qaboos had taken before his return to Oman might have broadened his mind, but this tour around his own country tapped deep into his soul.

Palms planted spaciously by the sea cast their shadows on the white town of Sohar. The breadth and openness of this town, caressed with fresh ocean breezes, was once attributed to Sindbad the Sailor, a native of Sohar. The young heir first encountered this name, a symbol of the enterprising and courageous spirit of Arab sailors, when he was learning to read a syllable at a time.

Inside the severe geometrical forms of the fortress, the last Imam of the Ya'ruba dynasty had ended his days and the star of the liberator of Oman, Imam Ahmed bin Said al-Busaidi, had risen. But it was also here that one of the darkest tragedies of Oman's history took place – on a dark February night, Sultan Thwaini bin Said lost his life. The powerful citadel of Rustaq nestled on top of the summit of Jebel al-Akhdar. As early as the primeval times of the *Jahiliya* there were battles here between the proud and warlike Azd and Persian warriors in armour. Strolling along the echoing halls which had once served as the ceremonial entrances of Ya'ruba Imams is tantamount to reading chronicles steeped in blood. Many thousands of people died for this stronghold.

Upon his return to Muscat on 9 August, Sultan Qaboos made a radio speech in which he declared his will to change the name of the country, which for half a century had personified a division into two inimical states. 'Muscat and Oman' were to disappear from the map, and the ancient name of Oman, which had glorified the land of seafarers, warriors, farmers and Bedouins, would return once again, this time for ever.

The Sultan announced the introduction of a new flag. Instead of the red banner of the Sultanate and the white one of the Imamate, a new standard of white, red and green was adopted, symbolising the fusion of the valuable traditions of the Imamate and the Sultanate through the single religion of Islam.

The main concern of the Sultan after the events of 23 July was to form a government capable of instituting rapid and effective reforms. Having dismissed the more rigid officials of the *ancien regime*, it was incumbent on Qaboos bin Said to replace them immediately with a team of people untainted by the methods of the past. Only a person well known to his countrymen, with wide connections among the tribal élite and a convincing air of international authority, could head the government.

Just one person was suitable for such a role at that time – the Sultan's uncle, Tariq bin Taimur. The Sultan had never met him; nonetheless he decided to ask him to accept the daunting post. The fact that the Sultan made one of his most important decisions, not on the basis of personal considerations but in the interests of the country, sent a signal to everyone that the new leader would cultivate a pragmatic style.

Every day Qaboos bin Said faced new problems in need of urgent attention. His father had led the state to a deep crisis, and it was difficult at times to decide which problem was the most pressing. Everything had to be dealt with at once – finances (a complicated and bureaucratic taxation system), communication (there was none outside Muscat), transport (there was no regular air communication with any state), health (only a few hospitals existed), education (three schools catering for the whole of Oman), the army (outdated weapons and insufficient strength). On top of all the internal problems, the country had to break into the international arena if it was to re-establish itself in the diplomatic field. The previous ruler had shunned diplomatic relations with every country except Great Britain, India and Pakistan.

Not surprisingly, Britain, Oman's main ally, was the first to offer support to the new administration; the government announced its official recognition of Sultan Qaboos bin Said on 29 July 1970. The first foreign leader to visit Muscat was the ruler of Abu Dhabi, Sheikh Zayed bin Sultan Al Nahyan, who arrived in October of the same year. The meeting of the two rulers was very cordial. They had seen each other for the first time in 1968, in Salalah, when Sheikh Zayed had come on the invitation of Said bin Taimur. It was the first and last visit of a foreign leader to Oman during the 38-year rule of the former Sultan.

Sultan Qaboos liked the dynamic and witty Zayed bin Sultan. The fact that this courageous and successful reformer was the first to show solidarity with the new Sultan, who was just beginning to work out plans for modernising his own country, was highly symbolic. Their affection for each other has never waned. Sultan Qaboos has more than once expressed his gratitude to Sheikh Zayed for the moral support that he gave to Oman at a difficult moment of its history. Moral support was precisely what the new leader needed to overcome the international isolation of his country.

One of the first actions of the new regime was to send missions of goodwill to Arab countries – in early 1971 emissaries visited Saudi Arabia, Kuwait, Jordan, Iraq, Yemen, Lebanon, Morocco, Algeria and Egypt.

Sultan Qaboos invited representatives of many other countries to visit Oman in order to see the country and to establish relations on an equal footing. Tariq bin Taimur met the Soviet ambassador in Kuwait and had long talks with him. But during that period, the countries of the Soviet bloc resisted the strengthening of contacts with Oman, preferring to coordinate their actions with the revolutionary Arab regimes, who long remained suspicious towards the Sultanate because of its close relations with Britain. For this reason it was not easy to overcome the negative attitudes towards Oman that had developed over the decades.

In March 1971 the fifty-fifth Session of the Arab League postponed to September discussion of Oman's request for membership. By that time the Sultanate had still established diplomatic relations only with Kuwait, and even that country looked to Cairo and Baghdad for approval – thus Kuwait, which had been the first to announce its recognition of Oman, excused its acquiescence in the Arab League's decision by saying that it expected a report from the Sultan regarding his foreign policy.

Nonetheless, the efforts of the Sultan's diplomats began to bear fruit. The Universal Postal Union became the first international organisation to open its doors to Oman in January 1971.

On 24 May of the same year Tariq bin Taimur asked the UN Secretary General to admit Oman to this organisation. Among the non-Arab countries that had recognised the Sultanate by the beginning of June 1971 were India, Pakistan and Japan.

Sultan Qaboos did not go abroad in the first months of his reign, though it was initially expected that he himself would travel around neighbouring countries with the objective of strengthening his international position. But the more the young monarch learned about the state of affairs inside the country, the more numerous and complicated proved the problems that had to be urgently resolved. The most acute and immediate issue was to form a competent government.

The management structures which Sultan Qaboos inherited could not respond at all to the task of rapid reform and, therefore, could not serve as the foundation for a governmental apparatus.

The first attempt to devise an effective instrument for carrying out the monarch's plans was the creation of a Provisional Consultative Council. For about three months, while negotiations were held on the formation of a new government, this Council was occupied with developing and executing priority measures in every sphere.

All oil revenue, which previously had been at the disposal of Said bin Taimur, was brought under strict control. Projects on the rational use of credits and aid, promised by some of the Arab countries, were drafted. Omanis and their wives were given permission to leave the country.

From the beginning of September, prices for all types of fuel were lowered. In the same month the first school for girls and the first school for nurses were opened.

Tariq bin Taimur was finally able to present candidates for ministerial posts at the end of autumn. Heads were appointed for the ministries of Internal Affairs, Justice, Awqaf (Religious Endowments), Health, Education, Labour and Social Insurance, and Information. The Sultan reserved for himself the portfolios of the defence, oil and finance ministries.

The Sultan and Prime Minister at first shared the role of Foreign Affairs Minister, although their respective responsibilities in this sphere were not clearly distinguished.

An acute shortage of qualified personnel was an obstacle to the creation of new government bodies and to the realisation of large-scale projects in health and education. Sultan Qaboos could see for himself the catastrophic situation in these two areas during his trips round the country. The high rate of illness and disability was evident everywhere, and most people were illiterate. Oman's infant mortality rate was one of the highest in the world. Many Omanis had received their education abroad, but almost none returned, preferring to use their knowledge for the benefit of the countries that had given them hospitality. These people formed the essential base of the young Sultan's ambitious plans to transform Oman into a modern state. But how could he convince them to come back?

When Qaboos bin Said asked his compatriots to return to their native land and take part in the process of renovation, the response was extraordinarily enthusiastic. Almost immediately Omani youth began to flock to Muscat. Moved by patriotic enthusiasm, recent graduates of European universities did not seem to be in the least daunted by the difficulties that awaited them.

The Omani Information Minister was one of those who returned from abroad after the events of July 1970. He remembers that there were not enough houses for the numerous returnees to live in, so tents were pitched for them right on the beach. Nobody grumbled at the discomfort; everyone was eager to work for the sake of their country. Months and even years elapsed before these young intellectuals could find respectable accommodation. 'Even now,' said the Minister in an interview in Muscat, 'when we get together, we remember that period as the happiest time in our lives.'

It is difficult to imagine what their country must have looked like to those who returned from the flourishing oil capitals of Kuwait and Manama, from Cairo, London and even Moscow. Probably the first thing they noticed was the absence of surfaced roads so that the handful of cars kicked up clouds of dust on the country roads and in the towns. Other signs of backwardness would then become evident – a dearth of electricity and water; the absence of televisions, telephones and public transport; the severe shortage of doctors and teachers. All the basic ingredients of civilised life were luxuries in Oman. Few people could afford an automobile, the means of communication or any of the everyday comforts that many in neighbouring Arab countries were beginning to take for granted. In a country where summer temperatures exceed 50° Celsius, an air-conditioner was something wondrous, affordable only by the rich.

The difficulty of the transformation that had to be undertaken lay in its urgency and the fact that everything had to be done simultaneously. It was impossible to overcome backwardness by stages. To satisfy both the demands of economic necessity and the suddenly unleashed expectations of his people, the Sultan had to ensure that change was not just revolutionary in its scope but that all changes took place at the same time. The most precious thing that the young Sultan had was the support of the fellow countrymen and he could not afford to waste this support through half-hearted implementation of the promised transformation.

The most spectacular projects, realised to a considerable extent in the first year of Qaboos bin Said's rule, included the construction of the Muscat–Sohar road, a modern airport in Seeb and a seaport in Matrah. By the end of 1971, 15 new schools, 6 hospitals and several dozen clinics had been opened, while 7000 schoolchildren, including 1100 girls, were attending school on a daily basis.

If one considers that under the previous Sultan there were only 900 pupils in the entire country, and no schools for girls at all, the pace of transformation in this field can be called revolutionary. And the effect of all these innovations was stronger than any propaganda could be. In Dhofar this was more evident than anywhere else.

# Struggle for Hearts

 IKE A GREEN WALL Jebel Samhan rises into dense clouds. From this impenetrable veil, sunburnt *qara* dressed in checked *wizar* would descend, carrying firewood on camels to the inhabitants of the town of Mirbat. Soldiers often searched these men for mines. Everyone knew that among these indigo-tinted mountaineers were members of the armed units of the PFLOAG (People's Front for the Liberation of the Occupied Arab Gulf), which the soldiers called *adoo* ('enemy' in Arabic).

They had supporters among the local people, who ferried provisions and medicines to the rebels. Government forces were powerless to stop them, since their support was limited. Even those who would have liked to help the government preferred to keep silent, afraid of reprisals from the insurrectionists, who had spies everywhere. From time to time special groups appeared in the mountain villages, sent by the leaders of the Front to wreak vengeance on 'traitors'. Rumours of this 'revolutionary justice' spread through the whole of Dhofar, paralysing potential backers of the Sultan.

This machinery of fear was not a native invention; it had been devised in the training camps of the Chinese secret services near Beijing. The Chinese were great masters of revolutionary tactics – their support for extremist movements had already borne sinister fruit from the Philippines to Peru.

In the jungles of every continent numerous groups of different persuasions were operating. In Europe the 'new Lefts', armed with Mao's quotes and Kalashnikovs were attacking capitalism – Red Brigades and

Red Armies organised massacres in the centres of well-to-do capital cities. Even many professors wore badges with the face of 'the Great Helmsman' and taught his 'Great Doctrine'.

The disciples of Beijing's ideological masters successfully used their 'brainwashing' technique in Dhofar as well. Revolutionary nihilism towards religion and tradition was drummed into the young in the schools. Boys and girls, dressed in identical khaki uniforms, learned by heart the sayings of Marx and Mao and repeated them in unison. They parroted that there was no Allah, that Mohammed was not a prophet at all, but simply a representative of the ruling classes who had thought up a means of ideologically controlling the working class. They parroted that only an armed struggle against the Sultan's authorities and the reactionary tribal élite would lead to a new society. But their minds were thoroughly confused.

Since they were unable to understand the concept of the proletariat, the ideologists of the PFLOAG invented a new revolutionary class – the 'Bedouintariat', consisting of young *kabili* (tribe members) isolated from their kin. They were supposedly the most progressive force of history at that stage. Those who succeeded better than others in assimilating the ideological concoction were sent to Yemen, where propagandists and commissars for insurrectionist units were being trained in special centres.

When soldiers and officers loyal to the Sultan first obtained samples of Bedouintariat propaganda, they were perplexed. They had always been taught to answer fire with fire. But how can one oppose an aggressor who has invaded the soul? Under the old Sultan the SAF had made no provision for psychological warfare – they had relied on force of arms and on the discipline of their soldiers. But in this battle one had to struggle both for territory and for men. The soldiers of the small Mirbat garrison discussed rumours that in Salalah they had thought up something extraordinary and unexpected for the *adoo* . . .

By the time the change of power occurred in the Sultanate, the pro-communist insurgents had seized most of the southern province and had even set up their own authoritative bodies in some parts. The insurrectionists divided Dhofar into four zones. The part bordering The People's Democratic Republic of Yemen (PDRY) was completely controlled by the insurrectionists and was called the Western Zone. The neighbouring region received the name 'Ho Chi Minh Zone'.

This was just when the war in Vietnam was at its height, and the leaders of the PFLOAG wanted to demonstrate that they too were in the front line of the struggle against world imperialism.

The zone where intensive fighting with the SAF was taking place was called the Red Line. The Eastern Zone was the name given to the part of Dhofar that bordered Mirbat; here the government positions were stronger, but confrontations with guerrillas were not unusual.

In August 1972 the PFLOAG adopted a decree concerning the creation of people's councils on the territories they controlled. These councils were to include representatives elected by the population and appointed by the People's Liberation Army, and they were designed to 'educate' the population more effectively and involve it in the revolutionary process. At the same time, membership of a council was prohibited to anyone suspected of political heterodoxy. To *qara*, cattle-breeders who lived in primitive huts and caves and knew only the rudiments of civilisation, the rebel leaders could seem to be benefactors, because on their orders schools were built and elementary medical and veterinary service was introduced. Naturally, literacy training first and foremost had a propagandistic objective.[11]

Said bin Taimur had never understood the source of guerrilla power and had for that reason consistently underestimated the threat it posed. His successor, who had received his military education when the tactics of communist insurrectionists and their psychological methods had become a subject of study in the West, had a better understanding of what was happening in Dhofar and a knowledge of the tactics required for combating it successfully.

He set his government the goal of defeating the rebels where they were strongest. Literacy, medical service and technical advances had to come to the mountains of Dhofar not from the other side of the Yemeni border, but from Muscat and Salalah. It was important to oppose the brainwashing of the tribes with real improvements to their lives.

[11] Alexsei Vassiliev, a Soviet journalist who visited Dhofar at the end of the 1960s, has left us a revealing account:
'A mountaineer, his torso bare, squatting under a lamp, was reading a book in a sing-song voice, making his way laboriously through laborious phrases. I listened, trying to understand. It was not possible!
"What is that you have?"
"Take it, comrade, have a look."
I took the shabby book in my hands and red the title, written in Arabic script: *Two Tactics of Social Democracy in a Democratic Revolution.* Just above it was written Vladimir Lenin.'

The Sultan's men did not shrink from ideological duels. Soon, the owners of transistor radios in the mountain villages could listen to a Salalah station and later on the literate could read leaflets dropped from aeroplanes. Thanks to this information offensive, the Dhofaris learned of the amnesty announced by Qaboos bin Said for everyone who took part in the conflict on the side of the PFLOAG. By August 1970, about 200 tribal representatives had allied themselves with the government forces.

The creation of *firqah*, irregular combat units formed from the *jebali* (highlanders) who lived year-round on the plateau, was one of the young monarch's most courageous decisions. Those who left the PFLOAG, disillusioned with Marxism, formed its core. Using their thorough knowledge of both the insurrectionists and the local terrain – they were familiar with the locations of rebel arsenals, their movements, their potential and their propaganda methods – the *firqat* performed reconnaissance and patrol tasks and were of invaluable assistance to the regular army. Their information enabled the SAF to inflict serious damage on the rebels and to seize the initiative. As the inhabitants of the mountain villages came to realise that the PFLOAG was not omnipotent, their fear of reprisals gradually subsided. More and more people went over to the Sultan's side.

The strategy behind the struggle against the guerrillas also changed. The SAF passed from defence to attack. Before, with the coming of *khareef* (the summer monsoon), when air support became problematic and supplying military units became more difficult because of the state of the roads, the government forces abandoned their positions and retreated to the Salalah valley, so that the rebels re-conquered lost territory.

Now, government positions in the mountains were consolidated on a permanent basis and the zones controlled by the SAF were gradually enlarged. According to the classic rules of anti-guerrilla warfare, the first *firqah* operation aimed at re-establishing government authority took place in the town of Sadah, on the coast. There, the position of the

He then describes a surreal scene he witnessed in an indigent village:
'A demonstration was coming towards us. Children in front, followed by women and, finally, men. A young boy with a rifle was shouting slogans; the others picked up his cries. "The administrative committee extends its friendship to the Soviet people, headed by the CPSU!" "Lenin is a great teacher, a fighter against Sultans and colonisers!" "Marxism–Lenism is a true lodestone for the working masses, for the struggle led by the working class against world imperialism." . . . We distributed badges picturing Lenin and the Kremlin. They accepted them joyfully and pinned them straight away on their chests.'
Alexsei Vassiliev, *A Difficult Pass*, Moscow Nauka (1977) p. 75.

insurrectionists was less secure and everything came down to an exchange of small-arms fire. Later on, the tactic of 'biting off' peripheral sections from a vast area controlled by the PFLOAG was successfully used and permitted government forces to exert more pressure on the rebel wings, which in turn allowed further attacks on the centre.

All the basic decisions regarding the conduct of operations against the rebels were taken by the Sultan after careful study of their tactics and the mood of the population in the regions they controlled.

Qaboos bin Said received the first group of *jebali* (literally, 'people of the mountain'), who had defected to the government, in the al-Husn palace in late November 1970. A participant in this historic meeting, Ahmed Suheil, who lived in the village of Shihait, still remembers the event vividly. When five ex-guerrillas arrived, the Sultan came out to meet them wearing a simple *dishdasha*. They were pleased to see that the ruler, who was their age, was indicating that he was just a Dhofari, as they were. In true *jebali* style, he had a thick black beard, and he addressed them in their native language, for his mother came from the same Maashan tribe as Ahmed himself. The attentive and friendly look of the Sultan at once encouraged the visitors to speak frankly. They sat on wattle mats, sipping Arab coffee.

The Sultan was convinced that one of the major tasks was to cut off supplies to the insurrectionists. The Sultan's army could strike at the insurrectionists, but it was unable by itself to find out who provided food to them, or to trace out the supply routes. Only local inhabitants could provide that information, so the monarch outlined the objective of creating an information network among the mountaineers. Because the first *firqah* was being formed, the organisation of military preparation, and the provision of ammunition and food were discussed. He agreed to a proposal not to store large caches of army food on the *jebel*, as they could be looted by the guerrillas, and promised to order the delivery of supplies in small batches. It was decided that a part of the foodstuffs would be used to help the population. As many of the guerrillas were accustomed to light and efficient Soviet-made submachine-guns, the English rapid-fire rifles used by the SAF seemed to them heavy and uncomfortable. Thirty years have passed, but Ahmed's memory still retains the words 'Kalashnikov', 'Simonov', 'Degtiarev'. The conversation was full of the names of reliable rifles, pistols and machine-guns.

For the tribesmen, who had been carrying arms their entire lives, security and ease of operation were the most important merits. Thus, the possibility of arming the *firqah* with weapons taken from the rebels was discussed at different levels. But though the advisers in the Sultan's army acknowledged the logic of the tribesmen's preference, it was considered incorrect from the political point of view. Instead, it was decided that a bonus would be paid for every captured firearm. Ahmed Suheil recollects that at the beginning the guerrillas were ubiquitous: there were stocks of arms and ammunition in almost every village and *wadi*. So at first, hunting for these trophies was one of the most important tasks for the *firqah*.

Meetings between the Sultan and the people were a powerful impetus for altering the psychological climate in Dhofar. Unlike his predecessor, who had confined himself to the palace for the last four years of his reign, and had kept his contacts with people to an absolute minimum, the young ruler was eager to hear of his subjects' troubles at first hand. Qaboos bin Said had an intimate knowledge of the organisation of his army and assumed personal control of the SAF units, improving conditions for the soldiers, visiting training centres and overseeing the implementation of new technology and weaponry.

His visit to the camps of Medinat al-Haqq and Qairoon Hairitti received an especially warm response. The Sultan arrived in a helicopter with some of his assistants and spent the whole day with the militiamen, sharing their simple meal, listening to their wishes and telling them in detail about his plans for the transformation of the country. The Sultan's audacious decision to confide in ex-rebels, among whom PFLOAG agents could easily hide, greatly increased his authority. The 'desert telegraph' immediately spread the news everywhere. The number of defectors from rebel ranks increased sharply. If the first *firqah*, which began operations in 1971, consisted of only a dozen combatants, by 1974 there were 17 units, with a total strength of 1500. When forming the *firqah* units, the tribal divisions were respected – a strategy which amply demonstrated the ability of the Sultan to grasp a situation quickly and to learn lessons from the rebels' mistakes. The first *firqah*, named after Salahadin, the bane of the crusaders, fell to pieces before it could even be deployed for active service, because of disputes between members of different *jebali* clans. This was taken into account when further combat units were created and the tribal groups proved more stable. On the other hand, the leaders of the Front, who blindly followed their own dogma prescribing the abolition of 'the remnants of tribalism', impaired the effectiveness of their own troops.[12]

Of course initiatives on the battlefield alone could not guarantee victory. The success of the armed struggle only became possible after the political strategy of the state was changed and after supremacy over the rebels in the ideological struggle was achieved. When planning their campaign for the mass media, SAF analysts adopted from the outset the principle that all information had to be absolutely truthful. Only news about real achievements could win the confidence of the mountaineers. In contrast to the communist propaganda disseminated by Aden, the broadcasts of the low-powered government radio station were an accurate portrayal of life in Dhofar. Realising that they had the strongest message, but that widespread tribal poverty meant few in the mountains could listen to the radio, the government authorities decided to organise the sale of low-cost radios on the local market, counting on the fact that something bought even for a small sum would be appreciated and not handed over to the commissars of the PFLOAG.

Clearly the opportunity to listen to broadcasts from Salalah undermined the rebels' monopoly on information. Even if there were only several hundred people who regularly listened to the news on the radio, that news gradually became common property. Among the tribes, word of mouth had always been the main method of communication.

As the information services of the SAF and the government were well aware of this fact, they used simple, intelligible methods to inform the population of Dhofar of all the Sultan's major decisions, especially his measures for improving the life of the common people. Therefore, in every strategic location in and around Salalah, huge notice boards were installed, on which the authorities posted everything they wished the *jebalis* to know. People could read these notices and then circulate the information when they returned to their villages.

---

[12] From the Soviet point of view this was *An Infantile Disorder* (the title of a famous book by Lenin: Left-Wing Communism: An Infantile Disorder)'Some functionaries of the PFLO[AG] made serious exaggerations typical of leftists at the end of the 1960s. Initially they manifested an incomprehension of the historical causality of the existing tribal formation and regarded it as "a counterrevolutionary" phenomenon. Trying to finish off tribal separatism and intertribal conflicts in one go, these functionaries "in the name of revolution" "abolished" tribes in Dhofar and announced that all the tribal territories, especially the pastures and the sources of water, were for everybody's use. Such a poorly

The government's message also sought to warn the *jebalis* against what the communists really stood for. One of the leaflets dropped from aeroplanes in 1971 told the people from Dhofar:

> *The communists do not serve your interests, do not fit in with your beliefs. The communists are your worst enemies; do not let them deceive you. Pay heed, my brother, to what the communists have said and done. Pay heed so that you may distinguish right from wrong. The communists say: 'There is no God, no Creator." The communists do not recognise the prophet Mohammed (blessed be his name) and other prophets of God. There is no place for rights among the communists, my brother; they allow illegal things and the abolition of the rights of man. These things are known to you. They kill fathers and leave their children as orphans.*
>
> *All these thing have been done by the communists before your own eyes. You protect them indirectly. You are their fuel and their slaves and later on you will be their target. Watch out for yourselves before it is too late. Join the party of God. The party of God will be the winners. The victory is yours for eternity, my Muslim brothers. Death is for God's enemies, for those who are also your enemies and against freedom, dignity and Holy Islam. Muslim fighters from all of Dhofar have joined the party of Islam, which is under Qaboos' leadership. Begin the difficult but honest task of finishing off the communists in order to satisfy God and to purify this country, which has been stained by the blood of criminals. Begin, my brothers, to link up with your brothers and to take your natural place in the service of your government and country, which is your service because you have the most to gain from this. Your government welcomes you, looks after you, protects you, assures you of your rights and defends all your rights.*

The appeal concluded with the words 'Islam is our way. Freedom is our aim'. These words became a sort of slogan, uniting around the Sultan everyone who cared for religion and the traditions of their ancestors. The older generation had long been worried by the fact that the young

conceived campaign, which ignored the reality that had formed over centuries, cost the Front dear. The combat units of the PFLO, composed artificially on a non-tribal basis, were losing their combat spirit; some of the tribes, influenced by their sheikhs, began to yield to a compromise with the enemy, who was actively taking advantage of this mistake of the PFLO in order to compromise it.' N.N. Vorobiev, 'The Role of Tribes in the Social–Economic Life of Oman (1950–1980)', in *State Authority and Social–Political Structures in the Arab Countries*, ed. I.M. Smilyanskaya, Moscow, AN SSSR Institute Vostokovedenija (1984).

people who had attended the schools of the PFLOAG were flaunting their atheism and were critical of the tribal customs. The secondary school named after Lenin, situated in the PDRY close to the border with Oman, was one of the main breeding grounds of atheism. Classes were held in tents and boys and girls studied together. The teachers, trained in the countries of the communist bloc, purposefully inculcated distrust of Islam and mocked all those who observed the prayers and fasts.

The PDRY province of Mahra, where the major bases of the PFLOAG were located, became a real hotbed for developing methods of communist infiltration in Arab countries. These methods included direct propagandist brainwashing and military training for the young *jebali*, as well as sweeteners for the older generation such as medical and veterinary care and food aid. The Cuban hospital, set up in the region of Hauf, not only treated wounded insurrectionists, but also provided free medical treatment for the civilians of Dhofar. For people who knew only one therapeutic method – cauterisation with a red-hot iron – the seemingly miraculous healings in Hauf were weighty arguments in favour of the Front.

In fact, nothing supernatural was happening: every tablet taken by a mountaineer had much more of an effect than it would have had on someone used to taking medicines. When the SAF doctors later began to treat the civilian inhabitants, they were struck by the powerful healing effects that simple antibiotics had on patients.

The bodies of the elderly, covered with scars from cauterisation, are living evidence of the times when an organism could rely only on itself to fight disease. As soon as the Sultan's government had set up a reliable health service, the people stopped thinking of medical aid from the PFLOAG as a blessing.

---

[13] One extremely important fact about the anti-guerrilla war was that the Sultan's objective was not the physical annihilation of the enemy. He constantly underlined that the people had to be persuaded, not cowed into submission. This specific feature of the Dhofar War is stressed in the memoirs of Major-General Tony Jeapes, *SAS: Secret War*: 'Because it was a war about people, a counter-revolutionary campaign could not afford to go in for booby-traps designed to kill or maim the enemy. Very little private enterprise was shown and no official support at all given for the sort of thing which goes on in most wars, leaving behind bullets which explode in the breech for the enemy to find and use, poisoning his water supply, booby-trapping dead bodies, etcetera. These are, in any case, measures troops tend to take when they are losing, when they cannot get to grips with the enemy in any other way. Booby-trapping is a recognized form of warfare but it should have no place in a counter-revolutionary campaign like the Dhofar War. First, there was always the danger that a civilian may suffer instead; blowing up Grandma is not a very good way of gaining the support of most families.

The establishment of schools, the building of roads and the organisation of basic trade on the tribes' own land gradually neutralised the PFLOAG's propaganda. As the support of the population ebbed away, the leaders of the Front became jittery and cracked down further on 'traitors' and dissidents, which lost them even more support.[13] Indeed, at the lower levels of the PFLOAG leadership, the number of renegades sharply increased. These were sheikhs and respectable tribesmen who desired a real improvement in the lives of their fellow countrymen and who believed in the sincerity of Qaboos bin Said's appeal to cooperate for the sake of the future.

On 12 September 1971 in the Eastern Zone of Dhofar, 40 Front commanders were arrested and money, transport and arms were seized. But the upper ranks of the PFLOAG managed to organise a counterattack, freeing their commanders and recovering what had been seized by the Sultan's supporters. Nevertheless, it had been shown that the insurrectionists were not all-powerful, and 'the attack of September 12' had a significant impact on morale.

Despite the PFLOAG's campaign of repression,[14] the people could not be prevented from defecting to the Sultan. The tangible improvements taking place under the new regime were highly effective weapons of persuasion – capable of implanting in people the resolve to resist the PFLOAG's bullying methods and inflammatory rhetoric. Civil Action Teams (CAT), established by the Civil Aid Department at the same time as the *firqah*, undertook the most urgent projects: digging wells, organising medical services and food supplies, etc. As the zones controlled by the government troops grew larger, so did the scale of development. Roads were built, electricity was installed, schools and mosques were constructed.

Second, the aim was to persuade the adoo to come across to the Government. Blowing one man to pieces, or worse, blowing pieces off one man, may remove an adoo soldier from the enemy's order of battle but it would harden the resolve of several more. Booby-trapping, in short, was counter-productive. A government cannot use all the means open to the enemy.' Major-General Tony Jeapes, *SAS: Secret War*, London  HarperCollins (2000) pp. 329–330.

[14] According to the data of Arab author Muhammad ash-Shuaibi, the terror was aimed not so much at the 'exploitative classes', as at simple *qabili*. He reveals such figures as the following: among the 76 persons executed by PFLOAG, there were 11 workers, 18 herdsmen, 6 camel drivers, 5 tradesmen, 2 clergy, 2 sheikhs, 1 fisherman, 2 porters and 1 farmer. Among those shot was even a madman who publicly cursed the 'bulls of the Front' (a play on the words *suvvar*, revolutionaries, and *as'var*, bulls). The muezzin of the mosque in Hauf, Said Yahtub Isa, who dared to criticise the actions of the PFLOAG in a sermon at Friday prayers, was killed immediately thereafter.

The Marxist leadership of the PFLOAG tried to halt the exodus by making some changes in its ideology. The pro-Beijing orientation was played down and contacts with Soviet communists strengthened. This was a consequence of a change in priorities for the PDRY leadership. For all their sympathy for the ideology of such national communist icons as Mao Tse-Tung and Ho Chi Minh, they saw that it was Moscow who had the real military and financial resources. Massive Soviet aid to North Vietnam, after all, was the principal reason why the half-million-strong American army had been defeated. As much as the revolutionaries believed in the strategy of 'surrounding the world's capitalist towns with the world's country', they understood that without the help of 'Soviet revisionists, walking the bourgeois path' (a favourite jibe in the Chinese propaganda of that time) they would be unable to create a modern army. In addition, it was noted that Aden's drift towards 'scientific socialism' was greeted favourably in the Soviet Union.

A flow of modern armaments plus a huge number of military advisers soon helped the South Yemeni leadership build up an army so powerful that it was considered the best on the Arabian Peninsula. Some of the Soviet generosity filtered down to the Dhofar guerrillas – large-calibre Shpagin machine-guns, light 60mm mortars, portable missile installations, anti-aircraft guns and a large number of modern rifles greatly increased their capability to wage war against the Sultan's army.

Dhofar in fact became a front line of the struggle not between a mythical Bedouintariat and world imperialism, but between the world communist bloc and an Arab state making its first steps on the way to overcoming its age-old backwardness.

For all their disagreement, Moscow and Beijing joined forces in the Dhofar War. Training camps on the territories of both communist superpowers and in the lands of their satellites – East Germany, Cuba, Bulgaria – prepared command staff for conducting guerrilla war by teaching military tactics and the use of modern arms. In addition, the PDRY directly interfered in the internal affairs of Oman by sending its military units into Omani territory.

But the balance of forces in the Arab world began to change little by little. The change of power in Salalah in July 1970 turned out to be only the first link in the chain of events that year which eroded the positions of the leftists and the extremist forces. In September, King Hussein of

Jordan managed to defeat armed Palestinian groups who had been hatching a plot to seize power.

In November, leftist Ba'athists lost power in Syria. Anwar Sadat, who became President of Egypt, took a moderate position and purged his government of pro-Soviet elements. In such circumstances, close contacts were established between Oman and many Arab countries. The most precious help against communist aggression apart from that given by the British came from King Hussein, who sent experienced officers and instructors to train reinforcements for the SAF, and also pilots for the new aircraft of the Sultan's Air Force.

A Jordanian battalion, stationed in Thamrait, protected the road connecting the plateau to Salalah and played a direct role in repulsing guerrilla attacks. Later, Egyptian military advisers also arrived in Dhofar. To be sure, this could not abruptly change the balance of power, but it was of great psychological importance – the Omani soldiers felt that their Arab brothers were in solidarity with their struggle.

At that time the future was quite unpredictable, given the many ominous incidents taking place throughout the world. Wars were raging everywhere; alliances were notoriously unstable. Victory in one battle was no guarantee of success in the next one, let alone of overall victory. Even when the Sultan's forces gained the upper hand in the Dhofar War, they had to strive their utmost to win it.

In a speech on 18 November 1974, on the occasion of the National Day of Oman, Sultan Qaboos said:

> *On the southern borders of this land there is a mobilised community of subversive groups, linked to secret organisations scattered throughout the countries of this region, working in league with international communism. This fact is self evident and undeniable. In spite of this, we stand firm and have succeeded in breaking the back of their offensive, as a result of which our brethren in the mountains now enjoy protection and security from their terrorism. The terrorists, on the other hand, have begun to lose faith in their masters, who goaded them into venting their terrorism on innocent people. 'They are like fire which burns itself when there is nothing to burn.'*
>
> *These days, new slogans are coined and new names mentioned. Some look on such tactics with indifference. I have warned that the safety of the region is all or nothing. Security is the responsibility of all states and people in the*

*area. Communism has no faith. It recognises no other doctrine. Should it retreat on one front for one reason or another, it does so solely in its own interest. It is one of their principles to take one step back so as to advance two steps forward. I frankly declare that any negligence in defending the faith of God will lead to disaster. There are no two ways about it – communism is dedicated to the extermination of all religions.*

In fact, Oman did become the front line against Marxist expansion for the entire Arabian Peninsula and even all of the Middle East. The escalation of foreign aid to the insurrectionists made the internationalisation of the conflict inevitable. Though the SAF had already become strong enough to oppose the forces backed by the power of the communist bloc alone, the struggle could still go on for years. The Sultanate could not afford to dissipate its energies in the war, spilling more and more blood to prevent the Sovietisation of the Gulf.

By 1971, if not earlier, every family in Oman had lost someone in the war. One could not talk about modernising the country while its lifeblood was draining away. Qaboos bin Said therefore searched for an immediate settlement of the conflict.

The Sultan's objective of cutting off food supplies to the Front was being achieved. *Firqah* and SAF garrisons stationed in mountain villages gradually pushed the bulk of the rebel forces out of the Eastern and Central Zones.

In November 1971, in the Central Zone of Dhofar on the road from Salalah to Thamrait, a network of fortified posts was created and minefields were laid along possible rebel routes. Thus did the 'Leopard Line' come into being, a prototype for the system of barriers that was ultimately constructed in Dhofar. These barriers eventually solved the problem of how to isolate the rebels from their supply bases in the PDRY.

In April 1972, parts of the Dhofar brigade even managed to take control of Sarfait, situated on the plateau a number of kilometres from the Yemeni border. But the situation continued to be rather unstable, since the 'Leopard Line' was abandoned by the troops with the arrival of *khareef* in the summer of 1972 due to the impossibility of organising supplies in persistent fog.

Rebel troops operated over the whole plateau, and sometimes they accumulated in large numbers and attacked the coastal valley. As long as the rebels controlled the main routes in the west, along which arms and ammunition arrived from Yemen, it was impossible to stop them completely.

Understanding what it would mean for their forces to be cut off from their main base in South Yemen, the leaders of the Front decided to conduct a large-scale offensive on SAF-controlled territory. The main strike had to be made against the garrison of Mirbat.

Early in the morning of 19 July 1972, as a monsoon shrouded the coastline like a thick blanket, from the northern hills at the foot of Jebel Samhan and from the bed of the *wadi* in the east, a hail of mortars and other projectiles came down on the old fort. The soldiers of the garrison, awakened by the alarm, found themselves under machine-gun crossfire.

The insurrectionists, who had secretly infiltrated the valley, were advancing from different directions, closing in on the defenders in a pincer movement. Counting on the fact that air support could not be provided for the surrounded garrison, the PFLOAG command was certain of success.

The SAF had not been subjected to such an onslaught in the whole of the Dhofar War. The walls of the Mirbat fort flaked away as they were peppered with large-calibre machine-gun bullets; dugout ceilings collapsed from repeated shell impacts. The fumes of foetid powder and burnt tolite (explosive) choked the defenders of the ancient bastion, which had been built in times when war was fought with smoothbore guns and swords. Dozens of dead and wounded lay about the half-destroyed fort. Smoke mixed with clouds of dust reduced visibility to almost nothing. Fiery flashes moved closer and closer to the fort along the slope of the *wadi*, which the submachine gunners were climbing to get to the rear of the besieged company. Knots of combatants with ammunition belts raced up to the barbed-wire perimeter fence, threw pieces of sackcloth over the top, and began to scale it. Even the hail of gunfire did not stop them. Many attackers were slain, but more replaced them. It seemed that the rebels would soon burst into the fort. Then suddenly, from the cloud ceiling just above the ground, the Strikemasters of the Sultan of Oman's Air Force (SOAF) emerged. Firing at points where the rebels were concentrated – the bed of the *wadi* and the slopes of the hills surrounding the fort – they halted the onslaught. And then helicopters appeared and landed in the outskirts of

Mirbat to offload the SAS troops. The reinforcements, armed with machine-guns and grenades, forced the rebels to retreat.[15]

The surviving defenders of Mirbat sat in the midst of the charred fortifications, smoking cigarettes and looking at the green slopes of Jebel Samhan. Veterans remembered how they had received the news of the removal of the old Sultan at the same fort two years before. Few had then believed that it was possible to win, for the insurrectionists had been growing more and more impudent by the hour. Scarcely a day had passed when their leaflets, which predicted imminent victory, could not be seen in the town. Many soldiers had felt hopeless. But now the situation was quite different. The land around the fort was covered with the bodies of *adoo* and the Omani flag flew above it. The warriors were overwhelmed with pride. Tears of sorrow for fallen comrades changed to tears of joy: they had won!

The initiative passed to the SAF. The leadership of the PFLOAG did not hazard any more operations similar to Mirbat. So the next objective of the Sultan's forces was to sever the terrorists' supply lines. From the coast near Mughsail (35 kilometres from Salalah) SAF troops started building a chain of fortifications and barbed-wire barriers and laid mines over a wide area. Every square inch of land on which this system of defence was built, all the way up into the mountains, had to be taken by force. The 'Hornbeam Line' stretched for almost 50 kilometres inside Dhofar.

The character of the landscape dictated a number of innovations. It was impossible to dig trenches on the rocky peaks, so the SAF made *sangars* from boulders – circular walls behind which soldiers hid and firing positions were concealed. Today, a quarter of a century has passed since the end of the Dhofar War, but the stone fortifications on the mountain tops remain as a reminder.

---

[15] Tony Jeapes writes: 'The battle of Mirbat was a milestone in the Dhofar War. The Front had to do something spectacular to counter the Government's successes during and since Operation Jaguar the previous year. The attack was well planned and well executed. By using the cover of the monsoon, the Front had calculated that the SOAF would not be able to fly. Similarly, having decoyed the *firqah* out on to patrol, they had anticipated that 250 hard-core fighters supported by all the Eastern Area's recoilless artillery and mortars should be more than enough to take out the defences that remained. From the enemy prisoners we learned that the aim was to capture the town, to hold it for a few hours only, possibly for a day, to denounce and execute the *wali* and his advisers, to subject the townsfolk to a propaganda harangue, and to retire once more to the jebel. And, had they achieved it, the effect on Government plans would have been disastrous. It had been hard enough to find a *wali* in the first place. After such a catastrophe nobody would have taken the job.

Some of the *sangars* represent real feats of engineering, stretching for hundreds of metres. They resemble medieval fortresses, and looking at them it is very easy to imagine the din of arms, the shouts and groans, the clouds of smoke every now and then hiding the lacerated standard. But erecting the Hornbeam Line resolved only some of the problems. The troops failed to move westward, to the Yemeni border, where the *adoo* were most entrenched and where their proximity to their bases in Yemen allowed the Front to shift reinforcements and ammunition. Qaboos bin Said thought it necessary to attack the terrorists' major strongholds. Yet it would be impossible to take control of the Dhofar plateau without a massive drop of parachute troops, which was precisely what the Omani army did not have at that time.

The Sultan therefore approached the Shah of Iran for help. The first Iranians, a Special Forces battalion, arrived in early 1973. In December 1973, a further 1200 Iranian troops landed in Dhofar and right away began fighting the rebels west of the Hornbeam Line.

Different nationalities took part in the Dhofar War. A host of soldiers and officers from several Arab countries served in the SAF with the Omanis. But the crucial element was Qaboos bin Said's talent as a military leader. His military education enabled him to conduct a difficult campaign in accordance with modern requirements and to foresee the actions of the rebels, which were planned under the guidance of major military experts from the communist bloc.

The Sultan directly supervised operations and the planning of specific campaigns. The commander-in-chief also constantly looked after the coordination of land units, of *firqah* units, of the airforce and the fleet, and of armaments and supplies. Military talent is the ability to manoeuvre with forces in order to overwhelm the enemy at a decisive moment, to disorient him and impose one's own terms. The recent Sandhurst graduate demonstrated all these capabilities.

Townspeople throughout the province would have been terrified into total non-cooperation with the Government, and the Front could have used the towns and villages as they pleased. Eighteen months of painstaking effort to build up the confidence of the Dhofari people would have been demolished in one day . . . Back on the jebel, the *adoo* looked about for scapegoats. The faith of the younger men in their leaders had been shattered. These resorted to terror in an effort to re-assert their authority and a number of kangaroo courts were set up on the jebel to judge and execute those considered responsible for the failure of the plan. The death of so many of their friends (the total number of deaths including those who died from wounds in the primitive jebel hospitals was just under 100) also had its effect. It was no surprise when August and September proved to be particularly good months for enemy surrendering to the Government.' Major-General Tony Jeapes, *SAS: Secret War*, New York, HarperCollins (2000) pp. 219–220.

But to wage war victoriously, military genius is not enough. Only a skilful foreign and domestic policy can ensure that the victories on the battlefields have not been in vain. The art of policy-making involves taking into consideration a great number of factors and predicting the acts of direct and indirect participants in a conflict well in advance. In this respect the Sultan was far superior to the rebels.

The rebel leaders understood perfectly that in Qaboos bin Said they were up against a modern, well-educated leader. Their propaganda techniques, which had served them well during the Sultanate of Said bin Taimur, rapidly became outmoded and inefficient. In a desperate effort to regain the support of the *kabili*, the leaders of the PFLOAG attempted to turn the population of the plateau against the Iranians by presenting themselves as patriots of Dhofar: in July 1974 they even resorted to renaming their organisation the People's Front for the Liberation of Oman (PFLO). But they did not succeed. The highlanders saw how rapidly their standard of living was rising – roads were being constructed, the CAT were drilling hundreds of artesian wells; numerous schools and medical centres were opened. Since there was a dearth of specialists, the government invited teachers, doctors and nurses from Egypt, the Lebanon and Jordan to work in Oman. Farm tractors made their appearance. The scale of reforms carried out by the government convinced the population that real improvements in their lives would not come from the other side of the Yemeni border. Besides, what was happening in the PDRY was sufficient to give pause to even the most enthusiastic Marxist.

First, private trade was prohibited. Then came food shortages, followed by rationing, the collectivisation of property and the compulsory creation of Soviet-style *kolkhoz* cooperatives. There were endless displays to distract the population from the country's countless problems. These trademarks of socialism scarcely inspired the confidence of the *jebali*, who could easily distinguish the phrasemongers from the people of action.

By November 1974, the rebels had lost control of the lands to the east of the Hornbeam Line and had moved all their heavy arms away from the region. Only isolated groups were operating over the territories that until recently had been a bulwark of the PFLO. Patrols of government troops, together with the *firqah*, methodically searched the *wadi* for arms depots.

As Dhofar is honeycombed with caves, the task was not an easy one. Nevertheless, they succeeded in finding sufficient to augment substantially the display of trophies in Salalah. With time the exhibition became mobile, transported in a specially equipped lorry through all the provinces of Oman.

At the beginning of 1975 the Iranians, supported by the Sultan's fleet, took the rebel capital, the port village of Rakhyut. The naval supply route to the insurrectionists was now cut off. After this key success, construction began on a new system of fortifications, called the Demavend Line. It ran 35 to 40 kilometres west of the Hornbeam Line. The desperate attempts of the PFLO to prevent the construction of the Demavend Line were to no avail.

At the same time, in January 1975, several companies of the SAF launched an offensive against the main rebel stronghold in the Western Zone, the Shershitti *wadi*. Thanks to land and air reconnaissance carried out at the beginning of 1973, it was known that sizeable arsenals and food stores were kept in the numerous caves of this deep mountain gorge, so the *wadi* was of considerable strategic importance.

The bloody two-week battle was indecisive, though the rebels suffered huge losses. But the operation made evident the Front's weak points of defence, and therefore laid the foundation for future success. The SAF offensives continued.

In February 1975, a major battle took place in Ashuwk *wadi*, 20 kilometres west of the Hornbeam Line and the rebels suffered heavy loss of manpower and arms, including large-calibre mortars and missile launchers. A month later, in the same zone, Guyper *wadi* was cleared of rebels. It was clear that they were being pushed closer to the border of the Sultanate. In an interview with the *Times of Oman* on 11 May, the Minister of State for Foreign Affairs declared that in the ranks of the revolutionary fighters operating in Dhofar there were about 200 soldiers of the PDRY army. This indicated that the human resources of the Front were badly overstretched and the Marxist leadership of Aden was trying to stave off defeat.

Many PFLO actions at that stage were not dictated by tactical or strategic considerations, and therefore amounted to little more than empty propaganda. Thus, on 9 June 1975 there was a violent mortar and missile attack on Sarfait to celebrate the tenth anniversary of the 'revolution'.

Nobody except the official Yemeni radio station acknowledged this jubilee. The nonsense of continuing the war for the sake of the Marxist clique of the PDRY became clear to more and more combatants. There was desertion on a massive scale: almost every day someone surrendered and handed over his weapons to the legitimate authorities. The summer *khareef* that had previously served as ideal cover for rebel actions was this time turned to good effect by the Sultan's forces. They created another chain of fortifications that cut off the Shershitti *wadi* – the Simba Line. It was not as solidly equipped as the Hornbeam and Demavend Lines. But it passed very close to the PDRY border. Not surprisingly, the end of the monsoon in autumn 1975 was marked by intense combat in the frontier zone. From the PDRY side there was a ceaseless artillery and missile barrage on the SAF positions.

While in previous months the rebels had fired about 30 shells each day, in October that figure leaped to thousands. There was a real possibility that they would capture the Simba Line. In response, the Sultan took a very risky decision. On the morning of 16 October low-flying Hawker-Hunter aircraft attacked military targets in Hauf. Artillery positions, the headquarters of the PFLO and the South Yemen police station were all destroyed. Omani soldiers, who had been afraid of venturing out of their fortifications, poured out on the plateau, greeting their Air Force with joyous salutations. Hauf disappeared in a maelstrom of smoke. At last the rebel guns were silent.

The leaders of the PDRY might easily have taken the raid as an excuse for invading the Dhofar region. Indeed, the next day their representative made a speech to the Arab League denouncing the 'aggressive actions' of the Sultanate. But that was the end of the matter. It was clear that the seemingly impetuous actions of Qaboos bin Said were not impetuous after all; the Sultan had calculated the consequences well. He had been keeping an attentive eye on the PDRY and knew that their regime was being torn apart by its own contradictions. Even in Hauf, just before the air attack on 16 October, there were heated arguments between the followers of Nasser and the devotees of 'scientific socialism'. Furthermore, the constant tension on their border with North Yemen, which more than once had erupted in large-scale fighting, did not allow sizeable contingents of troops to be posted to the remote province of Mahra.

Once the support bases of the PFLO had been destroyed, events moved swiftly to their conclusion. The SAF units on the western peaks blocked a rebel retreat to the plateau. The Sultan's fleet blockaded the coast. And Iranian forces advanced beyond the Demavend Line and closed off all escape from Shershitti *wadi* to the east. The main group of the *adoo*, together with their arms, were now trapped in a huge ravine, since the Simba Line prevented them from heading west for South Yemen. The Omani army was prepared to annihilate the rebels. But at that moment, the leader of the People's Democratic Republic of Yemen sent an appeal to the Sultan of Oman, via the Soviet leadership. Since the Sultanate had relations neither with Aden nor Moscow, the British government accepted the delicate mission of mediation. This was the first diplomatic contact Oman had ever had with the Soviet Union. The PDRY asked that about 200 of their soldiers be allowed to leave the ravine. The Sultan did not want to wreak revenge and told the British that he would agree to an exit corridor. It was clear to him that by showing mercy he would achieve not only a military but also a moral victory over the PFLO and its minders.

A ceasefire was declared on 1 December. When the encircled PFLO units and their South Yemeni allies left Shershitti *wadi*, the Sultan's troops moved in to search this broad, overgrown canyon. They found an extensive network of caves on the slopes filled with arms, ammunition and accoutrements, sufficient for equipping an entire army. With the loss of these strategic reserves, the PFLO could no longer hope to be a serious military force.

For the first time in years there was peace in the Dhofar region. On 11 December Qaboos bin Said announced that the war was over. On 11 December, about 100,000 people gathered for a victory celebration in Muscat, in a new stadium in the district of Alwatia. It was the largest gathering that Oman had ever seen. When the Sultan addressed the crowd, his joy and pride in the country and its people, who had demonstrated patience and tenacity for ten long years, was evident in his voice. At the end of the celebration the enormous throng, tears of joy in their eyes, sang the new national anthem, glorifying the Sultan:

> *O'Allah, protect for us His Majesty the Sultan,*
> *And the people in our land*

*With honour and peace.*
*May he live longer and supported,*
*Glorified be his leadership*
*For him we shall lay down our lives;*
*O'Oman – since the time of Prophet,*
*We are dedicated people amongst the noble Arabs,*
*Be happy – Qaboos has come,*
*With blessings, of Heaven*
*Praise him and commend him to the protection of your prayers.*

The final operation in the Dhofar War was a brilliant example of the strategic acumen of Qaboos bin Said. Not only in the military field, but also in political, financial and economic spheres the decisions that he was taking often looked like impetuous and elegant improvisations. But this impression was deceptive, belying the years Qaboos had spent thoughtfully absorbing all that he had experienced, both at home and abroad; the time spent in formal and wide-ranging study of history, theology, politics, economics and military strategy, the close observation of people and situations and his practical military training all supplied his analytical mind with thoroughly considered material from which to draw on coming to power in a troubled period of his beloved country's history.

The nature of the last operation in the Dhofar War – hastily conceived and risky, but precisely what the situation demanded – demonstrated a decisive, analytical skill that would be displayed again more than once by Sultan Qaboos in other, peaceful arenas. And the humane outcome of the battle of Shershitti revealed another of the Sultan's most important qualities – compassion.

Victory was achieved by the tireless work of the Omani military and political leadership, both commanded by the Sultan, who held the posts of commander-in-chief and prime minister. What was happening in the mid-1970s in south-east Arabia seemed to defy global tendencies. The overall world situation did not favour the West. The year 1975, after all, was the year of a communist triumph – in the wake of the communists' total offensive in Vietnam, the pro-American regime was collapsing. Half a million US troops fled the country, leaving their allies to the mercy of fate. In the course of that year, communist regimes arose in Ethiopia, Angola, Mozambique, Cambodia and Laos. In such a situation the West had few opportunities to render aid to Oman. The assistance of Oman's friends in the Middle East proved more substantial, thanks largely to the Sultan's talent for coordination.

The Sultan had to consider a host of factors when making the most momentous decisions during the Dhofar War. Since that war was unfolding on the boundary of two social-political systems, its consequences were inevitably far-reaching, affecting myriad distant capitals: Moscow and Washington, Cairo and Baghdad, London and Tehran.

The Dhofar campaign proved the efficacy of a strategy which recognised and tackled the underlying causes of political unrest; the Sultan's emphasis on eliminating the poverty and inequalities which had allowed revolutionary ideas to gain a foothold was crucial to his subsequent military successes. His attention to the physical and spiritual well-being of his people allied to his comprehensive modernisation of the state's infrastructure ensured a loyalty based on appreciation rather than on the fear which ideological revolutions tend to provoke. While the leaders of Aden tried to whip up a revolutionary war according to the precepts of foreign theoreticians, the Sultan gained solid support from the people by appealing to native values, especially Islam, and tribal traditions, though modernisation remained a government priority. In the People's Democratic Republic of Yemen, modernisation was also taking place – but modernisation based on Marxist prescriptions. Everything that connected people with their past was being rooted out; propagandistic clichés were being fed to the public under the guise of education. People of all social classes became equal victims of this 'Cultural Revolution'.

Their ideology of class struggle led them to see traitors and enemies everywhere. Regular clashes between cliques in the ruling Marxist party in Aden toppled one leader after another. The same was true in the provinces, where revolutionary terror ruled supreme. But in Dhofar, and indeed in all of Oman, it was clemency and forgiveness which reigned supreme – thousands of ex-guerrillas turned to a life of peace and serenity. All of them became participants in the building of a new Oman; many of them reached high positions in government and in business. Thus the Sultan's strategic objective – not to exterminate the rebels, but to win over the hearts of the people – was accomplished.

*A portrait of His Majesty Sultan Qaboos bin Said as a young child*

*Sultan Qaboos in his teenage years*

*Sultan Qaboos in military uniform at Sandhurst*

*Graduation at Sandhurst*

*Proclaiming victory following the communist defeat in Dhofar*

*Sultan Qaboos reviewing documents*

*Inaugurating the Royal Hospital, Muscat*

*Sultan Qaboos on 'Meet the People Tour,' one of many*

*Sultan Qaboos with a military unit*

*Sultan Qaboos on a military inspection*

*His Majesty Sultan Qaboos in military uniform*

*Sultan Qaboos greets a resident of a village during his annual tour*

*With Sheikh Zayed Al Nahyan, President of the United Arab Emirates*

*With King Fahad bin Abdulaziz of Saudi Arabia*

*With Sheikh Jabir Al Sabah, Amir of Kuwait*

*With Former Ruler of Dubai, Sheikh Rashid Al Maktoum*

*With Sheikh Hamad Al Thani, Amir of Qatar*

*With Hamad bin Issa, King of Bahrain*

*With Former King Khalid bin Abdulaziz of Saudi Arabia*

*Leaders of Gulf Cooperation Council in Muscat, 1985*

*With Crown Prince Abdullah bin Abdulaziz of Saudi Arabia*

*With Former Emperor of Iran, Mohammed Reza Pahlavi*

*With Former King of Morocco, Hassan V*

*With Former King of Jordan, Hussein bin Talal*

*With Former Egyptian President, Anwar Sadat*

*With Ali Saleh, President of Yemen*

*With Hosni Mubarak, President of Egypt*

*With King Abdullah bin Hussein of Jordan*

*With Former President of Syria, Hafez Al Assad*

*With Émile Lahoud, President of Lebanon*

*With Bashar Al Assad, President of Syria*

*With Palestinian President Yasser Arafat*

*Presenting a gift to Omar Hassan El Bashir, President of Sudan*

*With Rafiq Alhariri, Prime Minister of Lebanon*

*With Former President of Algeria, Chadli Benjedid*

*With Former President of Algeria, Lamine Zeroual*

*With Former President of Somalia, Mohamed Siyad Barre*

*With Former President of Djibouti, Hassan Gouled Aptidon*

*With Former President of the Comoros, Tajiddine Ben Said Massounde*

*With Former President of Sudan, Jaffar Numeiri*

*With Former President of Yemen, Ibrahim Al Hamdi*

*With Former President of Tanzania, Julius Nyerere,*

*With Former President of South Africa, Nelson Mandela*

*With Queen Elizabeth II of the United Kingdom*

*With Prince Charles of the United Kingdom*

*With Former British Prime Minister, Margaret Thatcher*

*With Former British Prime Minister, John Major*

*With Tony Blair, Prime Minister of the United Kingdomn*

*With Sultan Hassanal Bolkiah of Brunei*

*With Jacques Chirac, President of France, in Paris*

*With Former President of France, François Mitterand*

*With Former US President, Bill Clinton*

*With Former US President, George Bush*

*With Former US President, Ronald Regan*

*With King Juan Carlos I of Spain*

*With Former King of Malaysia, Sultan Salahuddin Abdulaziz Shah*

*With Former President of India, Shankar Dayal Sharma*

*With Pervez Musharraf, President of Pakistan*

*With Former Indian Prime Minister, Narshima Rao*

*With Former Indian Prime Minister, Rajiv Gandhi*

*With Maumoon Abdul Gayoom, President of Maldives*

*With Former President of Indonesia, Abdurrahaman Wahid*

*With Former President of China, Jiang Zemin*

*With Mary McAleese, President of Ireland*

*With Former President of Germany, Johannes Rau*

*With Former President of Austria, Thomas Klestil*

*With Former President of Turkey, Suleymen Demirel*

*With Mario Soares, President of Portugal*

*With Former President of Austria, Kurt Waldeheim*

*With Former President of Pakistan, Zia al-Haq*

*With Former King of Nepal, Birenda Bir Bikram Shah Dev*

*With Former President of the Philippines, Fidel Ramos*

*A portrait of His Majesty Sultan Qaboos*

*Sultan Qaboos with Government Ministers at the beginning of the annual tour*

*His Majesty Sultan Qaboos decorating an officer*

*People celebrating National Day in Salalah*

*Sultan Qaboos on horseback at a national celebration*

*Sultan Qaboos addressing the crowd at a military parade*

*Sultan Qaboos University, Muscat*

*A profile of Muscat, a capital with a long history*

*Alshumukh Castle in the interior of Oman*

*Sultan Qaboos Grand Mosque*

# Family of Peoples

VER SINCE SULTAN QABOOS brought about the end of Oman's political isolation, international relations have been one of his main concerns. As noted earlier, his father had put the country in an exceedingly difficult situation. Diplomatic services were practically non-existent; the Ministry of Foreign Affairs was minuscule and its few employees had rarely participated in international forums.[16] Thus, the first goodwill missions sent abroad consisted simply of pillars of the community – sheikhs, theologians, *qadi*s and a few intellectuals. Their efforts were very important in creating a new image of the country, but the establishment of constant contacts with foreign countries and international organisations was, of course, a task for professionals. Due to the understaffing of the foreign service, the Sultan and the prime minister had to take on an additional burden, and at first they actually divided the responsibilities of a minister of foreign affairs between themselves, but without specifying that division very clearly. Both went abroad on non-official visits, during which much of the groundwork was laid for the recognition of Oman by authoritative international organisations and leading countries. For example, in June 1971 Qaboos

[16] Neil Innes, Oman's Minister of Foreign Affairs under Said bin Taimur, has said: 'What did I do? A great variety of things, very few of which had a direct bearing upon foreign affairs, at least in the customary context of the phrase; fewer still which are generally associated with the duties of a minister. During the five years of my service the several duties which I did perform constantly evolved, which did not make their definition any easier. From time to time they covered responsibilities more naturally associated with the posts of military secretary, staff officer, liaison officer, political officer, passport officer, director of medical services, and secretary for development. They did not at any time include ministerial responsibility for Foreign or "External' Affairs." This was the case right up to the abdication of Said bin Taimur. Neil Mcleod Innes, *Minister in Oman*, Cambridge, Oleander (1987) p. 10.

bin Said travelled to London, where he attracted much attention with his openness and frankness. Of course, Arab monarchs frequently visited Britain, but usually they shunned the media and stayed away from public places. Sultan Qaboos, on the other hand, gave extensive answers to journalists' questions, and attended the theatre with the British Foreign Secretary, Sir Alec Douglas-Home.

The first stage of the struggle for the recognition of Oman as a fully-fledged member of the family of nations was completed in the autumn of 1971. On 29 September, the country became a member of the Arab League. On 7 October, the General Assembly of the United Nations voted to admit Oman into the organisation. There was only one dissenting vote – that of the People's Democratic Republic of Yemen.

In the same month the Sultan made his first official visit abroad. At the invitation of the Shah of Iran he arrived in Persepolis, where 2500 years of the Iranian monarchy was being celebrated on a grand scale. Amid the majestic ruins of the capital of one of the great empires of the ancient world, high-ranking guests from many countries gathered. There were troop parades and processions of actors in costumes depicting different events in Persian history, fireworks and luxurious receptions to display the power and wealth of modern Iran and of the Pahlavi dynasty, heirs to the glory of the ancient Achmeanids. Mohammed Reza Pahlavi, who had recently celebrated the thirtieth anniversary of his accession to the throne, was radiant with self-confidence and conviction. The official title of the Shah – His Imperial Majesty – emphasised his intention to play the leading role in the region.

Iran and its leader were of particular interest to Sultan Qaboos for many reasons. In just ten years Oman's closest neighbour had changed from an underdeveloped country into a nation with modern industry, a powerful army and rapidly expanding cultural potential. The 'white revolution' proclaimed by the Shah seemed an incarnation of the doctrine put forward by President Kennedy's administration at the beginning of the 1960s. It affirmed that the ruling élite should co-opt revolution, realising its most attractive ideals, to prevent pro-communist forces from seizing power in Third World countries.

The West considered Reza Pahlavi's modernisation programme to be virtually complete. The level of education of the population had risen sharply, medical care had improved, agricultural reform had been carried out and advanced centres of industry had been created. The rate of economic growth exceeded that of Japan and other dynamic economies in the Far East. In ten years the gross national product had multiplied more than tenfold.

Urbanisation was progressing very swiftly, a network of beautiful roads now covered the country, luxurious boutiques and supermarkets challenged the bazaar, which for centuries had dictated the nation's style and level of consumption. Sultan Qaboos thought the Iranian experience should be taken into consideration when choosing a model of development for Oman – the history and culture of both countries had much in common, and both belonged to the world of Islam. During the centuries they had often been rivals, but such a relationship often makes neighbours more interested in each other's experience. At this stage nothing overshadowed Oman–Iranian relations and Oman's views on the 'white revolution' were quite without any sense of rivalry.

In talks with the Shah many questions were touched upon, especially Britain's forthcoming withdrawal from the Gulf and the independence of its former colonies. At that time preparations for creating a federal state consisting of nine sheikhdoms, from Bahrain to Ra's al-Khaimah, were coming to an end. The Shah had many times declared his intention to fill the power vacuum that would be created when British troops withdrew. In Tehran, Iran's claim to sovereignty over Bahrain, which in 1957 had been proclaimed the fourteenth *ostan* (province) of Iran, was often reiterated. The Persians had occupied the archipelago in pre-Islamic times, and more than once thereafter re-established their supremacy over it. In 1860 the Sheikh of Bahrain acknowledged Iranian sovereignty over the islands. But just a year later the British Empire made them part of its Protectorate, taking advantage of the weakness of its rival after the British–Iranian war of 1857.

In March 1970, the British presented the question of the island's status for the consideration of the United Nations. The organisation sent a mission to Manama to conduct an inquiry, the results of which convinced the Security Council to vote in favour of independence. Iran accepted the results of the inquiry, but for a long time refrained from making an official declaration renouncing their claim to the archipelago. Even after the visit of the Sheikh of Bahrain to Tehran in December 1970 and the archipelago's declaration of independence the following August, Arab leaders were still suspicious of their powerful neighbour.

Qaboos bin Said was aware of all this, and tried to see matters from the Iranian point of view. Thus, he gave particularly careful consideration to the Shah's ideas regarding the conditions for forming a federation of emirates and for guaranteeing the military presence of the Persians on the Gulf islands.

Sultan Qaboos believed that in the new, post-colonial era one should not allow rivalry to escalate: the interests of all the countries should be considered and the positions of all countries should be coordinated. So his conversations with the Shah had a sincere and confiding character. The simplicity and dignity with which the Sultan conducted himself charmed the Shah and he responded in a like manner. Following these first meetings in Persepolis, a special relationship began to develop between the two rulers and for almost ten years they kept peace in a turbulent region.

A month and a half after his visit to Iran, Qaboos bin Said went to Saudi Arabia. In Riyadh he and King Faisal managed to a great extent to overcome the distrust and suspicion which for many decades had soured relations between the two countries. The King, wise with vast political experience, a skilful diplomat and an astute leader, received his young guest as his equal. The disarming sincerity and flexibility of the Sultan contrasted sharply with normal procedure in the Middle East. Local diplomacy was based on old-fashioned, commonsense principles: do not hurry, keep your thoughts to yourself and manoeuvre with subtlety. For years the fires of conflict large and small had burned, but the practitioners of traditional diplomacy refused to change their ways.

Sultan Qaboos was the first to understand that if the Arab hereditary rulers did not inject some dynamism into all the political and economic processes on the peninsula, others, with less savoury methods, would step in to resolve the problems that had been building up.

Two months before the Sultan's visit to Saudi Arabia, it was not clear how Riyadh saw future relations with Muscat. This was evident in the fact that Saudi Arabia abstained from the vote to admit Oman to the United Nations. Only after the two rulers became personally acquainted did trust between the two countries begin to form. Though no communiqué was issued as a result of this visit, the Arab world considered it a success.

An agreement on an exchange of embassies was reached; Riyadh promised to offer economic and military aid; and the Sultan accepted the King's proposal to resume discussions regarding the border dispute that had led to a break in relations between them in the mid-1950s.

Thereafter, contact between Oman and Saudi Arabia strengthened every year. Even a small amount of aid from the kingdom was of enormous benefit to a country just on the threshold of implementing major development programmes. Sending Saudi Arabian teachers to the Sultanate and offering Omani students the opportunity to study in Saudi universities made a considerable contribution to the resolution of top-priority modernisation issues.

In the first years after Sultan Qaboos came to power, he visited most Arab capitals, some of them more than once – besides Riyadh, his visits included Manama, Cairo, Abu Dhabi, Doha, Algiers, Amman and Tripoli. During the same period, the rulers and presidents of the United Arab Emirates, Qatar, Saudi Arabia, Yemen, Egypt and Jordan visited Oman. These visits were the foundation of the Sultanate's transformation from outsider status to that in which it was recognised as being an integral part of the Arab world.

In 1973, the country became a member of the Non-Aligned Countries. The Sultan, although in the front line of the battle against world communism, had a vision of a multi-polar world which would be based not on rivalry between military–political groups, but on multilateral partnerships.

The period of initiation into the community of nations proved surprisingly short. The Sultanate aspired to an increasingly autonomous role in the Gulf region and in the Arab world as a whole. Already in the mid-1970s, Arab leaders were experiencing the new ideas and the unusual diplomatic style of the ruler of Oman. What may have seemed at first an idiosyncratic style of negotiation turned out to express a sophisticated political view. The years spent in Salalah poring over historical volumes and spiritual treatises had sharpened his perception of history. He saw the need for changes similar to those that Said bin Sultan had brought about at the commencement of his rule; the resolve not to be imprisoned by regional conflicts, but to find their solution within the context of expanding dialogue with partners far and near; the clarity to repudiate stereotypes and the proliferation of empty ceremonies in order to accelerate the processes of rapprochement, reconciliation and collaboration.

In those years Qaboos bin Said was one of the youngest Arab leaders, and probably the best educated. His whirlwind tours and dynamic political decisions, such as the agreement with Iran on military collaboration, or the renunciation of territorial claims on the United Arab Emirates and revenge against socialist Yemen, made an impression all over the world. It was, metaphorically speaking, a 'fresh air' strategy. As a breath of fresh air can relieve an oppressive atmosphere, so imaginative political decisions can liberate international relations from painful and fatiguing confrontations. Moreover, these decisions can change the face of international politics, encouraging leaders, even those notorious for excessive circumspection, to act energetically to keep pace with the times. It is easy to believe that the Camp David agreements were made possible after President Anwar Sadat realised that in the Middle East quite a new model of behaviour had made its appearance.

In December 1972, Qaboos bin Said made his first visit to Cairo. Later, in May 1976, he met Sadat in Alexandria, and the Egyptian President visited Oman in August of the same year. More than once they met each other during the all-Arab summits. Probably the only other person with whom the Sultan developed such a close and lasting relationship was King Hussein of Jordan. Thus Sadat was better informed on the actions of the Sultan and on his political philosophy than most other Arab leaders. Both politicians came to power almost at the same time, having inherited a difficult situation; both had to struggle with an external enemy; both had to undertake a radical reform of their nation's economy. Of course, overcoming the problems of Nasser's socialist experiment was not quite the same thing as dragging a country from the Middle Ages into the age of technology, but both were equally difficult.

Undoubtedly, Sadat was influenced by the example of Sultan Qaboos, who shattered the Gulf states' stereotype of Iran as an eternal enemy of the Arab nations. In any case, the unexpected lightning visit by the Egyptian President to Jerusalem and the Camp David agreements which followed, are reminiscent of the rapid improvement in relations between Muscat and Tehran to the level of strategic partnership. Both Sadat and the Sultan understood the essential continuity of those revolutionary turns in Middle Eastern policy, as was indirectly shown by the continuation of their friendship beyond the Camp David agreement. Oman and Sudan were the only Arab countries not to join the boycott against Egypt.

Qaboos bin Said refused to take part in the Baghdad summit of Arab leaders in 1978, during which sanctions against Cairo were adopted; and the Sultan never wavered in his support for Anwar Sadat subsequently, despite the many political difficulties which resulted.

Sadat was no less a nationalist than those who ruthlessly criticised him. A life which included participation in an anti-British military plot when Rommel was eager to seize Alexandria, prison, escape, membership of Nasser's secret officers' organisation and an active role in the coup of 1952 made him a worthy revolutionary. But in the eyes of traditionalists, his refusal to see things in simplistic black and white rendered him unfit for Arab leadership. He was more farsighted than any of them; he realised that only by persuading America to renounce its unilateral support of Israel could the impasse be overcome.

It is hard to swim against the current. Only those with sound principles are capable of resisting the lure of momentary political advantage. In a speech delivered on National Day in November 1974, Sultan Qaboos declared:

> *Our people participated in the battle of the Arab nation in its struggle against the common Zionist enemy. They did this by the sheer belief in the oneness of the Arab nation – to which we also belong, sharing in its destiny and conflicts and also in the solution of its problems and causes. This was unequivocally demonstrated in the war of 6 October [10th Ramadan] when our Arab forces humbled the arrogance of the Zionist enemy, and the Arab forces broke through the barriers to victory. Such participation has since materialised into genuine common action – epitomising Arab unity in its real sense. This has caused immense disappointment to sceptics. Victory has been obtained. If you support God, He will support you and strengthen your position.*

The support for Sadat's actions expressed by the Sultan during the war coincided with the general position of the other Arab countries. But when the Omani leader also approved of the further actions of the Egyptian President (which were, after all, only corollaries of his military actions), those same countries demurred. Even after Sadat's death, Sultan Qaboos did not back down. Thus, in an interview with the Lebanese magazine *Monday Morning*, in December 1981, he declared that the Camp David agreement 'opened the doors to peace in the region'.

For many years the position of Sultan Qaboos on the question of Middle Eastern security did not find much support in the Arab world, but in the long run even his irreconcilable critics had to acknowledge his farsightedness. According to the Omani Minister Responsible for Foreign Affairs, Yousuf bin Alawi bin Abdullah:

> We supported the peace process in the Middle East from the days of Camp David, and have never changed our position in this regard. Though in the seventies some were against Camp David, we firmly adhered to our belief in the importance of peace in the Middle East. Then a radical change took place: a conference was held in Madrid, and those states that were against Camp David are now for it, and we have all ended up in the same boat. Multilateral and direct talks came about, once again confirming our position. Two years ago the Israeli government changed, the new government refused to stick to the old obligations in full, so our positions also changed – our relations with this government have cooled. But the general idea of supporting the peace process has remained. Starting from this, we support the Palestinian national administration and the efforts of the co-sponsors of the peace process. The modifications in our tactical course totally correspond to the modifications in the framework of the dialogue.

Ties with Arab countries have always remained a priority in the foreign policy of Oman. This is reflected in diplomatic documents – a traditional hierarchy has been enshrined in the following formula: 'the development of relations with Arab, Islamic and friendly states'.

Speaking at the festivities marking the fiftieth anniversary of the Arab League in 1995, Qaboos bin Said said:

> The Sultanate of Oman, since joining the Arab League on 29 September 1971, has acted in accordance with its well-known, frank and plain convictions in support of the efforts aimed at achieving joint Arab action. It also confirms the importance of activating the role played by the various bodies of the Arab League in all fields in order to come up with positive results in the interests of all Arabs. May God grant us success.
>
> As we celebrate with you today this great event at the Arab League headquarters in Cairo, Egypt, we are also celebrating this event in Oman with due pride and respect.

That last sentence is revealing: only national and religious holidays are celebrated on the same scale in Oman. But this does not mean that the Sultanate prefers Arab countries to all others. The spirit of Omani politics is not nationalistic; it is open to the best possible relations with all countries. The example of Iran expresses this spirit particularly vividly. Even after the overthrow of the Shah, who was a close friend of the Sultan, Qaboos bin Said did not build relations with his neighbours on the basis of personalities, but tried to preserve all the advances that had been made during the close bilateral contacts of the 1970s. Relations with India are equally indicative of the Sultan's unfettered policies. Religious and cultural differences have in no way impaired them, and the cordial and ever-deepening relationship between the two countries is closer than that which Oman enjoys with many Arab countries.

As for the major world powers, from the very beginning Qaboos bin Said adopted a policy of utmost openness. While continuing his country's close collaboration with Great Britain in all spheres, the Sultan realised that his traditional ally was gradually losing its position in the world. The United States, the new leader of the West, was strengthening its influence in the Arab countries, and a realistic politician had to take this into consideration. The influence of the Soviet Union was also growing. For all its pragmatism, Soviet policy was more ideological, and for a long time this prevented the establishment of normal diplomatic relations between the USSR and Oman.

The Minister Responsible for Foreign Affairs commented:

> We had always wanted to have good relations with the Soviet Union. And we undertook special efforts to send unequivocal messages to the Soviet leadership, using a number of channels – through the Shah of Iran, through some British politicians. But it was difficult to understand the politics of the Soviet Union. I think that Soviet politicians did not entirely believe in the sincerity of those messages. We thought that the obligations of the USSR toward the government of South Yemen was one of the major obstacles.
>
> 'And we thought that the propagandist misinformation campaign that was being conducted by the government of the People's Democratic Republic of Yemen was also one of the main obstacles preventing the Soviet leadership

*from understanding the sincerity of those messages. Also the interference of South Yemen in the internal affairs of Oman, and especially in those of Dhofar, was somehow probably backed by the Soviet Union, but our success in Dhofar made the Soviet leadership change its point of view.*

It took almost 15 years to establish normal relations. This seemed particularly anomalous amid the dynamic development of relations between Oman and every other advanced country. Apart from the Sultan's meetings with outstanding politicians during his private trips to Europe, from 1974 he maintained constant contacts with world leaders in the course of official visits. The first of these was a visit to France and discussions with Valéry Giscard d'Estaing, followed almost immediately by a meeting with President Gerald Ford in Washington. The Italian President Giovanni Leone, the Indian Prime Minister Indira Gandhi and Britain's Margaret Thatcher were received by the Sultan in Muscat. In February 1979, in the magnificent al-Alam palace, a ceremonial reception in honour of Britain's Queen Elizabeth II was given.

The first decade of Sultan Qaboos's foreign policy-making firmly established him as a leading figure of geopolitics, whose opinions deserved careful consideration and whose positions deserved the respect of both friends and enemies. This reputation was further strengthened in the penultimate decade of the twentieth century, when the Gulf became the epicentre of a protracted military and political upheaval.

Events in Iran were a prelude to a number of conflicts that threatened to escalate into global crisis. Just as the French and Bolshevik revolutions sparked a chain of bloody wars, the Islamic revolution in February 1979 triggered instability throughout the Middle East.

The 'white revolution' conducted by the Shah without regard for the interests of traditional social forces, disrupting ways of life that had persisted largely unchanged for centuries, provoked a powerful anti-Western backlash which swept away both the dynasty and the pro-Western élite. What the rest of the world saw as a political earthquake, threatening not only the whole region but also international stability, Oman from the beginning saw as Iran's own affair, and therefore not a pretext for interference. The Sultanate kept relations with revolutionary Iran as close as relations with a friendly Muslim neighbour. The good-neighbour policy, which was a milestone in the history of Oman, permitted it more than once to play the role of peacemaker in moments of tension that the West believed to be the fault of Tehran.

The revolution in Iran stirred up unrest elsewhere in the region. In 1979, a large band of extremists seized the Great Mosque of Mecca. The Saudi security forces managed to put down this revolt only at the cost of many lives. In 1981, a Shi'ite plot was uncovered in Bahrain which intended to establish an Islamic regime similar to that in Tehran. In 1983, a major conspiracy in the Saudi Arabian army was foiled and an attempted coup in Qatar was thwarted. A number of terrorists acts destabilised the situation in Kuwait.

The Soviet leadership, which was hoping to reinforce its position in the Gulf and the rest of the Islamic world, was delighted at the coming to power of the anti-American Khomeini regime. But in Moscow there was an influential group with a pro-Western, pro-Israeli orientation, which was secretly protected by the chief of the KGB, Yuri Andropov. Using the Soviet mass media, it attacked Khomeini and, taking advantage of dissension in the pro-Soviet People's Democratic Party of Afghanistan, dragged the Soviet Union into a military venture that caused friction with Iran and other Muslim countries.

In the last days of 1979, 'Alfa', the attack unit of the KGB, seized the palace of Afghan President Hafizu Ilah Amin. At the same time, there was a large-scale incursion of Soviet troops, which set off a ten-year war. These actions were interpreted by the West as evidence of the Soviet Union's intention to gain access to the Indian Ocean and thereby establish control of the main route for transporting oil from the Gulf.[17]

[17] Simultaneously with the Soviet invasion of Afghanistan, the so-called Carter Doctrine was formulated; its essence was expounded in the President's State of the Union address at the beginning of 1980. With respect to the Middle East, the Carter Doctrine was to be applied as follows: 'A refusal to supply oil would have jeopardised our security and would have provoked even more serious economic crises than the great Depression of fifty years ago, and this would have also led to a radical change of our way of life. Last year we began to enlarge our possibilities of transferring our armed forces in the region of the Persian Gulf and now we are studying a possibility of using more actively military objects in this region. We have increased our naval presence in the Indian Ocean. Our rapid deployment forces... could be used to support friendly governments in the Persian Gulf region and Southwest Asia, and also in other regions.'
A high level official responsible for Soviet policy in the Arab world, Karen Brutenz, notes in her memoirs: 'It was out of the question to overlap an oil artery to the West. In the talks "at the top" oil wasn't even mentioned. Ponomarev [head of the International Department of the Central Committee of the Communist Party and a member of the Politburo] simply said that the Arabs had such a powerful weapon in their hands, and he was surprised that

Khomeini's reaction to Soviet interference in Afghanistan was extremely hostile. A propaganda war against 'Soviet imperialists' began. Relations with the United States were also worsening; on 4 November 1979 students in Tehran took over the American Embassy; more than fifty of its employees were taken hostage and remained in captivity until January 1981. Iran was internationally isolated. In the circumstances, President Saddam Hussein of Iraq, who had recently come to power, decided to make the most of the fact that the Iranian army was partly trapped in the north and east and partly weakened by personnel purges and invaded Iran on 20 September 1980.

But although the suddenness of the invasion at first enabled the Iraqi army to score some impressive victories, their momentum soon petered out. The Iranians began methodically squeezing the occupation troops out of their territory. The fact that Iraq was being backed by the Arab Gulf states[18] naturally soured relations between these countries and Iran, resulting in the so-called 'tanker war'. Intent on inflicting maximum damage on its Arab neighbours, the Iranian Air Forces began to attack all oil-loading tankers going to and from their ports. Hostilities threatened to escalate sharply; there was a moment when Saudi Arabia was poised to join the war against Iran.

After a three-year lull following the Dhofar War, Oman was once again in a perilous situation. Qaboos bin Said felt that the previous methods of keeping peace in the region were no longer effective. Tensions between the north and south coasts of the Gulf were too strong to be handled with bilateral agreements between nations. While maintaining his efforts to keep relations with Iran amicable, Qaboos bin Said searched for a new formula for multilateral collaboration that could deal with present and future difficulties.

it wasn't being used effectively; he advised tightening the screws on the USA and convincing it to renounce its pro-Israeli position.' Karen Brutenz, *Thirty Years in the Old Square,* Moscow, International Relations (1988) p. 375.

[18] We can presume that the Iraqi action was approved by some of its neighbours and by some Western states. The pilgrimage of Saddam Hussein to Mecca in August 1980, immediately before his troops invaded Iran, sent a clear signal to the Gulf rulers: the revolutionary phraseology of the Ba'ath Party had been left behind, together with the people who exploited it; Saddam Hussein was standing up for values common to all Arabs, to all Muslims. The king and the sheikhs watched this demonstration with evident satisfaction, and their generous help permitted Iraq to conduct the war for eight years on a scale unprecedented in that region, without causing much hardship to the army or to the civilian population. The war cost Iraq almost US$200 billion – nearly half of which came from the oil monarchies of the Gulf. Saudi Arabia alone provided US$20 billion in the first two or three years of the war. Iraq, which in 1980 received US$26 billion from oil exports, had over $50 billion in foreign aid that year. By the end of the war, according to Saddam, it had a debt of US$40 billion.

In October 1979 he proposed a project for the defence of the Strait of Hormuz, to include the forces of the Arab countries as well as those of the United States, Great Britain and the Federal Republic of Germany. The plan envisaged a first tranche expenditure of US$100 million. But only President Sadat endorsed the Sultan's scheme.

Desperate for the release of the diplomats held hostage in Tehran, President Carter approved an ill-fated commando raid to free them, which failed to match that carried out by the Israelis at Entebbe, Uganda, in July 1976.

The Soviet invasion of Afghanistan created a disturbing undercurrent in world politics. The Sultan decided to secure his country's situation by strengthening its relations with the United States. On 4 June 1980 the two countries signed a treaty on the allocation of American heavy armaments at Omani military bases. A year later, when the war between Iran and Iraq was particularly bitter, a joint American–Omani military exercise, 'Bright Star 81', was conducted in Oman.

As with the Camp David agreements, Qaboos bin Said demonstrated his farsightedness. The Sultan had realised ten years in advance what the Arab countries of the Gulf would have to confront in 1990. Those who had criticised his military collaboration with the West had to appeal urgently to the international community. The collaboration of Oman with the United States and Great Britain was by no means tantamount to a missile aimed at the other countries. On the contrary, the Sultanate's relations with Tehran during the Iran–Iraq war were most constructive; while Oman's other neighbours gave generous aid to Saddam for his struggle against Iran, Oman served as a mediator, a role that was greatly appreciated on both sides of the Gulf. More than once the Sultan's mediation enabled warring parties to bring their positions to each other's attention.

In 1987, Qaboos bin Said proposed that negotiations be held in Muscat between Saddam Hussein and President Rafsanjani of Iran. In the event, such negotiations never took place, but the Sultan's efforts played a very important role in the conclusion of the armistice in 1988.

[19] After the war in Kuwait, during which the Soviet Union took a constructive position, Oman spoke out also for a Soviet military presence in the Gulf. This demonstrated better than anything the Sultanate's objective political strategy. In June 1991, the Minister Responsible for Foreign Affairs, in an interview with a TASS correspondent, said: 'The problem of security in the Gulf is not purely regional, because the stability of the international situation depends on the situation in this region. The Sultanate of Oman regards without prejudice the foreign

The countries of the Gulf showed extraordinary myopia in supporting Iraq throughout the longest war of the twentieth century. Having exalted by their own hands (or, rather, money) the 'saviour' of the Gulf, they suddenly found that without huge foreign armies they would be unable to defend themselves from the new Nebuchadnezzar. The position of Oman, always suggesting that limited military action by Western states was necessary to preserve peace in the region, proved much more moderate.[19]

The ominous events at the end of the 1970s and the beginning of the 1980s made Arab rulers abandon their sceptical attitude towards the idea of creating a regional organisation for maintaining peace. As early as the autumn of 1976, at a conference of the Gulf countries in Muscat, Oman had proposed a security plan for the region, but it had not been accepted. Only the full-scale battle along the Iran–Iraq frontier convinced the rulers on the south coast of the Gulf to reconsider the question of collective defence. But for a long time the road to this objective was strewn with obstacles: some leaders feared they would have to surrender their autonomy to the strongest states; others were dissatisfied with the vagueness of particular proposals.

During the Amman summit of Arab leaders in November 1980, Kuwait circulated a memorandum calling for a union of the Gulf countries. The document was approved and, on 4 February 1981, the ministers for Foreign Affairs from six countries in the region met in Riyadh. The decision to create an Arab Gulf Cooperation Council (GCC) was taken, and sealed with the ministers' signatures in March of that year in Muscat. At the same meeting a text of the new organisation's Charter, which expressed the aspirations for development and the strengthening of stability in the region, was approved.

On 26–27 May of the same year the rulers of the six countries – Saudi Arabia, Oman, Kuwait, Qatar, the United Arab Emirates and Bahrain – gathered in Abu Dhabi. The main purpose of the new organisation was proclaimed – comprehensive integration in economic, political, social and cultural spheres.

military presence in the Gulf zone. The very term "foreign military presence" belongs to categories from the previous world and the period before the reconstruction. For the time being, the oil-exporting Arab countries cannot defend their riches from outside threats with their own forces, which is why they have to ask for help from other states. In the conditions of a new world order the Soviet Union can become such a state. The military units of the USSR can also be an element of a "foreign military presence".'

Questions of military cooperation were initially posed only in the most general form, though Oman hoped that regional collaboration would be realised in the field of defence and internal security. The majority of GCC member states declared their interest in economic collaboration and saw the organisation as a kind of EEC.

Once again, the Sultan's point of view proved to be more realistic. For obvious political reasons, collaboration on defence was not going to be easy – the majority of GCC countries saw integration as a threat to their own sovereignty. But, as Sultan Qaboos had predicted, cooperation on defence was easier than economic cooperation. The economies of all the GCC states had a similar structure: all exported raw materials and imported machinery, equipment and foodstuffs. The main export – oil – could not be included in a mutual commodity agreement; other fields of industry were only in their infancy and therefore could not generate enough products for the Gulf market. Only a few Saudi Arabian enterprises were sufficiently developed and interested in exporting their goods.

With time, the GCC embraced more and more areas: commerce, transport, public health, education and information. The harmonisation of customs policy, the establishment of a common travel area for all member state citizens, the creation of investment funds for projects of importance to all members – all this reinforced the climate of confidence.

Political reality obliged the Gulf countries to seek closer union. An attack by Israeli warplanes on an Iraqi nuclear reactor in June 1981 showed that none of the Arabian countries could consider themselves remote from the Arab–Israeli conflict.

As disturbing events continued to unfold, GCC member states understood more and more clearly the need for close cooperation in military matters. The ideas of Sultan Qaboos on this issue, which had originally been rejected, began to find favour. In 1984, at the meeting of · the heads of the GCC states in Kuwait, the Sultan once again emphasised security concerns:

> At the level of current developments in the area, we emphasise the importance of the great efforts that are being made by the countries of the Council and their participation in the efforts which aim at finding a solution which will put an end to the Iran–Iraq war and achieve the peace and stability we all cherish for our area and all its countries and its peoples.

*The world around us is now witnessing a situation which is dominated by bitter events and conflicts which bring out new challenges every day. While we commend the solidarity shown by our countries for the sake of maintaining their stability, we wish to emphasise the special importance of pursuing our joint endeavour towards developing the coordination which exists between our efforts and capabilities, to enable us to spare our countries and peoples the dangers that confront us, and to enable them to overcome these challenges and difficulties, and to enable them to direct their energies and resources towards continuing to achieve the aims of construction and development. At the same time we must ensure that our countries continue their work and effective participation for the good of our area and our Arab Islamic nation and the entire international community.*

In 1985 the sixth summit of the GCC took place in Muscat. In the luxurious al-Bustan Hotel, built for the occasion, the rulers of the Gulf heard again the Sultan's insistent appeal to be on their guard against dangers which were evident only to the most attentive observers of the political scene in the Middle East:

*The important deliberations we have held on military and security coordination between our states, and on the prevention of terrorism, have helped take us forward another step, and this will have a positive effect on the maintenance of security and stability in our region.*
*Our work during this meeting has resulted in further gains which reflect our strong desire to develop our joint venture in a manner compatible with each stage of its implementation. It will then serve the vital interests of our states and peoples and reinforce our solidarity in the face of challenges.*

Throughout the war between Iran and Iraq, the Sultanate maintained friendly relations with Baghdad, but this did not in the least spoil Oman's relations with Tehran. When receiving Iraqi delegations of the closest associates of Saddam, Izzat Ibrahim and Tariq Aziz, the Sultan sincerely wanted to understand their position. But of course he could not forget the days when Iraqi-trained rebels spread death and destruction in Dhofar. This 'revolutionary' activity could not have occurred without the authority of Saddam Hussein. That same man also directed the frenzied propaganda campaign against his own neighbours – in the Iraqi press, for example, King Hussein bin Talal of Jordan was mockingly called 'Hussein bin Zen' (after his mother instead of his father). After gaining absolute power in the summer of 1979, Saddam liquidated part of his retinue and soon initiated friendly overtures towards the rulers of the Gulf, declaring his Islamic credentials by making a pilgrimage to Mecca.

But when the war with Iran broke out, the leaders of the Gulf countries quickly forgot the twenty-year period when Iraq called itself the vanguard of the Arab revolution. Whilst some Arabian rulers poured money into the bottomless pit of that senseless massacre, Oman took a more cautious approach, refusing to give unconditional support to Iraq.

Saddam's attack on Kuwait in 1990 came as a complete surprise to most of Baghdad's sponsors from the Gulf as well as to the rest of the world. The Arab world had never witnessed such perfidy and the attack resulted in a confusion of reactions by Arab leaders, ranging from reserved acquiescence to strong opposition. The most tangible consequence of the Iraqi invasion was the complete *volte face* of the Arab rulers towards the West. There were powerful calls for moderation by both King Hussein and the Sultan of Oman. The Sultan's political strategy was based on a rational evaluation of political leaders and their actions in the historical perspective. The solid pragmatism of the Omani ruler prevented him from succumbing to mood swings throughout that critical decade.

It has been argued that greater efforts by the GCC countries in the first ten years of that organisation's existence towards the creation of instruments of collective security might have prevented the invasion of Kuwait.[20]

Resentment towards Saddam was so great that the hope in many Arab capitals was that the 'Desert Storm' military operation would topple him. Once again passions prevailed. And once again the Sultan of Oman, in keeping with his policy of not allowing his actions to be affected by his emotions, urged moderation, calling for the conflict to be settled by peaceful means. Although he supported the UN resolutions and sanctions, he understood the destabilising consequences that a downfall of the Ba'ath regime in Baghdad could bring to the region. Even after the invasion, Oman did not break diplomatic relations with Iraq, believing that Iraq could be of great assistance to all the GCC member-states in the post-war period.

---

[20] The Saudi Prince Khaled bin Sultan, commander of the armed forces of the anti-Iraq coalition in 1991, writes about this campaign in his memoirs *Desert Warrior*: 'The crisis showed that the Gulf countries' system of defence, as it existed in 1990, proved absolutely incapable of coping with Saddam's aggression. "The Shield of the Peninsula", the defence

During the worst of the Kuwait crisis, when military activity was escalating hour by hour on both sides, Qaboos bin Said, with deliberate calmness, maintained his normal routine. His point was to show both his subjects and his allies that he thought the situation was under control. At the customary time he took his annual trip around the country and National Day celebrations passed off as usual. Of course, the crisis centre was extremely busy, continually providing the Sultan with information essential to his decision-making. Delegations from both Iraq and Kuwait came to Oman and the monarch listened attentively to their points of view; his suggestions helped to resolve the issue of the evacuation of Kuwaiti subjects from Iraq.

His political actions, intended to pour oil on waters troubled by the agitation of his adversaries' rhetoric, did indeed serve the cause of reconciliation and were aimed at ensuring minimal foreign presence in the region. But the huge military build-up which formed part of the international coalition rushed irresistibly forward, pre-programmed and unstoppable.

After Iraq's defeat and the introduction of sanctions by the UN, the Sultanate was one of the first countries to call for the abolition of these measures, which did more harm to the Iraqi people than to Saddam Hussein. As the Sultan had foresworn revenge even during the Dhofar War, his opposition to sanctions was convincing, and contributed to the gradual relaxation of tensions in the Gulf region after Desert Storm.

In 1991, at the meeting of the heads of the GCC states in Qatar, Qaboos bin Said was elected chairman of the Supreme Committee on Security Issues for the Gulf, which had been set up by the Council within the framework of a plan to create a united armed force. The formation of this committee was, in effect, an acknowledgement of the value of the Sultan's perceived wisdom on these matters.

During the first years of his reign Qaboos bin Said was considered the most constant ally of the West in the Gulf, although this reputation reflected not so much the reality, as the clichés that his opponents were feeding to the public. In a polarised world, where the shibboleths of the Cold War were dominant, the black-and-white typecasting of countries

system of the Arab Gulf Cooperation Council, did not have enough power to contain Iraq or to mount much resistance with its own forces when the invasion took place. Therefore, there was an urgent necessity to reconsider our approaches in the field of collective defence.' Khaled bin Sultan, *Desert Warrior,* Beirut, Dar Alsaqi (1995) p. 545.

and of political figures left no room for the concept of a genuinely independent foreign policy. Hence the establishment of diplomatic relations between Oman and the Soviet Union in 1985 was seen as illogical and abnormal. Indeed, at that time Kuwait was the only member of the GCC to have diplomatic relations with the USSR. But the Sultan's decision was natural enough, reflecting as it did his wish to conduct a truly non-aligned policy regionally and globally.

The Sultan's longstanding desire to involve the world's leading states in the affairs of the region reflected his understanding of modern geopolitics as the cultivation of partnership and not of rivalry: to link as many countries as possible by common interests meant reducing the possibility of confrontation. This was amply demonstrated by the GCC. Before its foundation, every conflict between states in the region was primarily the affair only of its direct participants; after 1981, any tension between individual states was an object of concern to all its members, activating a unified effort by the GCC to settle the conflict. One noteworthy example of this is the resolution of an acrimonious dispute between Bahrain and Qatar over sovereignty of the Hawar islands. Oman took the role of mediator, but other states also contributed to the peacemaking efforts.

The first serious contact on a high level between the Sultanate and the Soviet Union took place in 1984. Eugeny Primakov, then leader of the Institute of the World Economy and International Relations, arrived in Muscat with a special message from the Soviet leader Andropov, which he delivered to the Sultan in person. During a long talk, the desirability of establishing normal relations was discussed and it was agreed that their respective ministers of foreign affairs would draw up papers enabling diplomatic relations between the two countries. Unfortunately, health problems on the part of Andrei Gromyko, head of the Soviet Ministry for Foreign Affairs, led to a postponement of the finalising of the Muscat agreements. Only with the appointment of a new minister, Edward Shevardnadze, did the signing of an agreement on the establishment of diplomatic relations become possible. This took place at the end of 1985 in New York during a session of the General Assembly of the UN.

Qaboos bin Said has never let ideology cloud his understanding of inter-state relations. Even the People's Democratic Republic of Yemen, which long served as a base for hostile soldiers and had hosted Soviet military bases, was not seen as an enemy by Muscat.

Although demonisation of the other side was characteristic of the time (recall Reagan's condemnation of the USSR as 'the evil empire' and Khomeini's branding of the USA as 'the great Satan'), major politicians found points of contact and often made considerable progress.

Under the mediation of the GCC, talks between neighbouring Gulf states began, and on 15 November 1982 an agreement was reached between Oman and the People's Democratic Republic of Yemen on the normalisation of relations and on mutual respect for sovereignty. The agreement explicitly recognised an obligation on both parties not to allocate territory for foreign military bases or for the preparation of attack and provocation by foreign states; it also recognised the need to refrain from hostile propaganda campaigns in the mass media and to establish diplomatic relations.

Normalisation of relations with the PDRY happened with the seeming rapidity and air of improvisation common to the Sultan's other major foreign policy decisions. But, as in the past, the decision was merely the visible result of a long analytical process in which the situation and the consequences flowing from any possible action had been scrutinised minutely. Had the Sultan's decisions been mere improvisations, they would have remained local actions without pattern or meaningful consequence. But each action of Qaboos bin Said on the international scene turned out to be one in a series of steps, and with time even an outside observer began to see a definite plan in that sequence. However, it was only after decades that the logic driving the Sultan's foreign policy became fully evident, and only then was he acknowledged as one of the most skilful diplomats of the Middle East.

One can already speak of the fulfilment of the principles of foreign policy which the Sultan formulated at the beginning of his reign. The Minister Responsible for Foreign Affairs, responding to the question as to whether there exists a document defining the Sultan's main foreign policy objectives, commented:

> The first document is a speech by His Majesty on 23 July 1970. Though that document is rather short, it contains the basic principles of the internal and foreign policy of the State. The basis of our relations with other countries became principles of mutual respect for sovereignty and non-interference in internal affairs. These principles are reflected in the fundamental documents of the UN. [21]

Then, emphasising the Sultan's personal participation in foreign policy decision-making, the Minister said:

> *One problem in which His Majesty took a direct political decision was in the regulation of border questions and disputes with neighbouring states. This decision was taken by the Sultan himself based on lengthy strategic planning. Border questions were solved on the basis of principles of mutual understanding, dialogue and positive collaboration with neighbouring states. And mutually acceptable outcomes were found – because one of the basic principles His Majesty affirms is that relations with our nearest neighbours should be positive and fruitful, and that these relations in no case should be hostile or confrontational. It is well known that territorial and border problems are usually the most difficult and sensitive.*
>
> *Though we have certain obligations to preserve our sovereignty in certain points and in certain regions, in order to honour our principles of cooperation with neighbouring countries we even gave up our claims on certain territories. Oman is the only state in the Middle East that has settled all its territorial problems by peaceful means with all its neighbours. This confirms the long-term and farsighted nature of the Sultan's strategy.* [22]

When Sultan Qaboos took the throne, Oman, comprising Muscat, Oman and Dhofar, was depicted on world maps in a rather arbitrary way. The outlines of the country looked as blurred as the outside world's idea of what was going on in Oman. Only the coast was indisputable and looked the same on all maps. The borders with Saudi Arabia and Yemen were represented by broken lines, located according to the cartographer's whim and varying between atlases by up to several hundred kilometres.

The document which initiated the long process of border definition was an agreement with Iran signed in 1974, which marked the continental shelf. In 1990 a border agreement on frontiers was signed with Saudi Arabia and in 1992 one was signed with Yemen. Since then the borders of Oman have been as sharply defined as the image on the medal that has become the symbol of the nation and the era.

[21] Interview with author.
[22] Ibid.

Stability in a broad regional context remains a fundamental concern for Sultan Qaboos. Soon after Desert Storm, he proposed initiatives to unite previously hostile nations in a comprehensive security system and therefore limit the possibility of fresh conflict spiralling out of control.

At the end of March 1993, the Kuwaiti newspaper *As-Siasa* published an interview with Yousuf bin Alawi bin Abdullah, where he echoed one of the Sultan's most perceptive observations.

> *Understanding the difficulties of the consequences of the Gulf War for the states of the region, especially Kuwait, and for Arab countries and for the whole world, one cannot forget that a new world order is being formed and quite different forces are uniting in large blocs and groups.*

According to the Minister, Iran and Iraq should participate in the new regional security pact. The Arabs could follow the example of Europe, where after the Second World War the victors and the losers cooperated within the framework of new organisations.

The policy of Qaboos bin Said regarding the Arab–Israeli settlement has also remained consistent. Oman was one of the first nations to establish economic relations with the Jewish state, and this was where the pragmatism of the Sultan and his freedom from ideological blinkers was most evident. In this sense the ruler exemplifies the tolerance peculiar to the Omani ruling dynasty, a dynasty founded by the member of a family of merchants (the great Said bin Sultan described himself as 'just a merchant').

At the end of 1994, Israeli Prime Minister Yitzhak Rabin visited Oman. Commercial missions were opened in Muscat and Tel Aviv. But when the Netanyahu government refused to honour a number of the previous agreements, Oman suspended the normalisation of relations with Israel – in complete accordance with the decisions of the Arab League and in accordance with the principles of its own foreign policy.

The overall policy of the Sultanate of Oman is thus a dynamic and constantly developing process. As goals are reached, the Sultan sets others which are more ambitious. And in relations with other countries, he constantly aspires to new levels of achievement. The history of Oman's multilateral contacts with India, China and other countries of south-east Asia illustrates the increasing success and sophistication of the Sultan's foreign policy. The same is true for relations with Russia. During a meeting with the author on 9 November 1999, Sultan Qaboos bin Said said, regarding the prospects for increased Omani–Russian collaboration:

> *Our relations are excellent. At first they developed slowly, but subsequently they acquired a dynamic of their own. They are moving in a positive direction and I am sure they will continue to strengthen in the future.*

In November 1994, Russian Prime Minister Victor Chernomyrdin visited Muscat. High ranking governmental delegations, groups of members of parliament and heads of large Russian companies have also visited the sultanate and an agreement on commercial and economic cooperation has been signed between the two countries. Consultations take place annually at deputy level within the ministry of foreign affairs. As new strategic realities becomes clearer, interest in Oman is growing. Although still at a formative stage, Russia's desire to develop multilateral contacts with China, India, Iran and the Arab world will inevitably give a new impulse both to bilateral and to multilateral relations in the region.

The Sultan's approach to conflict resolution has earned him the respect of both East and West and his pragmatic attitude on many international disputes is widely acknowledged and admired. An excellent example of his approach can be seen in the role he played during Allied discussions on whether to conduct large-scale bombing of Iraq in February 1998. Oman, together with Russia and others, did its best to forestall military action, but also demonstrated an understanding of the limits beyond which it could no longer negotiate peacefully. A skilful leader will recognise that there are certain realities which cannot be changed and will learn to operate within those realities.

Omani diplomats think that Qaboos bin Said is the founder of a new school of international relations, which is based on a single principle: the world is moving towards multilateral collaboration and regional limitations will soon be removed. The Sultan declared in an interview with the monthly magazine *The Middle East* that:[23]

> *The world is growing smaller, and I firmly believe that all countries should follow these precepts and seek to understand each other, to cooperate with each other, and to work together for the benefit of all mankind. There have,*

---

[23] *The Middle East* (November 1995).

*incidentally, been encouraging signs in recent years that conflict between states is becoming recognised as utter foolishness, and that disputes between countries must be settled by means of negotiations, and not war.*

Diplomats say that the Sultan has always regarded dialogue as the only route to ensuring mutual interests. In the more than three decades since this diplomatic school was founded, we can see that its ideas are becoming stronger, not only at the regional but at the international level. The prime confirmation of this was the end of the Cold War, the first step in the trend towards globalisation.

The World Trade Organisation (WTO), which succeeded the General Agreement on Trade and Tariffs, is more all-embracing and capable of solving more large-scale problems. Oman, which is now a member of the WTO, believes the main trends of the twenty-first century will be towards a lessening of the sovereign powers of individual states through increasing economic interdependence. When commerce frees itself from the fetters of regulation – for example, customs regulation – then frontiers between states will become more transparent. The more closely-knit states become, the less important are issues of individual sovereignty and the more likely will be a world of global citizenship. The Sultan had a sense of this three decades ago.

Europe seems to be on the verge of comprehensive integration and the world as a whole is moving toward greater unity. The hope is that economic and not political theories will govern human conduct in the future. The new school founded by the Sultan embraces these looming changes. Moreover, the ruler's philosophy attracts major researchers and diplomats. Oman sees regional conflicts and regional struggle as a preparatory stage for this new style of organisation of international relations. A huge flow of information technology now connects the West with the East, the South with the North, but international relations are still based on the formulae of 70 years ago.

Qaboos bin Said received the International Peace Award in 1998 from several leading American institutions as an expression of the high regard for his contribution to modern politics and his peacemaking role in the most volatile region of the world. The award was voted by the twelve largest American political and strategic research centres and two dozen US universities, and the fact that it was the first occasion on which the

Peace Award had been conferred gave the event a special significance. At the gala ceremony in Washington, former President Jimmy Carter presented the Award to the personal representative of the Sultan and he received the congratulations of many heads of state and prominent politicians from all over the world.

Oman has established diplomatic relations with 135 countries. Flags of all colours flutter above the embassy district in the capital area. None has yet been lowered as a sign of a rupture in relations: in this, the Sultanate is also unique – in recent decades all of its neighbours have from time to time resorted to this extreme measure. Beautiful white residential houses facing the ocean, tranquil roads shaded by palms and acacias, the respectability and serenity of this part of Muscat serve to convey a sense of political stability and trustworthiness.

# Renaissance

HE WAR IN DHOFAR was an enormous drain on the country's finances, with military expenditure accounting for more than 40 per cent of the country's budget. The main task faced by Sultan Qaboos during the first years of transformation was the social and economic development of his country. Many of those who write about Oman have claimed that the Sultanate started this task from scratch and have cited plausible figures – for example that only 5 per cent of the population was literate, or that the entire country contained only three small schools with a total of 900 pupils, and one hospital.

In fact, matters are not that simple. If Oman had actually been a *tabula rasa*, the Sultan's work would have been far easier. It is far more difficult to transform a society with ancient traditions and an established spiritual authority.

The period that began in Oman in 1970 would be better called '*nahda*' (renaissance). This term describes very accurately the essence of what happened – the country returned to its former flourishing state. And this meant that the political authorities had to overcome the overwhelming stagnation into which the country had sunk not only because of external circumstances, but also because of the century-long conflict between the traditionalist tribes and the enlightened central powers. Were it not for external challenges, the thirst for modernisation would not have remained so keen, with part of the ruling élite understanding the reasons for the country falling further and further behind.

A great merit of Qaboos bin Said is his respectful attitude toward the customs and culture of his country. In the absence of a 'spiritual

infrastructure' the reforms could not have had a solid social base. Qaboos
has recalled the times when he was formulating his reform plans:

> *Each country goes through periods of progress and decline. Oman was*
> *in difficult circumstances. Its resources were insufficient for development.*
> *We had to find a way of renewal, but funds from the sale of oil alone*
> *could not ensure that. Education is a key to success. It is not an end in itself;*
> *it is a means, first of all to self-knowledge. The problem of education*
> *occupied me from my very youth. Without education, people cannot*
> *distinguish good from evil, cannot take care of themselves.*
>
> *I felt strongly that a country such as Oman, which has a long, rich history,*
> *did not deserve to find itself in such a difficult situation, that it could and*
> *should get back on its feet. I was deeply disturbed by the fact that my*
> *country had lost the magnificence and popularity it had had in the past.*
> *In my youth, most foreigners didn't even know where my country was.*[24]

The literacy programme and the establishment of schools turned out
to be not only the basic ingredients in Oman's development, but also
important steps towards reforming the country's political system.
The monarch was convinced that without education, all attempts at
liberalisation would degenerate into anarchy – only informed subjects
could consciously participate in the rebuilding of society. Another aim of
these measures was to liberate the populace from Marxist dogma in
the southern regions, which had for long been under the control of
the insurrectionists.

Even before the realisation of the first development projects, schools
and centres for adult literacy were created throughout the country.
Often classes were held in the shade of a large tree, with no textbooks.
Many teachers were expatriates, and those from other Arab countries
were not always sufficiently versed in the local dialect. Yet the resulting
improvements in education were impressive. By 1975, literacy had
increased to 30 per cent of the population. State spending on education
comprised 1.8 per cent of the total budget. The following year, the first
year of peace after the long Dhofar War, it rose to 2.2 per cent and the
rate of growth has remained constant ever since. By 1980 it was 4.1 per
cent, by 1990, 6.9 per cent, and today it exceeds 10 per cent. Numbers of
educational establishments, pupils and teachers have also grown

[24] Interview with the author (9 December 1999).

markedly. In 1975 there were 214 schools, 56,000 pupils and 2000 teachers; by 1980 there were 377,950 pupils and 4000 teachers; in 2002, there were 1187 schools with 629,000 pupils and 33,614 teachers.

The state provided generous support for Omani youths to study abroad. Thousands of students went to universities and colleges in Arab countries, Europe and America. This enabled the country to satisfy an urgent need for qualified specialists and start the process of Omanisation, as the Sultan called his programme for the gradual replacement of foreigners in key government positions.

In 1982, by decree of the Sultan, construction began on Oman's first university. A British firm won the contract to construct an ultramodern educational complex 50 kilometres from the capital. About US$500 million was spent on the construction of lecture halls, libraries and living quarters, and on extending communications and planting trees.

In four years a piece of desert was replaced by a magnificent campus. Speaking at the opening of the university on 9 November 1986, Qaboos bin Said declared:

> *The university has the particular responsibility to preserve Omani values and traditions and to preserve the valiant and exemplary Omani heritage as an incentive to our young people to serve their country by carrying forward what has been achieved in the past. We look forward to seeing the theoretical and applied research of the university in the service of Oman and in developing solutions to our social and economic concerns.*

Within another four years the first graduates were to receive their degrees from Sultan Qaboos University. This event was noted by the Sultan as a major landmark in the history of modern Oman. Addressing the university's first graduates, he said:

> *The knowledge and expertise you have acquired will qualify you to play a vital part in building a modern Omani society preserving the gains of the Blessed Renaissance, and achieving greater progress for the present and coming Omani generations, within the framework of the eternal values we all share. These values represent virtue and truth, tolerance and integration, selflessness and sacrifice, and decent conduct in one's dealings with others. These are values inherited from our fathers and forefathers, and absorbed by Omani society over generations.*

In the decade since then, the university has expanded in every respect. The number of students has more than doubled to almost 11,635, more than half of whom are female. In addition, the Ministry of Higher Education funds almost 500 students to study abroad, and another 5000 Omanis study in foreign countries either at their own expense or on grants. As is clear from the Sultan's speech at the inauguration of the university, education and progress are indelibly linked in his mind: 'We live in an age of science and education. Education and work are only means of progress and development within the context of our Islamic civilisation.' Given the country's pressing need for specialists in all areas and the high cost of educating students abroad, the government has very positive views on the possibility of the opening of private universities in the Sultanate.

Over the past few years another tendency has become noticeable in the field of education – the number of independent schools is growing. This increases parental choice, creates healthy competition with state schools and broadens the range of teaching methods. The network of independent schools links technical and commercial schools, schools of Islamic teaching, teachers' colleges and schools of medicine and commerce.

The Sultanate's youth policy also includes a sports programme. One only has to look at the groups of runners and footballers who throng the parks and beaches of Muscat every evening or the hordes of flag-waving fans at the stadia to see the success of the years of government effort in this area – sport has become a necessity for young Omanis, an indispensable part of life for the new generation.

Every provincial centre – Nizwa, Sur, Ibri, and so on – has a modern sports complex, or 'youth centre', which is kept in perfect condition. These complexes provide training for all kinds of sport. Many villages have their own football team and businessmen consider it an honour to sponsor them. Every year the football clubs of Oman compete for the national football trophy. The final is played in the capital's marvellous stadium in the presence of dignitaries and statesmen, and the cup is presented either by the Sultan himself or by a member of his family.

Even figure skating has become popular and a newly built arena with artificial ice provides facilities where promising skaters can train from an early age. Traditional sports are also being developed – camel races are especially popular.

Another top priority for Oman has been the creation of a modern health service. Before 1970, few Omanis had any knowledge of vaccination, pharmacies, or effective preventive medicine. In just a few years a revolution in medical care has occurred. Omanis have literally and metaphorically been given a new lease of life – the average lifespan in Oman nowadays is 72 years, whereas 30 years ago it was a mere 50 years.

The publication of statistics did not occur until some years after the initiation of reforms, with health statistics being the last to appear. Official figures on public health spending generally date from 1975, by which time the situation had already improved considerably since 1970. Even so, the measured achievements are impressive.

In 1975, public health spending made up 2.9 per cent of the budget. Today this figure is about 7.6 per cent. In 1975, there were 24 hospitals with 1000 beds, now there are 49 hospitals with 4494 beds; there were fewer than 150 doctors, whereas now there are over 3536. Figures for child mortality show a spectacular improvement. In 1970 a high proportion of newborn babies died, now there are only 16.7 per cent deaths per 1000.

Considering that from the first day of the Sultan's reign all education and medical care has been provided free of charge, the scale of change is unprecedented in the country's history. The speed of technological transformation is equally impressive. It took only a few years to progress from mud-houses strewn with mats to today's snow-white multi-storey buildings filled with modern furniture, equipment and home appliances.

Every major facility built in Oman in the first years of Qaboos bin Said's rule caused a revolution in some sphere of life: an international airport in Seeb built in 1973; a television station in Muscat with the first programme broadcast on 17 November 1974; power stations and desalination plants; modern roads connecting the capital with the cities of the Batinah and Inner Oman. All this swiftly and dramatically changed a lifestyle established over centuries.

Raising the standard of living was a basic requirement of the government's drive towards economic development. Immediately after the war in Dhofar, Sultan Qaboos declared that the further improvement of his subjects' living standards would be his top priority.

Oil revenues soared from the end of 1973. The increase in energy prices after the Arab–Israeli war in 1973 lasted until 1981. It enabled the state to fund social programmes and led to a rapid increase in income for every family.

But big money can, of course, create big problems, such as runaway inflation, social stratification and corruption. Many Third World countries experienced social instability connected with the sudden influx of petro-dollars. Nigeria, Iran and Indonesia, all of whom received colossal revenues from oil, have also faced monumental social crises. These, and others, including some Arab countries, have been plagued by leaders whose megalomaniac plans to build gargantuan armies led them to squander the nation's wealth on military adventures. For such leaders, the Omani proverb, 'His name is renowned, but his stomach is hungry' is a fitting epitaph. Only stable political leadership and a clear programme of action can make money work for the benefit of the nation and prevent the unhappy side-effects of sudden riches.

Oil has been the basis of economic development in Oman from the very beginning of the Omani renaissance. Having begun in 1967 with average daily production of 300,000 barrels a day, by 2000 the average daily production had risen to over 900,000 barrels. Until 1982, when the first oil refinery was brought on stream in Mina al-Fahal, fuel and petroleum products had to be imported. Now the country's domestic needs are fully satisfied by its own industry.

Currently the Sultanate produces more than 306 million barrels annually, a figure which could be considerably increased. But the Ministry of Oil has set an annual limit of 6.5 per cent of recoverable reserves, at present about 734 million tonnes (5.7 billion barrels). The present production of nearly 800,000 barrels per day falls within this limit and fulfils the desire to preserve for as long as possible the country's main natural resource.[25]

The figures for explored oil reserves show that, in contrast to most of its neighbours, Oman could never count on massive profits from oil and must therefore husband its resources carefully in order to fulfil its development programme. The sellers' market in oil that arose in the 1970s was not exploited to the full by many oil-exporting countries. For some, the intoxication of the petro-dollars was followed by a painful

---

[25] The overall oil reserves of Oman are much greater than the figure for explored reserves. But extraction with present methods is still problematic. Sultan Qaboos explained the problem in an interview with the Spanish newspaper *Tribuna*: 'At present, the known reserves which may be drawn upon stand at 5 billion barrels, which are economically saleable at present world prices. Approximately a further 45 billion barrels have also been identified, but their economic extraction will depend upon future world prices and advances in the techniques required for their exploitation.' *Tribuna* (26 January 1996).

hangover when prices subsequently fell. Mexico's economic catastrophe was characteristic of such a development, while in the Soviet Union the fall in oil prices from as high as US$38 per barrel in 1981 to US$9 in 1986 led to a deep crisis.

The Sultan of Oman has always considered the country's oil to be the fuel for other sectors of the economy. He has been active in creating new fields of industry and in ensuring that Oman becomes self-sufficient in food, especially since the difficult year of 1986.

Oman's copper deposits in the Sohar region, already known to the ancients, returned to the fore at the beginning of the 1980s but were depleted by 1994. The copper-smelting plant near Sohar, completed in 1984, where imported copper is refined and then re-exported, has brought the country six million riyals (over US$15 million) from the export of cathode copper.

Government projects for the creation of an aluminium smelter at Sohar, making use of Oman's natural gas, for platinum, gold and silver mining, (small quantities of gold and silver are already produced from copper oxide deposits) for a construction materials industry and for fertiliser production reflect the country's ambition to develop a diversified economy that is not at the mercy of fluctuations in the price of oil. Some of these projects have already been realised; others are being considered. The country produces and exports marble, limestone, gypsum, salt, chromite and cement. The medium-sized industrial estates, the first of which was established at al-Rusayl in the foothills of the Hajar al-Gharbi range, are pioneers of modern industry. More and more consumer goods are labelled 'Made in the Sultanate of Oman'.

For the time being, the export of oil accounts for about 70 per cent of total revenues. This is a considerable improvement in comparison with the first decade of Oman's renaissance, when dependence on oil was absolute. But the Sultan is not satisfied with the present situation; he has concentrated his efforts on the task of accelerating the diversification of the country's economy. Before the oil runs dry, alternative sources of income have to be found.

In many of his speeches Sultan Qaboos reminds his fellow countrymen that 'the glory of oil is a perishable thing'. He encourages his people to search for alternatives that can protect the economy when oil prices fluctuate, as they did in 1986 and 1998.

On both sides of the rough, dusty road along the mountainous coast of the Gulf of Oman from Muscat to Sur, the landscape seems wild and inhospitable. The fishing villages do nothing to dispel this impression; goats huddle in doorways, seeking refuge from the scorching heat of the sun; nets dry on palm fronds; everything is almost as it was centuries ago. But for the telegraph poles and the odd car or motorboat, it would be easy to imagine oneself in the distant past.

This is equally true of the ruins of Qalhat, one of the ancient capitals of Oman. An unearthly silence hangs over the remnants of the fortifications. But walking slowly to the sea, you glance above the fortress wall and notice silvery cylinders towering above interlaced pipelines and industrial plants towering above the ash-grey rocks. A long viaduct, like a gap-toothed saw, plunges into the smooth, sun-drenched sea, and the juxtaposition of the ancient ruins and the industrial complex gives a sense of unreality. It is as if a gigantic spaceship, an envoy of an unknown world, has descended to earth in the times of the caliphs.

Such contrasts are characteristic of Oman, with its reverence for the past and its openness to the future. A brand-new gas liquefaction plant near the ruins of Qalhat, a town which was destroyed in ancient times by an earthquake, is a symbol of the country's economic progress.

Hopes are high for the development of the gas industry in the Sultanate. Oman has become a world leader in the exploitation of this new resource. The 283 billion cubic metres found by geologists to date can meet the country's domestic and export needs for the next 60 years. Total proven gas reserves at the beginning of 2000 stood at 29.3 trillion cubic feet, of which 25 tcf was non-associated gas.

The Oman NLG plant, a modern industrial complex recently constructed near Sur in the vicinity of Qalhat, cost US$9 billion. Raw materials are transported there by a pipeline across the desert. After liquefaction, the gas is loaded from a sea terminal into special tankers. The first tankers left the terminal (Port Qalhat) near Sur in April 2000. A market for the product had been secured as early as October 1997, when the government signed a deal with the Japanese agreeing an annual supply of 660 million tonnes of liquid natural gas (LNG) over 25 years. By 2002 gas production accounted for 15 per cent of Oman's GDP.

Sultan Qaboos considers development in this field a strategic direction for the future economy:

> *I am pleased to say that very substantial reserves of liquid natural gas have been found and are being exploited; these reserves promise to augment Oman's income in the future to a level which could well be comparable to our present-day earnings from oil.*[26]

The significance of the Sultanate's industrial development projects is not limited to the economic sphere. It is giving impetus to changes in the social structure and creating a new style of life. In a speech on National Day on 18 November 1996, the Sultan specifically mentioned the opportunities that would arise after the Sur complex was opened:

> *Our LNG project . . . is one of the major steps which aims to find diversified sources for our income. The implementation of this project will result in substantial economic returns, one of which will be the attainment of additional financial resources for our future development plans, and an additional injection of strength to our national working capital. It will also provide broad support for the people of the city of Sur and neighbouring areas, in the fields of public services, property, tourism, banking, industry, the acquisition of new skills and employment.*

Another project recently completed in Oman that can serve as an example of long-term planning and careful development is the construction of one of the biggest container ports in the world, in the vicinity of Salalah. The US$250 million spent on this facility is just the first phase of a significant flow of investment into the local and national economy. Dozens of companies, ultimately providing employment for thousands of young Omanis, will eventually locate in the industrial zone of Raysut.

The building of the container port was inspired by research into the sea-freight market in the region. Salalah is situated only 150 miles from the main shipping lanes between the Far East and Europe and America. Through these lanes moves the highest volume of goods traffic in the world. Most of the transportation of goods and industrial equipment is effected by huge container vessels, which can unload in more than one port along their journey; once unloaded, the containers are delivered by small ships to all the ports of the surrounding region.

[26] *Tribuna* (26 January 1996).

The countries of the Gulf are the major recipients of cargo shipped via this great East–West lane. In the past, ships had to make a detour of several thousand miles to enter the Gulf and also incurred extra insurance costs (the Gulf is considered a high-risk zone and insurance premiums are growing markedly). By unloading their containers in Salalah, shipping companies can make considerable savings. For Oman this has created the potential to develop an important regional commercial centre, similar to Dubai.

From the moment the first ship was unloaded at the Salalah container terminal in November 1998, Oman and her neighbours have reaped substantial benefits. In the first year alone about 500 ships docked there, unloading more than half a million containers. Clearly, the planned capacity will not be reached immediately. Six of the biggest port cranes in the world, supplied by Japanese firms, are capable of unloading and storing an enormous amount of goods on four cargo piers, and then loading them again onto small ships or lorries.

Lorries can cover the 1000 kilometres from Salalah to the United Arab Emirates in one day – matching the speed of delivery to the end-user from the other Gulf ports. A fine road linking Dhofar with the eastern provinces of Yemen has made it possible to deliver containers to this country as well.

The vast Yemeni market (there are almost 15 million people in this, the most populous country of the Arabian Peninsula) naturally catches the attention of Arab businessmen. In the frontier region of Dhofar a free economic zone, which will attract traders interested in developing this potential market, will soon emerge. The private sector will become the main participant in all projects connected with the zone. The government sees support of the private sector as one of its main aims – indeed, it has been a priority of Oman's economic policy for some years.

During the first phase of Oman's renaissance only the state had the necessary resources to invest in the infrastructure, mining industry and energy facilities. Private capital was scarce and was normally invested in commerce, residential construction and the financial markets. But today there are a significant number of businessmen whose fortunes enable them to operate in the public sector.

Sultan Qaboos, in accordance with his vision of the country's future, aspires to the creation of a true market economy, where the state plays a regulatory role and public citizens become the main agents.

The successful launch of a stock exchange in the Muscat Security Market in 1989 shows that conditions in Oman are ripe for the development of financial services. New large-scale projects are being carried out with the support of both domestic and foreign capital. For example, 20 per cent of the funds for the Salalah container port came from the government, while 19 per cent was provided by private Omani investors. The first private power station, not only in Oman, but in the Gulf states, the Manah Power Project, was constructed near Nizwa.

Private sector participation in the oil and mining industry also continues to grow, as the Sultan stressed in a speech on National Day in 1998:

> *The private sector now, more than at any time in the past, is required to redouble and accelerate its efforts, with confidence, and utilising all opportunities in promisingly productive avenues. This will have, with God's permission, positive and tangible effects on our economic and social life in the coming years. In addition to this, it will have to be fully aware of contemporary international circumstances, which are based on freedom of trade and investment. This necessitates that our economic enterprises should be at the highest level of efficient administration, productivity and marketing in order to have the strength to compete, especially since we are entering the World Trade Organisation.*

Creating favourable conditions for foreign investors is one of the high-priority tasks which the Sultan has set the government and legislative bodies. At the same time the state itself participates in major investment projects abroad. Thus, Oman became one of the participants in the Caspian Pipeline Consortium, founded to construct and manage the oil pipeline from the Kazakh oilfield of Tengiz to Novorossisk on the Black Sea. There are also plans to construct a sizeable oil refinery in Thailand, which, together with Japan and China, is one of the largest customers for Omani oil.

Beginning with the first five-year plan (1976–1980), Sultan Qaboos has striven to achieve realistic goals. The President of the State Council of Oman says:

> *Economic planning was based on flexibility, because we know that we live in a difficult world, where different interests and influences are interwoven. Planners should not think that they work in a vacuum, that they work only*

*with black and white and that nothing will happen that can make them change their plans. Planners must have a clear idea of the possible regional and global consequences. Planners in Oman always consider it necessary to be prepared for change. We keep an eye on what is happening in the world economy; we are not afraid of changes.*

*Notwithstanding the difficulties we have overcome in thirty years, the Omani economy progresses step by step and does not retreat. We accelerate forward when we can, when conditions are right; we slow down when there are difficulties.*[27]

The economy of Oman has avoided major crises, though for a country that almost completely depends on world oil price fluctuations it has not been easy. In the last quarter of the twentieth century, the Sultanate had the world's second highest rate of economic growth. According to World Bank data published in the spring of 1999, the average rate of growth from 1965 to 1997 was 9.7 per cent.

In the twenty-first century diversification and strengthening the role of the private sector remain the main objectives of Oman's economic policy. Sultan Qaboos sees the country's development as a guarantee of its stability. In a speech in his Royal camp in Dhofar the Sultan said:

*Consider what happened to certain countries where the citizen depended wholly on the State. Those countries collapsed and poverty and instability prevailed. No country in the world can eliminate the role of the individual, nor can the individual depend wholly on the State.*

*This is also against the teachings of our religion, which recognises and respects private ownership and urges the individual to work. When he works, he gains wealth and gives others a chance to work with him to earn their living. Thus the bounty of God is well distributed among individuals and societies and thereby increases in their midst. He who is capable gives a chance to another who is capable, and the latter gets the opportunity and the means to feed his family so that all can benefit.*

The nation's tasks for the next two decades are formulated in the document *Vision 2020* and in several five-year plans. Private owners will have to create the majority of jobs, which will help the young generation of Omanis to find their place in life.

[27] Interview with the author (22 December 1998).

The problem of employment is directly connected to the problem of Omanisation. During his annual tour of the country in 1998, Sultan Qaboos gave a speech before the leaders of the Batinah, in which he focused on the problem of employment for young people:

> *All over the world foreign labour is used. It is a normal phenomenon. But when it is not a necessity, and a great deal of money goes abroad and local people consider certain jobs shameful socially, this is not acceptable. Omanis have always been hard workers and Omanis also go abroad to work; it is a normal practice, it is a mutually beneficial affair. And God orders human beings to go around for the sake of earning a livelihood. Our reliance on foreign labour, however, must have reasonable limits.*

The Sultan emphasised that it was necessary to educate young people not to look down on some professions as lacking prestige, and to make them understand that what is important is the quality of labour and a responsible attitude to work.

The government is making efforts to create acceptable living standards in the countryside to halt the depopulation of agricultural localities. Modern villages with comfortable houses, equipped with all the benefits of civilisation, are being built with state funds. Equalising the standard of living in urban and rural areas has reduced the flow of labour from the countryside.

The traditional occupations of the people of Oman – agriculture, cattle-breeding and fishing – remain an object of constant government concern. In these spheres fundamental changes have also taken place. The following snapshot of life in Dhofar epitomises these changes.

On the side of a road a Japanese limousine comes to a stop beside a herd of grazing camels. A *jebali* in a snow-white *dishdasha* leaves the air-conditioned atmosphere of his car and, with a bucket in his hand, milks one of the camels. He returns to the plush velvet interior of his car, escaping the burning rays of the sun, and speeds away to the next herd, loud music blaring from his car stereo. It is hard to recognise in this sleek young man the son of a sun-blackened shepherd, wearing only a towel who 25 years ago climbed the rocky slopes of the mountains in bare feet, searching for errant cows and camels.

Fishermen go to sea in high-speed boats, throw out nylon seines and deliver their catches to refrigerators, to be sent to domestic or foreign markets. What a contrast with the days when mountains of unsold fish would rot on the beach, or be dried for camel fodder.

Palm groves and crop plantations today receive water from wells and distilling plants distributed by powerful electric pumps. Tractors, cultivators and other agricultural machinery are commonplace. Further development of irrigation systems will permit a considerable increase in yields, as well as the exploitation of new arable lands. Currently, of the 7.5 per cent of the Sultanate's land that could be utilised, only 1 per cent is given over to agriculture.

Oman now has every right to be called a modern society. And it has avoided the pitfalls of societies which have experienced rapid and far-reaching change – especially depersonalisation and standardisation. This is what makes the renaissance initiated by Sultan Qaboos unique. His personality, his aesthetic inclinations and his loyalty to historic traditions and religious values have been the most important factors of this velvet revolution.

In the process of renewal, care has been taken not to damage or harm the natural environment. Hundreds of historic forts, mosques, palaces and public buildings have been preserved. Yet it is not only the conservation of old buildings that enables the country to preserve its distinctive architectural identity: the modern architecture of Oman also pays the greatest respect to its own national traditions. Muscat, Salalah, Sohar, Nizwa and other important centres of Oman have managed to avoid even a hint of American style – a trend in the modernising Third World countries – which has left its mark even on the architecture of the ancient European capitals. When asked about his architectural preferences in an interview with *Figaro* magazine the Sultan said: 'I particularly hate glass buildings . . . But of course we don't interfere with the interior decoration'.[28] The authorities will not grant permission for new constructions until the plans are agreed by the architectural inspectorate, who take great care to preserve the traditional appearance of towns. While the size of buildings erected and the construction methods used have changed radically, aesthetic principles remain and in modern Oman, houses continue to be decorated with carved doors and windows are covered with patterned wooden gratings.

In all probability, there are few countries in the world whose architecture is determined to such an extent by the taste of its ruler.

[28] *Figaro Magazine* (30 April 1994).

The Sultan Qaboos prize for architecture was first awarded in 1999, but it could be claimed that everything constructed or restored in Oman since 1970 is a monument to the Sultan.

Protective zones have been created around major historic monuments. The ruins of the lost city of Ubar and other ancient cities are being excavated and conserved. The ruined city of Sumurham, at the port village of Khor Ruri near Taqa, and the site of the ancient settlement of al-Balid in Salalah, probably the ancient town of Dhofar, have been dug out from centuries of detritus. Also in the care of the state are the ancient fortress of Bahla and the ruined prehistoric necropolises of Bat and al-Ain. All are landmarks on UNESCO's World Heritage List.

Reverence for Oman's past is expressed not only in the maintenance of its historic monuments, but also in the creation of new structures that pay tribute to their memory. The ultra-modern naval base in Wudam was named after Said bin Sultan. The newest combat ships are named after vessels which distinguished themselves in the naval battles of past centuries. The guards proudly wear traditional uniform, though they are armed with submachine guns instead of swords and smoothbore guns.

The process of transforming a nation threatens more than just monuments and the historical face of the urban landscape. Nature itself can suffer grievously from the influence of modern technology. While the Batinah was for centuries the country's granary thanks to its substantial reserves of fresh water, today the future of the region's arable lands is fraught with anxiety. From time immemorial a system of wells and *aflaj* (plural of *falaj*) had been used for irrigation, but since 1970 almost every farmer has used electric pumps. The water table has been disturbed and soil salinisation has begun. Considerable sums of money are being spent to combat this problem.

The Sultan is deeply concerned to avoid the catastrophic consequences of environmentally unsustainable development. At the time of the Rio Environment Summit in 1992, he said: 'We must set a limit to haphazard methods and protect what is left of our grazing lands and water resources against desertification and drought.'

In the course of meetings with his people, the monarch constantly exhorts them to treat the environment with respect. During his trip to Dhofar in January 1995 he said:

*It is important to preserve the environment and avoid overgrazing because if grass does not produce enough seed, it will perish. We have seen how well grass grows in fenced-off areas. Let us benefit from the mountains that God has bestowed on the region and protect their flora. The owners of grazing animals will have less need to use them because there is a plan to shift fodder crops from the plains of Salalah to the other side of the mountains.*

In 1973, after long years of ruthless exploitation of nature and the resulting impoverishment of flora and fauna, some of which are unique to the area, the Sultan introduced an absolute prohibition on hunting and other trades which threatened the environment. Oman became the first Arab country to create a Ministry for Protection of the Environment.

In the 1970s, although the country was a long way from achieving the Sultan's development targets, substantial resources were devoted to the preservation and restoration of native fauna. Birds wintering over in Oman – pink flamingos, geese and many species of duck – were given protected status; protection was also extended to the green turtles living on the coast. For the first time in many years the unique Omani mountain goats that had become a rare sight had no need to fear the rifle, and a major project was implemented to reintroduce and establish a population of Arabian oryx – once a symbol of Arabia.

The recovery of the Arabian oryx has been dramatic. Small herds used to inhabit the vast peninsula and Bedouins on camels with regular smoothbore guns did little to reduce their numbers. But with the coming of Land Rovers and the development of long-range rifles, the situation abruptly worsened. In 1972, in the Jiddat al-Harasis desert, the last wild oryx was killed. Three years later Sultan Qaboos decided to restore the oryx to Oman. Through the agency of other Arabian rulers, the World Wildlife Fund and the London Zoo, a few of the last remaining Arabian oryx were caught and given refuge in Kenya; from there a herd of nine were delivered to Phoenix Zoo in Arizona, US, where the climate is similar to that of Arabia. There the Arabian oryx began to breed.

In 1982, a plane with five of these offspring landed at Seeb International Airport and they were transported to the place where wild oryx had last been seen – the territory controlled by the Harasis tribe. The Sultan agreed with the sheikhs that the tribe would take them under its protection. The animals were kept in an enclosure and in due course became accustomed to their new home. Shortly thereafter they were joined by two more groups of young oryx from Phoenix. By special decree of the Sultan the National Park of Jaaluni was established as a centre for rearing oryx for the wild. Initially the park employees fed them with alfalfa and hay and watered them. Only after completion of the first stage of 'Operation Oryx' were the animals released into the wild. Their numbers climbed to some 400. Today their population totals only something over 100 – the reduction of these swift, gracious inhabitants of the desert being attributed to poaching by the tribal neighbours of the Harasis. However, numbers are growing once again.

Green turtles may not have come quite as close to extinction as the oryx, but poachers still hunted them for their meat and egg collectors raided their sand covered clutches of eggs. In June 1977, the Sultan announced an ambitious project for the protection of these unique marine creatures. A natural park was created near the cape of Ras al-Hadd, where ideal conditions exist for the nesting of the huge marine reptiles.

To watch the turtles return to the same shores they left as hatchlings to lay their eggs, one must take up position on the beach (as advised by the environmental protection services) on a moonlit night, and wait motionless and soundless until a wave deposits on the sand something that, from a distance, looks like a military helmet. Gradually, the dim form of a turtle, up to a metre in length, can be distinguished as it crawls slowly from the sea leaving a wide furrow, like the tyre track of a tractor, in the sand. At about 20 metres from the high water mark more and more turtles heap up little piles of sand with their flippers and excavate deep pits in which they lay some one hundred or so eggs. These enormous, phlegmatic creatures live for up to 400 years; quite possibly there are among them some that emerged in the same silent way in the days when the Portuguese were masters of the land, and when the star of the Ya'ruba dynasty rose and set. An involuntary tremble overtakes you to see a living creature that was possibly born in the days of Imam Ahmed, who was alive at the beginning of a great dynasty – to touch its hard armour is to touch living history. And as the giant reptile disappears back into the waves, leaving the eggs alone to incubate in the heat of the nest she has prepared, you hope that the measures being taken to secure the future of the green turtle will, with time, be wholly successful.

Sultan Qaboos has more than once stressed in his speeches that preserving the natural environment cannot be left to individual nations. Only broad international cooperation can restore the earth's environment. The creation of the Sultan Qaboos International Award for Nature Protection in 1989 testifies to his sincerity on this point. Distinguished recipients of this prestigious award include a Mexican research centre (1991), a Czech scientist (1993), a conservationist organisation in Malawi (1995), the University of Alexandria and a Sri Lankan agency for the protection of forests (1997) and the Darwin Natural Park on the Galapagos islands (1999).

# Facing the Future

HE STATE APPARATUS that Sultan Qaboos inherited in July 1970 was an obstacle to reform. Even with the means for development, progress cannot be achieved without the appropriate administrative structures. The young Sultan knew how government and municipal bodies functioned in Europe and he recognised that while the chain of command in Oman had to be built on traditional lines, he also had to consider the experience of the world's leading nations. In 1970, however, there were just 1750 state employees in the whole country. Even the creation of new ministries was a serious problem, let alone the formation of management bodies. Some months passed before a government could be formed.

Previously, the management of the country had been in the hands of the Provisional Consultative Council, composed of the old Sultan's confidants and given no freedom to act independently. The Council lacked the time to implement any plans for economic development. Its functions passed partly to the government, partly to special bodies whose task was to coordinate development projects. But because the philosophy of reforms was at a rudimentary phase, the development councils proved to be short-lived. The Tenders Committee was the first body to come into being, but shortly afterwards its functions were transferred to a newly created Interim Planning Council, which existed for just six months. In September of the same year a Supreme Council for Economic Organisation was formed, but this body also proved ineffective, and in April 1973 it was replaced by the General Development Organisation, which was dissolved at the end of the year.

The Ministry of Development which succeeded all the above-mentioned groups was itself subjected to a reorganisation after less than a year. At the same time (in late 1974), the Sultan created both a Finance Council and a Development Council. All these reshuffles demonstrated the difficulty of creating efficient working structures in a vacuum. Notwithstanding the enormous problems – the dearth of management, lack of infrastructure and the diversion of resources to the war in Dhofar – in the first years of its existence the new government apparatus managed to find its feet.

The Sultan thought it necessary to involve the people in the country's reconstruction. But from the beginning he realised that the traditional system of government, with its reliance on the tribal structure, should not be totally demolished. It was his opinion that everything valuable from the past ought to be brought forward into the future.

Therefore, in that momentous radio appeal on 9 August 1970, Qaboos bin Said reassured the tribal sheikhs that they were an essential part of the country's future. As far as the monarchy as a political institution was concerned, the Sultan had no doubt that it was absolutely essential – Oman could not survive without it. It was, however, clear to him that flexibility and efficiency must be an integral part of the role he had taken over from his father if Oman was to be protected from the unrest that threatened to envelop it. The war in Dhofar was undertaken in order to secure for Oman a future that was not based on the destruction by outsiders of all that gave the country its unique character and meaning – but in conducting the affairs of his country during those difficult years, Sultan Qaboos benefited greatly from his ability to distil from his knowledge of Western civilisation those aspects which would benefit the development of Oman. As he once commented on this mission of an hereditary ruler:

> The role of a monarch in modern times is that of a guide who should act as a resource and a reference in a changing world. He should play the role of arbiter and outline policies to be carried out by the government in the interests of the people.[29]

In every society that passes through a period of profound change, opinions will differ on the content and pace of reform. If a radical point

[29] Ibid.

of view prevails, economic reforms accompany political and social transformation. If the advocates of a cautious approach gain the upper hand, changes are initially instituted in the sphere of economics, while social changes are permitted only after an economic base is created.

Liberalisation in politics which is not bolstered by serious economic achievement usually provokes a rapid disintegration of the state and triggers social revolution. So it was in France at the end of the eighteenth century and in Russia at the beginning of the twentieth. Having lost a precious instrument in autocracy, the reformers lost the possibility of influencing events and became hostages of rapidly changing circumstances. But history also knows other varieties of societal coups. Some rulers, bewitched by the idea of rapid progress, played the role of revolutionaries themselves – Peter the Great in Russia and Mohammed Reza Pahlavi in Iran, for example. Both set their nations the objective of catching up with Western countries practically overnight; both knew that the inertia and conservatism of their subjects were the main impediments to achieving this. The interference of the state in all spheres of life became appallingly burdensome. Even secular customs and morals were often ridiculed for the sake of what seemed progressive to the supreme leader. The leader of the 'white revolution', the Shah of Iran, ordered the purchase of a multitude of foreign breweries and distilleries and encouraged the spread of European fashions. He was flattered when Iran was likened to the countries of southern Europe.

Sultan Qaboos was very conscious of the fact that the promise of uncompromising progress without any accompanying action poses the danger of stirring up violent political extremism even amongst those engaged in the process of attempting to bring about such a development. The people of Oman had to see, and be involved in, action implementing change for such a potential catastrophe to be averted. He well remembers how his plans for reform began to mature. After years of studying the history of Oman and other countries, he came to the conclusion that all societies pass through ups and downs, and he felt certain Oman's lack of development was only a temporary phenomenon.

Government was the major instrument for bringing about the most urgent transformations. In the initial stages, when management structures were being created, the energy and authority of Tariq bin Taimur played a significant role. After Sayyid Tariq left office in

December 1971, the Sultan reserved for himself the post of Head of Government and Minister of Foreign Affairs, Defence and Finance. He thus assumed full responsibility for the success or failure of restructure. This was a very courageous step, given the many difficulties strewn upon the path to reform.

The Sultan defined the essence of that important period as follows:

> *The main difficulties I encountered – in addition to the grave military situation that existed in the south of our country – were the widespread and vital needs that confronted me on all sides. But, in a sense, we were lucky that Oman's development occurred later than that of some of the other countries of the world, and particularly in the region, and so we were able to learn from the mistakes of others and have the opportunity to use our financial resources to the best possible ends.*
>
> *I am pleased to think we have succeeded in this. Of course, errors were inevitably made in the crash programme that was required for many of the areas of our development, but these were soon corrected and became fewer as we gained experience and as the oil revenues increasingly flowed.*[30]

The government developed along with the increasingly complicated tasks the country had to face. If in the autumn of 1970 some ministries with rather fuzzy competence were created, several years later their respective responsibilities had become clear and firmly fixed, and their operation more efficient. As the country attained the goals set by the political leadership new tasks arose and new ministries appeared with clearly defined areas of responsibility.

Thus, for example, the Ministries of Regional Municipalities and Environment, Legal Affairs, and the Civil Service were established. Their creation was motivated by the fact that Oman's social structure was becoming more complicated and by a new understanding of development problems. Today the Government of Oman consists of three dozen experienced ministers, each with considerable authority. Every minister reports directly to the monarch. They occupy their posts for many years, working ably together – a sign that the Sultan has chosen astutely. But it does not mean that he is undemanding. Not only administrative errors but violations of professional ethics incur very serious consequences for the highest-ranking officials. The law is the

---

[30] *Leaders* (October–December 1995).

law, Sultan Qaboos believes, and no one can put themselves above it. He himself strives to set an example in this regard. In Oman there cannot be one law for the powerful and another for the populace. When the Sultan drives a car, he waits as patiently as anyone else for the lights to change.

The country's rapid growth in all spheres prompted an increase in the number of state employees. This stratum of Omani society increased ten-fold in the first seven years of reform, and it has since grown several time more. Now a large corps of functionaries manages the administrative structures and also the public property of the Sultanate – thousands of schools, medical institutions, cultural artefacts and industrial hardware. The three-coloured national flag is flown above every establishment that belongs to the state.

When Sultan Qaboos took the first steps to create modern management structures, the administrative system, organised into wilayats, was retained without significant changes. They were headed by the *walis*, who in turn relied on tribal sheikhs. Later, while making modifications to procedures for forming local authorities, Sultan Qaboos was careful to preserve their basis. Although the administrative heads of the wilayats used to be appointed directly by the Sultan, this is now done through the Ministry of the Interior.

According to the former Minister of the Interior:

> *A wali heads the government institution of a wilayat. Very often he acts as an arbiter, if he can resolve a dispute peacefully. If he cannot it is referred to the courts, or to the police, or to the relevant municipality. A wali often received requests from tribal sheikhs representing the interests of citizens regarding services and other problems.*
>
> *As for local representation bureaux of those ministries involved in development, as a rule the wali is in charge of them. The role of the wali consists in working with sheikhs and explaining to them the particulars of governmental plans.*

The tribal autonomy which for many centuries was a source of instability, especially in Inner Oman, is gradually becoming a thing of the past. A modern state with an administrative mechanism at its disposal that is able to guarantee law and order, the collection of taxes, and the smooth functioning of socially important structures, has narrowed the sphere of influence of many traditional institutions.

But Sultan Qaboos never made the mistake of attempting to force modernisation on the tribal structure. On the contrary, the authority and experience of tribal leaders were eagerly sought by the Omani state throughout its period of radical transformation. The Minister further noted that: 'At the beginning of the 1970s we didn't have identity cards, or birth certificates, or any other proof of identity'.

Only the sheikh of a tribe could furnish information on the date of birth and origin of a person. In 1970 the Sultan insisted that every Omani citizen should have a document confirming his nationality. The sheikhs, working directly with the *walis*, played an indispensable part in this scheme. The cooperation and local expertise of sheikhs remains particularly important for the less developed regions of Oman, where there is as yet no organised structure for dealing with the everyday problems of road building, health and education. In some cases the sheikh of the tribe acts as a mediator in conflicts.

The political wisdom of Sultan Qaboos is evident in cases such as these. In contrast to reformers of many other countries, he had always aimed to draw out the creative potential of the traditional structures, whose roots reach deep into the past.

Qaboos bin Said ended the centuries-old practice of awarding top government posts to the tribal élite. All Omanis now have equal career opportunities. But the sheikhs did not demur, since their power over their fellow tribesmen quite painlessly mutated into other forms – now their moral authority provides support for the Sultan's innovations. The tribes of Oman (there are about 200 of any significant size) long had a social welfare system – about 10 per cent of their members were unmarried women (including widows and divorcees) who, according to Islamic tradition, could not earn their living and were therefore the responsibility of the community. Aid was also granted to the infirm. These enlightened moral traditions are carefully preserved and they inspire all of the Sultan's decisions on social questions.

When reform plans were being conceived at the dawn of the Omani renaissance, one of the greatest obstacles to modernisation was the complete absence of modern legislation. The first legislative acts in Oman were introduced in conjunction with the formation of the first government. They were established by the Sultan's decrees, or those of the Council of Ministers. Over the past quarter of a century, numerous laws and codes defining relations in the economic and social spheres have been adopted. And although *shari'a* has remained the foundation of Omani legislation, arbitrage in the field of business is conducted by the Committee for the Regulation of Commercial Disputes. The promulgation of the Basic Law completed the creation of the legislative system.

In a National Day speech in 1996 in Sur, Qaboos bin Said declared: 'Crowning the efforts of a quarter of a century of fruitful work, we have issued . . . the Basic Law of the State, which is the distillation of the experience gained over the past years.'

The Basic Law bestowed by the Sultan defines the fundamental principles of state policy, and also the system of forming authoritative institutions. For the first time in the nation's history the Sultan's prerogatives, as well as the mechanisms for the functioning of the monarchy and for the transfer of power, are outlined. The activity of the supreme ruler has therefore become subject to legislative regulation; thus, obligations to the country have been codified.

The rights of citizens to privacy, to possess property and to express their opinions by legal means are declared; everyone is guaranteed religious freedom and the right to create organisations or associations and participate in them. It would not be an exaggeration to say that this document is the cornerstone on which Omani society and the Oman state are built.

Sultan Qaboos chose an opportune moment to draft a constitution. In contrast to the majority of analogous legislative acts, the Basic Law of Oman came to light not as the result of competition between social forces, but at the moment when society was in accord on all of the basic political questions. In Russia, by contrast, in the period of intended reform prior to the revolution the battle over the constitution was highly divisive and the fact that the Tsar agreed to adopt it in a moment of political conflict aggravated the divisions. The situation in modern Oman is quite the opposite – here the Basic Law plays a consolidating role: it does not weaken the monarchy but reinforces it; it removes the monarchy from the ambit of tradition and the minutiae of law, while keeping it at the centre of the political structure.

Soon after the Basic Law was adopted, the Sultan promulgated a decree forming the Council of Defence. The Sultan himself heads the council, whose other members are the Palace Department Minister, the Police and Customs Inspector, the head of the SAF, the commanders of the other armed services and the head of the Security Service.

The most brilliant reformer in the history of the dynasty, Said bin Sultan (1806–1856), realised that the state could only be strengthened by enlarging the base of political power. He therefore created the Sultan's Council (Sultani) which included representatives of different classes.

Sultan Turki bin Said, who ruled in difficult times (1871–1888) when Oman had to adapt to a new disposition of geopolitical power, also spent much of his time meeting tribesmen and always tried to stay in touch with the mood of the people. The grandfather of Qaboos bin Said, Taimur bin Faisal (1913–1931) undertook long trips round the country, during which he settled disputes and listened to the opinions of religious authorities and sheikhs.

The experience of Taimur bin Faisal proved similar to that of the young Sultan – both searched for an effective method of consulting with the people. Taimur bin Faisal knew the history of his country too well and loved its traditions too much to follow the advice of those who saw the Western parliamentary system as an ideal model. After all, he instigated his reforms not to elicit the applause of London or Paris, but to improve the everyday life of his people, who for many centuries had lived under tribal democracy. Qaboos bin Said found another way – the whole country became his parliament.

After his first brief trip around the interior of Oman, the Sultan firmly resolved to become acquainted with all the regions as thoroughly as possible, to get to know the leaders personally and to listen to the needs of the people.

When he ascended to the throne, Qaboos bin Said had hardly travelled within his own country, but within a few years his knowledge of Oman was encyclopaedic. Tours lasting several weeks became standard, developing into a series of consultations with local people from all walks of life. The Sultan, well aware that in an autocracy the real power belongs to those who have access to the ruler, decided to make himself as accessible as possible. As he himself has remarked, 'These meetings with my people are of paramount importance to me. The tradition of our country is that each Omani should be able to meet his Sultan directly.'[31]

[31] *Figaro Magazine* (30 April 1994).

The new Sultan's approach was in stark contrast to that of his father, who had not left the palace in Salalah for many years and was completely inaccessible to the people over which he wielded authority. Methodically visiting one region after another, and listening to countless requests and proposals during his meetings, the Sultan formulated specific tasks for ministries and local authorities, ensuring that matters were efficiently followed up and that the lines of communication between himself and his people were kept open.

In the 30 years of his rule, the Sultan has elaborated his own ceremonious annual 'meet the people' tours, making the event a holiday for all concerned. Improvised triumphal arches decorated with banners and portraits of the Sultan greet the enormous cortège as it passes through. One of the Range Rovers is driven by the Sultan himself. Rows of white-robed men line the roadsides, waving in greeting; schoolchildren mass to welcome their ruler; now and then women leap from the crowd to shower the Sultan's car with rose petals and the Sultan waves to the crowds. When something catches his attention, the Sultan stops, gets out of his car, and chats to his subjects. He drives into villages and visits the barasti of Bedouins and he examines new developments.

On the outskirts of desert settlements or in the villages of the foothills, camps are organised, and a mobile military unit guards the Sultan's temporary residence. At a distance, under the shade of acacia trees, groups of people sit all day long in the hope of seeing the Sultan, or submitting their requests.

On the day of the Sultan's arrival, hundreds of vehicles arrive at the camp. The pillars of the local society, armed with machine guns and carrying *assas* (slim canes) enter a large parade ground walled with benches. The Sultan arrives and is warmly greeted. A presentation ceremony follows, during which the monarch shakes countless hands and accepts numerous requests in envelopes. He then addresses the gathering, an unrehearsed speech in which he tells them of the government's plans.

As night falls, birds flash black against the lingering trails of colour emanating from the horizon, and slowly the stars begin to glimmer. The people gather closer to have their say. The Sultan sits on a bench, leaning on his *assa*, the dignitaries in their *dishdashas*, *khanjars* in their belts, keep a respectful distance. One by one the people approach their ruler.

He listens carefully, occasionally asking questions of a minister or assistant. Many of his decisions and decrees have been formulated after such meetings.

The meeting ends with a recital by local poets or tales of the glories of the homeland. Sometimes small festivities follow; the sound of flutes and drums fills the air and the men sing songs of battle from long ago. In the flickering firelight blades glitter and dancers leap and brandish their swords.

During these trips the Sultan usually visits three of the eight provinces, passing a week or two at each location. Ministers and dignitaries in his entourage visit the neighbouring villages and nomadic encampments, asking people what they need, sometimes remedying complaints on the spot, sometimes initiating more complex solutions through discussion with local officials. Many projects involving both the ministries in Muscat and local institutions have been the result of such discussions.

Though such direct contact with people is very fruitful, annual tours around the country have not become a substitute for permanent institutions of popular representation. The Sultan had no intention of reneging on the promise made early in his reign of developing a more democratic basis of power. As soon as the war in Dhofar ended, he began to plan a people's assembly similar to the Sultani. Later, in a magazine interview, he affirmed the importance of representative institutions.

> Of course popular participation is conducive to national stability. To fail to give one's people a voice in their destiny, to regard them as automatons fit only to be directed and not consulted, is a sure way to disaster. This has never been the Omani way, and I have every intention of ensuring that this popular participation is further developed to the benefit of my people and country.[32]

At first there were plans to create a representative body appointed by the head of state, assembling at his request. In 1981 the Sultan promulgated a decree establishing the State Consultative Council (*Majlis al-Istishari*) made up of 17 members representing the wilayats, 17 state officials and 11 representatives of the private sector.

---

[32] *Middle East Insight* (November–December 1995).
[33] According to the President of the *Majlis*, 'The Islamic principle of *shura* means the participation of everyone in the administration of state affairs. This principle does not have an exact definition in Islam and can be interpreted very broadly. As a rule the most influential and authoritative members of society, who can give their opinions on the most vital questions of social life, take part in the process of *shura*. The principle of *shura* in Oman is based on this concept, and in keeping with this concept we are flexible towards

On 3 November the same year, the members of the new Council gathered in the al-Alam palace for their first ceremonial meeting. In his speech to them, the monarch stated the duties of the Council:

> *While we entrust your Council with the duty of giving opinions and advice, it should also be the framework for a joint effort between government and public sectors for studying the aims and dimensions of our development plans, the priorities fixed for their projects and the obstacles which stand in the way of implementing these plans, and suitable solutions to them. For this reason, it is our intention that both government and the public sectors be represented on this Council – a representation in which the public sector will be the majority so that the Council is equal to the noble aim for which it has been established, namely to take the wishes and needs of the citizens into consideration in forming our national policy in the economic and social spheres. The Council shall also be a vital field for interaction between and integration of the opinions of its members, and for full cooperation between the government and its citizens, in carrying out the duties and obligations of the current stage of the development.*

The membership of the SCC was completely replaced every two years. Its members made many tours of the country, meeting the *walis* and other representatives of the people, a strategy which permitted an objective analysis of the government's actions and an evaluation of the efficiency of the development programme. The Council also became a kind of school of politics for the subjects of Sultan Qaboos, as television eventually began to broadcast sessions of the SCC, and everyone had a chance to follow their discussions.

In 1991 the State Consultative Council was replaced by the Consultative Council (*Majlis al-Shura*). The change of name meant alterations to both its principles and spheres of operation. The Islamic principle of *shura* was made the foundation of its activity.[33] The most authoritative people in the Sultanate were permitted to vote for nominees to membership of the Council.[34] Representatives of the

everything new and towards all changes that respect the principle of *shura*. We are open to new experience.' Interview with the author (26 December 1998).

[34] The Minister of the Interior informed the author that according to the voting law of *Majilis al-Shura* each citizen has the capacity to vote in the elections that take place to choose a representative from each wilaya. Wilyas with a population of 30,000 or more are represented by two members. Candidates with the highest number of votes become members of the *Majilis*.

government were no longer automatically granted seats on it. The ultimate right to approve candidates was reserved for the Sultan – from the four elected by the population of a wilayat, he appointed two. The number of members was increased to 59.

The Council assisted the government in studying problems and working out recommendations in the field of economic and financial policy. Council sessions were usually held four times a year and lasted a week.

The permanent bodies created by the members did the bulk of the work. Several committees were formed for this purpose. Their task was to examine draft laws submitted by the ministries before they were put into effect in the form of a decree by the Sultan. Ministers had to answer questions at committee sessions so that the members fully understood the proposed legislation.[35]

Discussion between deputies and their constituents takes place more often in the deputy's house over a cup of coffee, rather than in an office, a practice reminiscent of the gathering of fellow tribesmen in the tent of their sheikh. A millennium of democratic tradition in Oman is a major contribution to the idea of rule by the people, and is evident at every turn. One has only to glance in the telephone directories, where the office, home and mobile telephone numbers of all high-ranking officials and all members of the ruling family apart only from the Sultan himself, are listed.

Three years later elections for the second *Majlis al-Shura* were held. In a major break with tradition, two women entered the chamber of people's representatives for the first time. The Council was enlarged to 80 members and for the first time women were admitted – in line with the results of the first ever census in Oman, completed in December 1993.

Royal Decree 101, issued on 6 November 1996, put into operation the Basic Law, an important milestone in the history of the nation. In an interview, the Sultan recounted the creation of this document.

> *As I approached my Silver Jubilee, I said to myself: this is the time! I got together four of my most trusted people – all Omanis. I sat with them and told them exactly what I had in mind. I gave them a year to formulate it*

[35] The president of the *Majlis al-Shura* defined the main directions for the activity of the Council thus: 'The *Majlis* has the authority to present initiatives to modify certain laws currently in force. The *Majlis* studies the social and economic situation of the country and drafts initiatives regarding these questions. The *Majlis* also has authority to propose recommendations on the most important questions regarding the development of Omani society. The Majilis takes part in the preparation of five-year development plans for the

*in a legal document. Then we had a second review, and then a final session.
I announced it on my annual 'Meet the People' tour while encamped in the
desert in the heart of Oman. Then I waited for the reaction, which was very good.
Now the Basic Law is being implemented through laws and regulations.*[36]

Article 52 of the Basic Law defined and brought into existence a new
body of popular representation – the Council of Oman (*Majlis Oman*).
The *Majlis al-Shura* became the first chamber of this council, the newly
created State Council (*Majlis al-Dawla*) the second.

The third *Majlis al-Shura*, elected in 1997, included 82 deputies. At the
same time 41 members of the State Council were appointed by the
Sultan. He selected the former President of the State Consultative
Council and a number of ministries to head the second chamber.
The President of the *Majlis al-Dawla* defines the purview of the second
chamber of the Council of Oman thus:

*The creation of the Majlis al-Dawla is the last phase of building a system
of organisation. Each of them played its role at a certain period of time.
And each state organisation was created only when it was needed. In 1970
we had to create a government from scratch, and we created it.*

*There was a need for a body that would evaluate the results of the
government's activity, that would help the government. Then came the
moment for a specialised independent body that would evaluate what had
been done over the previous thirty years, the positive and the negative
results from this period, in order to use the positive results for future
development and to avoid the negative ones in future. Everything which,
according to the Sultan, needs to be evaluated, analysed and worked out so
that we can continue building on our achievements, becomes an object of
consideration. All such questions will be within the competence of the
Majlis al-Dawla. The most prominent, well-prepared and well-educated
representatives of Omani society make up the Council. These people have
worked in all spheres of statecraft: they have been ministers, vice-ministers,
ambassadors, they have served in the army and in the security service and*

country. When such a plan is worked out by the government, it is passed on to the *Majlis;*
from there it is submitted to the economic committee where government ministers
participate in the discussion of the plan. After the plan has been discussed and approved,
it is passed to the Sultan for approval. Five-year plans are prepared, taking into
consideration the geographical divisions of the country.'

[36] *Foreign Affairs* No. 3 (1997).

*have made a positive contribution to social and economic development. They are assembled here to ensure a smooth transfer of power from one generation to another. The authority of the Majlis al-Dawla is increasing.*[37]

Like the first chamber of the Omani Council, the *Majlis al-Dawla* has five women members, including a university professor and the editor of a women's weekly magazine, both of whom have considerable experience of working in various commercial and state structures and take part with the men in discussions of political and economic strategy. In no Arab Gulf country do women participate in the running of the country to the same extent.

By Royal Decree, two women have been appointed as undersecretaries, two women hold ministerial rank, and there are many women in the state and private sectors of the economy. Women are also represented in the air force, army and police.

The ruler attaches special importance to the involvement of women in all spheres of activity, thereby adhering to the teachings of Islam and the customs of his country. The Sultan notes that, 'The Prophet, praise and peace be upon him, has instructed us as to the role of women. This role was very significant in the early days of Islam.'[38]

There are no statements in the Qur'an that could justify discrimination against women. And the history of Oman gives many examples of women who have played a prominent role in society. In the times of the Ya'ruba dynasty, Queen Shamsa, famous for her wisdom, ruled the nation. Later, during Oman's struggle for independence, Asila bint Hamyer, who fought alongside the men, gained renown. Two experts in religious law Najia bint Amir al-Haji and Khadija bint Said al-Kindi are also enshrined in the memory of grateful descendants.

From the day he ascended to the throne, Qaboos bin Said has always stressed the necessity of granting women the same opportunities as men for study and work. Schools opened during the initial phase of reforms allowed equal educational opportunities for boys and girls. And at Sultan Qaboos University, women now make up more than half the student body. There are structures in ministries and local authorities devoted to the affairs of women, family, childhood and maternity. There are no gender restrictions in the nation's legislation.

[37] Interview with the author (22 December 1998).
[38] *Telegraph Magazine* (12 August 1995).

The Sultan's plans reflect his solicitude for the future of his people. Many of his decrees over the years are, in one way or another, the fruit of this solicitude.

Qaboos bin Said acknowledges the truth of the old aphorism that history is the tutor of kings. And history has taught Oman many bitter lessons. Few of today's ruling heads of state pay such close attention to the past as Qaboos bin Said. Careful examination of the past can illuminate the safest path into the future. In his speech on 3 November 1981, at the opening of the first body for popular representation, the Sultan said:

> *All our activities and experience should originate from within and be consistent with the values and traditions prevailing in our Islamic community. This is because human experience has shown, and is still showing, that the method of abstract imitation, overlooking reality, will always lead to great dangers.*

The creation of the State Council is not only a logical step in the development of representative bodies, but also an original mechanism for meeting conflict between generations. It is not by chance that it has been created now, when the generation of statesmen who created the new Oman have reached an age where they must think of handing on power to the next generation.

The President of the *Majlis al-Dawla* nicely expressed in 1999 the basic principles for passing on this responsibility:

> *Those who are 35 to 45 now begin to take leading positions: all of the director generals, all undersecretaries, almost every minister, all members of the Council of Oman, the army command. After the year 2000 those who are over 65 will make room; they will be replaced by the generation of those who are now 40 to 60, without any conflicts related to relinquishing power or trying to obtain power. One can compare our attitude to the situation with the point of view of a man who stands on the shore and watches the waves roll one after another onto the beach. And there is no wave that turns back, there is none that doesn't reach the shore. Everything happens on the basis of real estimations, planning and research. If there is no sound philosophy in society, no clear leadership founded on sound principles, the most unfortunate consequences ensue.*

*And if the old generation cannot transfer its power to new generations, new generations that want more power and more responsibility, the new generation will rebel. Civilisations perish this way. If the old are not ready to pass on power to the young, there is discord and previous achievements begin to be doubted. Therefore, development will not reach its aim . . . In 1970 the Sultan said that he intended to create a modern government that would be based on state bodies developing in a natural way, and on continuity.*

*The Sultan spoke about this on the day of the opening of the Council of Oman a year ago. He said: you will be responsible to the future. He addressed us, the generation that had been occupied with state affairs since 1970. The most important thing is to get and give away power correctly. Consider the laws that have been adopted since 1995, taking as their point of departure the necessity for the passage of responsibility from one generation to another – for example the law on pensions. This contains a principle that doesn't exist in any law on pensions elsewhere in the world. A person who has served the state for 15 years and who has reached the age of 55 can get an early pension. This ensures the smooth passage of responsibility from the elder generation to the younger.*

*This policy has yielded excellent results, so everybody wants it to continue. The person who takes part in passing responsibilities personally makes this choice; after that he won't criticise or declare something unfounded.*

Although by 1999, the formation of a system of state organs could well have been considered complete, events in the very next year showed how open Oman is to continuing modification and change; the elections of 2000 to *Majlis al-Shura* were conducted by a board of electors, but on the basis of direct voting by the people.[39] Democracy in Oman is based on long-term strategy, the scope of which is to make the structure of power stable and involve the people in administration. This deeply organic process, rooted in the ancient, spiritual Arab–Muslim culture, does not frighten the Sultan. He says:

*The observance of our religious and cultural traditions is deeply embedded in the life of our country and people, and it provides them with a*

[39] By law all citizens male and female, who reach the age of 21 years can vote to elect members of Majlis al-Shura. The first popular election took place in October 2003. There are 83 elected members.

*comprehensive reference and guidelines within which to lead their lives –
both with respect to religious observance and in their secular day-to-day
existence. Many years ago I told my people they should be ready to accept
what is good from the modern world, but reject those influences from it
which are bad; this I feel we have been successful in doing.*[40]

It has been Oman's great fortune to have been ruled by a hereditary
monarch as progressive yet, at the same time, as mindful of the beneficial
aspects of tradition as Qaboos bin Said; his skilful leadership has ensured
the country an orderly passage into the new era. The gradual changes to
the political system have demanded patience and tenacity not only from
society, but from the leader himself. Rather than plunging the country
into immediate and far-reaching political changes without consultation,
he has waited for the agreement of the people of Oman – and his strategy
has borne fruit. In the words of an Omani proverb: 'Who has the
patience to wait, receives a reward'.

Three decades of the Oman renaissance have enriched all the elements
of society; state structures, the economy, culture, science and education.
Every year the health system becomes more comprehensive, every year
the country and its citizens become more closely integrated with the rest
of the world, and all without social unrest. The policy of reconciliation
conducted by Qaboos bin Said from the very beginning of his reign cut
the ground from under the feet of those who dreamt about a violent
transformation of the society. Oman is united now as never before.

The Sultan's peaceful revolution has deprived his opponents of all
support, and his shrewd and humanitarian act of amnesty for political
opponents has achieved what no persecution could have done. In this he
has followed the precedent of Imam Nasir bin Murshid, who won the
hearts of his contemporaries by pardoning the vanquished enemies and
thus uniting a country exhausted by civil war and laying the foundation
of its future glory. It is difficult to avoid the conclusion that this man, so
devoted to the history of his country, has reached back to grasp what is
best from the most admired figures of his past in order to create his own
personal vision of what a good ruler should be.

The Minister of the Palace Office declared to representatives of the
Omani press in November 1999:

[40] *Tribuna* (26 January 1996).

*Forgiveness is a characteristic of the great and it should not be considered a weakness; thus when His Majesty issued the amnesty, it reflected the firmness of the state and its solidarity. There are no political prisoners in the Sultanate and the state is on alert against those who attempt to spoil the achievement of this country.*

In reply to a question of how he sees the future of his country, His Majesty responds with one word: 'bright'. He adds, 'Oman enters the twenty-first century with solid foundations. But we cannot stand still; we have to work constantly. While taking one step, we have to think at the same time about the next one.'

# The Conductor
# and his Orchestra

T HE TEMPERATURE NEAR NIZWA was 34° C on 9 November 1999 –
no more than a pleasant summer's day to the Omanis in their
loose clothing, but uncomfortably hot for me in my wool suit
and for the Iranian ambassador in his formal attire. We were seated in a
large green tent awaiting an audience with the Sultan, and everyone was
in high spirits.

It was not the first time the Sultan's camp had been pitched here, in
the Saih al-Barakat area (in the Omani dialect *seeh* is the narrow flat strip
between the desert and the mountain, and *barakat* means blessed).
Opposite is Nizwa, and it is within easy reach of Muscat by a good road
through the mountains.

The placename *barakat* probably attests to the fact that this is a place
where in past centuries people gathered to pray and talk with the
spiritual and secular leaders of Oman. It remains such a place. In the
numerous tents, equipped with the most up-to-date communications
systems, ministers and generals are at work. A steady stream of
information flows in and out. Elsewhere, the oil flows constantly
through a network of pipelines, the lifeblood of the nation. Hundreds of
thousands of kilowatts course through copper cables, providing energy
for the nation, and the armed forces are on the alert, all united as if
under the control of a single will.

The might of this modern nation is commanded by a man sitting out
of sight in his crimson tent. In this austere setting where long ago Imams
judged tribal disputes and discussed the finer points of *fikh*
(jurisprudence/religious law) with lawmakers, investment projects worth

hundreds of millions of dollars are today being considered. They include plans for a large-scale domestic Internet network, the development of modern metallurgical and chemical production, and the laying of a gas pipeline on the bottom of the Indian Ocean.

As the sun sets, the desert grows cool. I look out from my tent as the sky to the west gradually acquires its flamboyant evening colours that so startle the senses after the calm expanse of drained afternoon light. The colours of the Omani landscape are mainly pastel – bare hills, sandy dunes, ancient villages all blending almost imperceptibly one into another, and sand-coloured camels appearing as no more than faint suggestions of themselves against this subtle backdrop. The amazing similarity of colours is not even broken by foliage, for the paleness of those leaves that look dusted in ash merely add another layer to the muted palette. But the evening sky has other colours, like the reflection of a blaze upon a blade, the mysterious gold patches of light from a woman's bracelet . . . by the time a guardsman enters our tent in a cream *dishdasha,* the day has burned out and stars litter the sky. I pick out a familiar word in his rapid speech – Sultan. This means that one of us will now see the monarch. I am given the signal that it is my turn.

Our jeep takes us over a rutted dirt track, its headlights picking out the rocky soil. Then suddenly the headlights are extinguished and the darkness closes in. Our guide's torch shines and we get out and follow him. Through the darkness I see a tent and in the light of its overhead lamp I see a small linen peak trimmed with braid. On the carpet outside the tent stands a slim figure in a white dishdasha. His face is still indistinct, but the short beard that frames it is instantly recognisable.

An energetic and heart-felt handshake. The Sultan greets me with a gentle smile and a warm but penetrating gaze. How little he resembles the pictures I have carefully studied! He looks at least ten years younger in the flesh and there is a nobility of bearing and a brightness in his eye which cannot be captured by the camera. The bearing is of a man whose ancestors have sat upon the throne for 200 years.

We sit in easy chairs, with a thin Persian rug on the floor and a small round table between us. From time to time during the conversation the Sultan waves his right hand. He has a narrow palm, long fingers and a silver ring on his little finger. His movements are gracious, understated yet full of resolve. His manner is dignified, yet he smiles easily and sits in a most relaxed way. It is impossible to define his bearing other than as regal simplicity and I feel I am in the presence of an exceptional figure. I had occasionally seen Sultan Qaboos on television and had always been struck by the perfection of his posture – his is a frame to put one in mind of those that can be observed on the walls of Egyptian temples, where the pharaohs of thousand year dynasties are depicted.

The conversation moves smoothly from His Majesty's childhood to his studies and military service, touches on his views on Oman's historical past and its current problems, his musical preferences and favourite books. Everything I hear adds to my knowledge and makes me re-examine the facts. But most importantly, my interview with Sultan Qaboos animated everything I had gathered from books, newspapers, interviews and other sources about the man; my research now had a cohesion that could not have come from anything but this personal face-to-face meeting with the remarkable human being whose life I had been studying for so long. As I listened to the warm intonations of his voice when he spoke with sincerity and passion of people and policies he holds dear, it was as though I was experiencing that moment when a shake of the kaleidoscope finally produces, from the maze of colours and shapes, a perfect pattern.

Sultan Qaboos has done much to preserve and enrich his country's natural and manmade assets. The beautification of Oman is evident everywhere, from mass restoration of the country's rich architectural sites (castles, mosques, bazaars) and modern construction (strictly controlled by architectural reference to the past) to the creation and organisation of symphonic orchestras and female national costume shows. In everything lies something of the Sultan's personal taste. Muscat, with its ancient forts and white palaces cradled at the base of a formidable mountain range, represents, in contrast to most Arab capitals, a classic city of the Muslim east, and reflects the Sultan's respect and love for tradition.

The spiritual basis of modernisation is Islam. Four thousand mosques, built and restored during the reign of Sultan Qaboos, are filled five times a day with devoted Omanis, following all the teachings of the Prophet as their ancestors did. Their devotion to national traditions is so great that there are probably few other countries in the Arab world where the everyday customs inherited from the past are maintained to such an extent.

The national costume is preferred by all without exception, from students to ministers and every official is armed with a *khanjar* when fulfilling official duties.

Qaboos bin Said's love for Omani traditions has made him sensitive to the importance of traditions in other countries. He is therefore careful to study the protocol of each country that he visits – a practice which must endear him to his hosts and which certainly ensures that he is comfortable and at ease wherever he goes. He is a refined person, in the best sense of the word, and his charm, dignity and wisdom make it easy to understand why so many world leaders have visited Oman during his reign. His guests have included King Fahd; King Hussein; King Birendra; Queen Elizabeth II; Prince Charles and Princess Diana; Shah Mohammed Reza Pahlavi; Sultan Bolkiah; Sheikh Zayed; Mubarak, Bashar Al Assad; George Bush (senior), then a Vice President; François Mitterrand; Indira Gandhi; Atal Behari Vajpayee; Tosiki Kaifu; Kurt Waldheim; Margaret Thatcher; Victor Chernomyrdin and President Clinton. In addition to the dignitaries listed above, the heads of most major international organisations have visited Muscat. Probably the words of Prince Khaled bin Sultan of Saudi Arabia best sum up the general impression the Sultan gives to his guests: 'I was favoured with a private conversation with the ruler of Oman, Sultan Qaboos – a correct, highly educated and very informed person, worthy of every respect.'

World leaders are naturally not simply drawn by the Sultan's charm. Above all they value the opportunity to exchange opinions with one of the most shrewd and experienced politicians, a worthy bearer of his unofficial title, 'Wise Man of the Gulf'. His great knowledge of the domestic situation in Oman and his deep insight into the situation in other countries have enabled him to create realistic domestic and foreign policies, which together validate some of the most difficult actions he has had to take during his reign.

Just by seeing and listening to the Sultan in person you begin to understand the nature of his policies more deeply. His is a personality which brings artistry to everything he touches, from the colourful annual tours around the country to his military and political decisions with their heady combination of swiftness and foresight, their apparent effortlessness all reflecting a brilliant and analytical mind.

It is said that sometimes the Sultan drives around the capital and its environs to visit objects of interest and to evaluate the work of the city parks and street-cleaning services. These trips take place under cover of darkness, avoiding pomp and ceremony, following a tradition of ancient Islamic leaders. It is a method of keeping in touch with his nation that was practiced by Harun al-Rashid, the fatimid ruler of Egypt Hakim, and in our times was also followed by King Hussein of Jordan, who often posed as a taxi driver so that he could travel incognito amongst his own people. But few other modern leaders have made dialogue with his people such an essential foundation of government. In the 30 years of his reign, Sultan Qaboos has probably visited every village in his country and spoken to all those with authority in their district, or at least shaken their hands.

In describing the Sultan's attitude to his life's work, Pushkin's words about Peter the Great come to mind: 'as an academic, a hero, a navigator, a carpenter, he was an all-embracing soul on the throne, an eternal worker.' Qaboos Said is a man of such prodigious output – the list of posts he has filled indicates the volume of business he has to attend to each day. In an interview he complained:

> *Papers, papers, papers! They even bring me papers after dinner. I delegate, but they still want my comments. It gets worse all the time. In the beginning there was only one ministry, that of the Interior – but now . . .*

The Minister of the Diwan confirms that: 'A very large volume of documents goes to the Sultan. Decrees, edicts, letters of reference, decorations. Some issues are postponed for the second, third time. It is characteristic of His Majesty to make a balanced decision. But if matters are urgent, the document is quickly signed.' The Minister knows better than most the amount of business the Sultan has to deal with. It is the Diwan who organises his daily affairs, receiving applications from ministries and from other countries, and preparing daily and long-term programmes for the Sultan to approve.

Asked about the Sultan's working day, the Minister said that it is usually pressured. The Sultan values human contact and tries to meet people as often as possible. He also reads a great many letters. It is quite usual for him to write notes on them – he even corrects grammatical errors and circles words he wishes to have explained. In most cases the Sultan makes his own decisions, and his orders are executed promptly.

Sultan Qaboos goes out almost daily to talk to his subjects, and sometimes twice a day if many people have gathered. He is never accompanied by a bodyguard and during these informal sessions, as in his annual tours around the country, he deals with questions that are as wide-ranging as they are frank. Often decisions on complaints are taken immediately. Sometimes requests are handed over to the court for further examination. If a complaint is made about an official, the matter is thoroughly investigated. The Sultan's style is one followed by civil servants, who like to have as much contact with the people as their busy office lives permit, knowing that to keep the Sultan as fully informed as possible they must be in touch with the general mood.

When I spoke with female members of the State Council, I learned that widows and other women in need often turn to the Sultan for help, and he will give the appropriate instructions for the Diwan to disburse aid.

The Sultan deals with a wide variety of questions from his ministers. But he does not limit himself to reading material selected for him. The Minister Responsible for Foreign Affairs, told me that 'He reads a lot and makes his own decisions. The Sultan personally keeps abreast of the news with the help of modern means of communication, including television.'

It is difficult to separate those moments when the monarch is busy studying documents from those when he is simply watching broadcasts, and just as difficult to distinguish the days or hours that he sets aside for rest. The Minister of the Diwan says: 'The Sultan's leisure time is very limited. It is impossible to switch off completely from work. In the summer when the Sultan is in Salalah we follow the custom of announcing that His Majesty is on holiday, but work also catches up with him there.'

Even when the monarch goes on a private trip to Europe, which happens every three or four years, he is unable to escape the affairs of state.

In his rare moments of leisure, Qaboos bin Said reads books on history, politics, science and the art of war.[41] He is an experienced equestrian and

[41] In an interview with *Middle East Policy* the Sultan said, 'I have had the advantage over the years of reading the political and philosophical views of many of the world's foremost thinkers. In some cases, of course, I have found myself in disagreement with the ideas they have expressed, but this disagreement in itself has proved valuable in the evolution of my formed opinions and in my recognition of the need to consider all sides of a question.' *Middle East Policy* (April 1995)

delights in spending time at his stables near the palace at Seeb, riding and training his horses. The Sultan also enjoys sailing and, when time permits, takes to the sea in his yacht, which is equipped with all the means of communication necessary to keep him in touch with his ministers. He also enjoys shooting.

But the Sultan's greatest passion is music. It is more than a hobby and almost as important to him as politics. It is a subject on which he is most knowledgeable. When asked which of the Russian composers he especially likes, he immediately answered, 'Tchaikovsky, Rimsky-Korsakov and Rachmaninov.' He added:

> *I like many European composers, for example the Finn Sibelius. Also Brahms, Bach, Elgar, Olson. Mainly classical. But I also enjoy folk music from different countries and continents – Polish, Romanian and Arab melodies. Unfortunately, standards of performance of traditional Arab music have fallen considerably. The continuity has been broken and few performers can maintain the purity of our classics. In Oman, we try to preserve our musical heritage. I cannot give preference to just one direction or to separate works. I like the music of Andalucia, Turkish and Iranian music, a lot of Indian and African music. Of course, I love music from other Arab countries, and in particular from Yemen. The music of Oman developed under the influence of many other cultures, for example India and Africa. Our music is extremely diverse and expressive. Fortunately, Oman has maintained its tradition very well and I try to help its development. But it does not end there; we also have all the main types of orchestra – symphonic, military, jazz and so on.*
>
> *I hope that all these efforts to develop music will lead to the fulfilment of my goal – to raise the cultural level of the people in general and musical education in particular.*

The Oman Symphony Orchestra, formed by the Sultan, has reached maturity and its musicians have studied at a number of prestigious European centres, in particular in London. Fine military orchestras have also been created and enjoy international recognition.

The Ministry of Information has established a centre for the study of folk music. It publishes serious works on this topic, including an encyclopaedia of traditional music, and many radio and television programmes are dedicated to folk music.

The former Minister of Information, said that he who knows good, *is* good. This sage remark can serve as a key to the personality of the monarch. The Sultan's love for the highest achievements of human culture, his vast knowledge of religion and history, cannot but create an aura of goodness around him.

When he has a moment to himself he improvises on his lute, and on rare occasions plays the organ. In an interview Sultan Qaboos was asked which music he would take to a desert island, and he chose Beethoven's Sixth Symphony. The Sultan is clearly a man of balance and self-knowledge, his political style in tune with his artistic tastes. If we liken the leader of a nation to the conductor of an orchestra, then his primary task is to coax the best out of each performer – utilising individual strengths, minimising individual weaknesses, while allowing each performer sufficient space to develop their own sense of what the work demands. In the 33 years of Oman's renaissance, Sultan Qaboos has conducted his nation in such a way, with harmony, beauty and concord.

The Sultan usually starts his speeches by saying, 'Esteemed countrymen', or 'My dear people'. These are not empty phrases but the expression of deep affection. More than anything the monarch values the mutual trust of his nation, which can be likened to a large, harmonious family. As he said to an English journalist:

> *I feel responsible for all my people. A monarch should see himself as father of the entire nation. A monarch is a mirror. He reflects his people's history and their culture. They can understand their collective identity much better through him. He must always understand them, inform himself of their needs. He should do things in their interest before they ask him to. Young people get bored with old kings. They think they know better, so the system cannot stand still; it must improve all the time and you must never allow cracks to develop. Never.*

As befits a man of the calibre of Qaboos bin Said, he has found within himself the generosity to forgive his father for those six years of unjustified confinement and has, perhaps, come to place the fears which drove his father to such a radical action in a historical and psychological context which makes them comprehensible and, to some extent, depersonalises them.

For his part, Said bin Taimur, who has lived in his favourite London hotel, the Dorchester, for several years, is said to be proud of his son and is known to have written him a reconciliatory letter from there, full of warmth and tenderness. According to the former foreign minister of Oman, Neil Innes, who saw Said bin Taimur frequently, the ex-Sultan has accepted the situation very philosophically, and was in some respects very happy to have been relieved of his former responsibilities, and able, at long last, to relax. 'At least his son succeeded him without the more drastic revolution which he had feared, and which might have overthrown the Sultanate altogether. I think that in his heart he was proud of his son.'

The remarkable Said bin Taimur mosque in the Khuwair district of Muscat, built on the order of Sultan Qaboos in the late 1990s, will always serve as a symbol of this historic reconciliation between father and son.

Qaboos bin Said always had a particularly warm relationship with his mother. During his most difficult years Sayyida Miyzun helped him find strength and faith in the future. When he became Sultan he continued to value her advice and practical mind and he suffered a huge loss when she died on 12 August 1992. She was buried in her homeland Taqa, not far from Salalah. There, in the old cemetery around the mosque, are several identical marble tombstones, where the Sultan's uncle, grandfather and mother lie. Upon the tombstone of Sayyida Miyzun is an epigraph from the Qur'an (89, 27–30):

*Oh soul that art at rest!*
*Return to your Lord well-pleased (with Him),*
*well-pleasing (Him),*
*So enter among My devotees,*
*And enter My heaven*

Those from the Maashan tribe that live in Taqa say that sometimes, late at night, a jeep stops at the ancient cemetery and the familiar figure of the Sultan steps out. For a long time he stands by his mother's grave. The Sultan comes at night when the city sleeps because he does not want a crowd to gather around him. Only the whisper of the ocean waves can break his silent conversation with that person he holds so dear who has left this world forever. Perhaps he recalls those years when the beautiful and wise Sayyida Miyzun would come to talk with him in his small house by the palace, her visits giving him the courage not just to survive, but to grow during his years of confinement.

Just before sunrise in Taqa the wakening birds shatter the silence. Rays of the rising sun reach across the sea to outline the silhouettes of numerous fishing boats upon the surface of the water. Here and there the ocean's smooth surface suddenly flares with thousands of tiny fish leaping from the water to save themselves from some unseen predator. The tide slowly recedes, leaving behind it a line of rich debris on the sand. Looking at the eternally repeating cycle of life which Qaboos bin Said saw from the windows of the al-Hisn palace or during trips to his mother's birthplace, one feels in the presence of one of the sources of his personality. One can feel that his composed, harmonious and independent character was formed not only under the influence of his family and nation, but under the influence of the rhythmic, inexorable ocean movements, at once a symbol of freedom and of eternal existence.

Omani Arabs have long been open to the world. Their caravans carried the earth's precious gifts of myrrh and frankincense for thousands of miles through mountains and deserts. Their ships anchored in distant shores, populated by different races and cultures. In the rustle of the sand and the crashing of the waves they tried to hear the call of eternity and to decipher God's behest. Those who best comprehended God's call were those chosen in history – leaders, religious figures and wise men. These fathers of the people became the pride of subsequent generations and with time the symbols of national honour, worthiness and heroism.

Years, decades and centuries will pass. Poets from other ages will contemplate the eternally repetitive patterns of ocean life and try to penetrate the sense of never-ending sagas and the emotions which fuelled them, and, as I have done, some will search anew for the key to the dedicated ruler of this land, who has brought it so triumphantly into the new millennium.